THE MEDICAL MALPRACTICE MYTH

Tom Baker

THE MEDICAL MALPRACTICE MYTH

The University of Chicago Press

Chicago and London

TOM BAKER is the
Connecticut Mutual
Professor of Law and
director of the Insurance
Law Center at the
University of Connecticut
School of Law. Coeditor
of *Embracing Risk:*
The Changing Culture
of Insurance and
Responsibility, published
by the University of
Chicago Press, Baker
has also worked as a
consultant with insurance
companies and law firms.

The University of Chicago Press, Chicago 60637

The University of Chicago Press, Ltd., London

© 2005 by The University of Chicago

All rights reserved. Published 2005

Printed in the United States of America

15 14 13 12 11 10 09 08 07 06 05   1 2 3 4 5

ISBN: 0-226-03648-0 (cloth)

Library of Congress
Cataloging-in-Publication Data
Baker, Tom, 1959–
    The medical malpractice myth / Tom Baker.
        p. cm.
    Includes bibliographical references and index.
    ISBN 0-226-03648-0 (cloth : alk. paper)
    1. Physicians—Malpractice—United States. 2. Actions and
defenses—United States. 3. Insurance, Physicians' liability—
United States. I. Title.
    [DNLM: 1. Malpractice—trends—United States.
2. Economics, Medical—United States. 3. Quality of Health
Care—United States. 4. Insurance, Liability—economics—
United States. 5. Jurisprudence—United States.
W44 AA1 B126m 2005]
KF2905.3B35 2005
346.7303'3—dc22

                                                2005014065

Contents

1 THE MEDICAL MALPRACTICE MYTH

Medical malpractice premiums are skyrocketing. "Closed" signs are sprouting on health clinic doors. Doctors are leaving the field of medicine, and those who remain are practicing in fear and silence. Pregnant women cannot find obstetricians. Billions of dollars are wasted on defensive medicine. And angry doctors are marching on state capitols across the country.

All this is because medical malpractice litigation is exploding. Egged on by greedy lawyers, plaintiffs sue at the drop of a hat. Juries award eye-popping sums to undeserving claimants, leaving doctors, hospitals, and their insurance companies no choice but to pay huge ransoms for release from the clutches of the so-called "civil justice" system. Medical malpractice litigation is a sick joke, a roulette game rigged so that plaintiffs and their lawyers' numbers come up all too often, and doctors and the honest people who pay in the end always lose.

This is the medical malpractice myth.

Built on a foundation of urban legend mixed with the occasional true story, supported by selective references to academic studies, and repeated so often that even the mythmakers forget the exaggeration, half truth, and outright misinformation employed in the service of their greater good, the medical malpractice myth has filled doctors, patients, legislators, and voters with the kind of fear that short circuits critical thinking.

This fear has inspired legislative action on a nationwide scale three times in my lifetime. The first time was back in the mid-1970s. I remember sitting at the dinner table listening to my father report what he'd heard at his medical society meeting: "Medical malpractice insurance premiums are going through the roof. Frivolous litigation and runaway juries will drive doctors out of the profession." The answer, the medical societies and their insurance companies said, was medical malpractice tort reform—to make it harder for misguided patients and their lawyers to sue.

What the medical societies did not tell my father, or almost anyone else, was that their own research showed that the real problem was too much medical malpractice, not too much litigation. In the mid-1970s the California Hospital and Medical Associations sponsored a study on medical malpractice that they expected would support their tort reform efforts. But, to their surprise and dismay, the study showed that medical malpractice injured tens of thousands of people every year—more than automobile and workplace accidents. The study also showed that, despite the rhetoric, most of the victims did not sue. But almost nobody heard about the study because the associations decided that these facts conflicted with their tort reform message.

Two years after they achieved their goal of enacting restrictive medical malpractice tort reform in California, the associations printed the results of the study, but only as an association report.[1] All that was published for outside consumption was a technical summary, which did not feature the dramatic findings.[2] The report was not widely distributed, and it was written in exceptionally dry and technical language.

The next time I heard about frivolous litigation and runaway juries driving doctors out of practice was while I was in law school in the mid-1980s. Medical malpractice premiums were back through the roof. And, once again, the answer from the medical societies and their insurance companies was tort reform: raise the bar on getting into the courthouse and, in many states, limit what juries could do once victims got inside.

That time, more people were skeptical about the claims of the medical societies. But this was the 1980s, and organized medicine still knew best. Nobody had pulled together enough facts about medical malpractice litigation. And hardly anyone knew about, or could have easily understood, that buried California report.[3] The result was a virtual avalanche of restrictive tort reform legislation proposed—and often enacted—in legislatures across the county.

The third time began in 2002 and continues today. This time around we have a lot more information. But you would not know it from the tort reform remedies that the medical societies, the hospitals, and their insurance companies are pushing.

What do we know?

First, we know from the California study, as confirmed by more recent, better publicized studies, that the real problem is too much medical malpractice, not too much litigation. Most people do not sue, which means that victims—not doctors, hospitals, or liability insurance companies—bear the lion's share of the costs of medical malpractice.

Second, because of those same studies, we know that the real costs of medical malpractice have little to do with litigation. The real costs of medical malpractice are the lost lives, extra medical expenses, time out of work, and pain and suffering of tens of thousands of people every year, the vast majority of whom do not sue. There is lots of talk about the heavy burden that "defensive medicine" imposes on health costs, but the research shows this is not true.

Third, we know that medical malpractice insurance premiums are cyclical, and that it is not frivolous litigation or runaway juries that drive that cycle. The sharp spikes in malpractice premiums in the 1970s, the 1980s, and the early 2000s are the result of financial trends and competitive behavior in the insurance industry, not sudden changes in the litigation environment.

Fourth, we know that "undeserving" people sometimes bring medical malpractice claims because they do not know that the claims lack merit and because they cannot find out what happened to them (or their loved ones) without making a claim. Most undeserving claims disappear before trial; most trials end in a verdict for the doctor; doctors almost never pay claims out of their own pockets; and hospitals and insurance companies refuse to pay claims unless there is good evidence of malpractice. If a hospital or insurance company does settle a questionable claim to avoid a huge risk, there is a very large discount. This means that big payments to undeserving claimants are the very rare exception, not the rule.

Finally, we know that there is one sure thing—and only one thing—that the proposed remedies can be counted on to do. They can be counted on to distract attention long enough for the inevitable turn in the insurance cycle to take the edge off the doctors' pain. That way, people can keep ignoring the real, public health problem. Injured patients and their lawyers are the messengers here, not the cause of the medical malpractice problem.

JESICA AND JEANELLA·

No one who follows the medical news is likely to forget Jesica Santillan, who died after a receiving a heart and lung transplant at Duke University Hospital in February 2003. Brought to the United States from a poor Mexican town in search of better medical care, she inspired her new North Carolina community to raise money for a heart and lung transplant, and she inspired people to care about the problem of the medically uninsured.

When she received the transplant, it turned out to be the wrong blood type—a basic, easily avoidable, and tragic mistake. Her body began rejecting the new organs even before the transplant surgery was over. Her supporters launched a national public relations effort to find a second, compatible, set of heart and lungs, while accusing Duke of trying to stifle their efforts to avoid publicizing the mistake. She died shortly after receiving a second transplant, less than two weeks after the first, while the whole world watched.[4]

At the same time, doctors, hospitals, medical liability insurance companies, and their trade and professional organizations were mounting a fierce campaign for tort reform all over the United States. Beginning in about June 2002 and reaching a peak in early 2003, the medical malpractice crisis dominated the medical news. This, too, contributed to the attention on Jesica: a public and almost impossible to understand mistake at a leading medical center, at a time when doctors claimed that frivolous medical malpractice lawsuits and outrageous jury verdicts were the problem.

Fewer people know that Jesica Santillan was actually the second girl in seven months to die after receiving a transplant with the wrong blood type at a prominent medical center. Jeanella Aranda was the first. She received a transplant of part of her father's liver at Children's Medical Center in Dallas in July 2002, allegedly after a surgical mistake in an earlier operation had destroyed her own liver.

Due to a "laboratory mix-up," according to the *New York Times*, doctors thought that her father's blood type was a good match, when it was actually her mother's who matched. "The blood type mismatch was not detected until Aug. 5, 19 days after the surgery, when Mrs. Aranda, who was aware that her husband had type A blood, noticed that Jeanella's transfusions were Type O, and asked whether the transplant had been a mis-match."[5] Jeanella died on August 6, 2002.

Shortly after Jesica died in February 2003, the *Los Angeles Times* linked her story to Jeanella's while criticizing medical liability reform proposals in Congress. "Communication errors of the sort that doomed Jesica and Jeanella are all too common in medicine," the *Times* reported. The *Times* quoted Carolyn M. Clancy, director of the federal Agency for Healthcare Research and Quality, who said, "There's more double-checking and sys-tematic avoidance of mistakes at Starbucks than at most health-care insti-tutions." And the *Times* cited a survey published in the *New England Jour-nal of Medicine*, reporting, "Only 30% of patients harmed by a medical error were told of the problem by the professional responsible for the mis-take."[6]

Jesica's and Jeanella's stories became even more tightly linked to the medical malpractice debate when the families of both girls brought med-ical malpractice claims. As far as I have been able to tell, no one called those claims frivolous. Quite the reverse. Duke Hospital publicly apologized to Jesica's family, offered to fund a new program in her name, and announced that it had changed its organ transplant procedures. Children's Medical Center appointed a new medical chief for its organ transplant program and announced that it had adopted new policies and procedures "designed to improve every link of the quality control chain." Both cases settled.[7]

Throughout the medical malpractice crisis, leading newspapers carried accounts of other obvious medical mistakes. Like the *L.A. Times* piece on Jesica and Jeanella, the accounts often linked the particular mistakes to the larger story about the extent of medical malpractice in U.S. health care. The report by the Institute of Medicine of the National Academy of Sci-ence, *To Err Is Human*, was a common source. That report summarized research showing that nearly 100,000 people die in the United States each year from medical mistakes—more than die from automobile and work-place accidents combined.[8]

Because of that research and reporting, public opinion is coming around to the view that, distressingly, Jesica's and Jeanella's problems are not unique; our health care system has a serious medical-injury problem. But at the same time, public opinion remains firmly anchored to the view that we have an explosion of what President George W. Bush calls "junk lawsuits" and that medical malpractice lawsuits contribute significantly to the high cost of health care in the United States.

Stories like Jesica's and Jeanella's helped shift public opinion about medical malpractice only because they were linked to research and reporting that reframed medical malpractice as a public health problem. But their stories did not shift public opinion about medical malpractice lawsuits, because they were not linked to research and reporting that reframed malpractice lawsuits as a public good.

Like any durable and effective myth, the medical malpractice myth can accommodate almost any number of real-life examples that conflict with the myth—by classifying those examples as exceptions. Nobody but a researcher has the time or inclination to go out and take a systematic look at medical malpractice lawsuits in order to evaluate what is the rule and what is the exception. Everyone else has to take individual examples as they come.

As a result, lawsuits like Jesica's and Jeanella's do not pose a serious challenge to the myth. No one says that all the lawsuits are frivolous. But everyone "knows" that most of them are. Even a regular drumbeat of contrary examples does not call the myth into question, because the myth provides the context in which we understand the examples, not the reverse. It is time to change that context.

THE POWER OF THE TORT LITIGATION MYTH

The medical malpractice myth is part of a larger story about the litigation explosion, the litigiousness of Americans, and the debilitating effect that lawsuits have on the U.S. economy.[9] I have often encountered this larger story in my work directing the Insurance Law Center at the University of Connecticut School of Law in Hartford, Connecticut. We try very hard to get university and insurance industry people to talk to each other. People in universities call on me to find out what is happening in the insurance industry, and people in the insurance industry call on me to find out about the university research.

One good example came in the summer of 2003 when I was invited to speak to a meeting of insurance company CEOs in London. My assignment was to provide an overview of the academic research on how the U.S.

tort system really works and, in particular, to report on the substantial research debunking many of the claims about the litigation explosion.

My host invited me to come to the whole meeting, even though my session was near the end. For me, the chance to spend two days with dozens of insurance company CEOs was quite an opportunity, so of course I accepted. An extra day in London is no hardship.

I used the time to meet and talk with quite a few of the CEOs, to see what they were like and also to get a sense of what they were expecting to hear from me. They were smart, hard-working people. They were at least as well read and informed about current events as most of my university colleagues, and on the whole they were more informed about what was happening in countries other than their own.

I was surprised and a bit concerned, however, to find that almost everyone assumed I was there to provide them with the latest research on the extent of the litigation explosion and the particular ways in which the U.S. tort system was out of control. At first I worried that they thought I had been paid to tell them whatever they wanted to hear. (I had not been paid and, even if I had, I would not have done that.) So I checked with my host to make sure he knew what they were in for. He did. In fact, he was rather looking forward to the fireworks.

My concerns addressed, I put on my participant observation research hat and resolved to find out why the CEOs expected that from me. What I learned was that they assumed I was there to talk about the out-of-control tort system not because they thought I was paid to tell them what they wanted to hear, but rather because they believed, intensely, that chaos was the real situation.

That was interesting. I had always harbored a suspicion that insurance industry leaders promoted the tort litigation myth despite what they really knew to the contrary. Maybe some do, but not these people.

The CEOs were well informed about political and economic matters generally. They were especially well informed about things that affect their business. And the U.S. liability situation affects their business. So, as far as they were concerned, if they thought that there was a tort litigation explosion in the United States and if they thought that the U.S. tort system was out of control, then that was how it was.

Whatever else anyone might think, their support for tort reform was not a cynical effort to make money at the public's expense. While the CEOs did in fact think that tort reform was in their industry's interest, the emotion that fired them up came from belief—a belief that is *not* rooted entirely in self-interest. The debate over the other major issue for which they brought outside experts to their meeting (new international accounting standards) was pale by comparison. Yet, in financial terms the accounting issue would have a much bigger immediate impact on their business than liability reform, especially for the life insurance CEOs, who are not even in the liability insurance business. The CEOs tried to get fired up about it, but they could not. Accounting rules simply do not plug into beliefs about right and wrong in remotely the same way as tort liability.

They were concerned about the litigation explosion, not just because it affected their business, but also because of the impact they expected it to have on the larger economy and society. They were concerned about the United States, where they saw the explosion originating, and Europe, where they saw signs that it was spreading. They were looking forward to hearing from me so they could better understand and treat this American disease.

In this regard at least, I am sure that I disappointed my audience. As I reported to them, except for auto accidents and the occasional "mass tort" situation like asbestos, Agent Orange, or breast implants, Americans actually do not bring tort claims all that often, especially compared to the number of accidents and injuries there are. We now have two decades of solid research documenting this fact. What is more, the rate of auto lawsuits—the most frequent kind of tort lawsuit—is going down.[10] And, despite the media focus on mass torts, products liability, and medical malpractice, those kinds of cases are far less important in dollar terms than either auto accidents or workers' compensation.

In 2003 U.S. businesses paid $27 billion for auto liability insurance premiums, $57 billion for workers' compensation insurance premiums, and less than $5 billion for products liability insurance premiums. Doctors, hospitals, and other health professionals paid only about $11 billion in medical malpractice insurance premiums. This means that the real insurance money and the real claiming action for U.S. business does not lie in high-profile areas like products liability and medical malpractice. The real action lies in routine, below-the-radar areas like workers' compensation and automobile lawsuits. U.S. businesses paid less than half as much for products liability and medical malpractice insurance, combined, as they paid for auto insurance, alone, and only a quarter of what they paid for workers' compensation insurance.

Products liability and medical malpractice insurance look even less significant compared to what ordinary Americans paid for personal auto liability and no-fault auto insurance: $115.5 billion in 2003.[11] That is more than U.S. business paid for auto, workers' compensation, products liability, and medical malpractice insurance combined. Adding all the premiums of all the different kinds of liability insurance together results in a big number—about $215 billion in 2003—but that number is hardly exploding, and the medical malpractice insurance share—$11 billion— looks pretty small by comparison. It looks even smaller next to the $1.5 trillion plus (that is more than 1,500 billion dollars) we spent on health care that year. Something that amounts to less than 1 percent of health-care costs simply cannot have the impact on health care that the medical malpractice myth would have us believe.

Even on a per doctor basis, that medical malpractice insurance number is not as high as many people think. There were nearly 900,000 doctors in the United States in 2003.[12] That means that medical malpractice insurance premiums were about $12,000 per doctor, and of course hospitals, dentists, and other health-care professionals buy malpractice insurance, too. So the average premium doctors paid was less. Some kinds of doctors have to pay much more. Obstetricians are the best-known example. But there is a simple insurance reform that will solve that problem, as I will explain in chapter 8.

Where Americans do excel in litigation is in the area of business lawsuits. If you read the business section of the newspaper, you know that B2B—business-to-business—sales are hot. So is B2B litigation. Some of the business executives who complain about the litigation explosion must be thinking about their own behavior. In one indication, the proportion of lawyers who bring personal-injury lawsuits has remained steady since 1975, while the share of lawyers involved in business litigation has more than tripled.[13]

I enjoyed the London presentation, and, as predicted, we had some vigorous debate. Did I persuade the CEOs that the tort litigation explosion is a myth? They did not get to be CEOs by lacking confidence, so they were not shy about telling me what they thought. Some argued with me then. Some continue to argue with me. But we are still talking. And their people are reading the research.

I also told them, and I continue to repeat every chance I get, that they should be careful what they wish for. What other industry asks the government to reduce the demand for its product? Tame the tort system, and hospitals and other big businesses will decide that they do not need liability insurance. Take away the risk of a really big lawsuit, and a line of credit is nearly as good as an insurance policy, and, with a line of credit, you pay only for the credit you use. Once businesses can predict their liability losses with enough certainty, a monthly savings plan is even better, and it costs even less.

Who knows how long it will take me to convince them, if I ever will. But I have already noticed a change in the rhetoric, from complaints about the *number* of lawsuits to complaints about the *size* of the lawsuits. Complaints about the size of lawsuits represent a real improvement, because at least they have some basis in reality. Medical malpractice claims are getting bigger. So are auto claims and workers' compensation claims. Of course, the fact that claims are getting bigger does not mean that the tort system is out of control. Tort claims are getting larger mostly because health care costs more than ever before.

PUTTING THE MEDICAL MALPRACTICE
MYTH IN A POLITICAL CONTEXT

My interest in the medical malpractice myth grows out of a variety of experiences that have nothing to do with politics. My father and father-in-law are both doctors. I regularly teach tort law, the branch of law that includes medical malpractice law. My field research on personal-injury litigation introduced me to many lawyers on both sides of medical malpractice lawsuits. And my role as the director of an insurance education and research program virtually guaranteed that I would want to understand the medical malpractice insurance crisis that broke out in 2002.

Despite the fact that my interest in medical malpractice is not political, there is no avoiding the fact that medical liability reform has become a very partisan issue. With some exceptions, Republican legislators favor cutting back on tort liability and Democratic legislators do not. And over the course of the last thirty years, tort reform has become one of the top political objectives of groups like the Chamber of Commerce, the American Manufacturers Association and other traditionally business-oriented trade associations. These groups support medical liability reform as part of their effort to limit tort law more broadly.

The effort currently underway in Washington to include pharmaceutical companies and medical device manufacturers under the umbrella of national medical liability reform shows how medical malpractice reform can pave the way for broader efforts to limit liability. Pharmaceutical companies and medical device manufacturers are not the target of medical malpractice lawsuits. Instead they face the same kinds of product liability claims as any other manufacturer. But their products are used in the medical field, and therefore the medical liability reform tent may be big enough to hold them, too—or so their Washington, D.C., lobbyists contend. From there, it is a small step to limit liability in other areas, so that all defendants receive equal treatment.

Doctors have conflicting interests in the larger political struggle over access to the courts. On the one hand, efforts to limit medical liability serve their long-term interest in self-regulation and professional autonomy. As researchers from Harvard Medical School have explained, "Physicians and their societies are actively resisting the legitimacy of the law as a means of controlling and regulating the practice of medicine. . . . The profession's organizations have invested extensive financial, cultural and political resources to resist what both rank-and-file practitioners and the professional collective regard as infringements on medical work."[14]

On the other hand, doctors are consumers and, increasingly, employees and independent contractors who work for large organizations. In these roles they have a strong interest in maintaining access to courts.

These conflicting interests are playing out right now in my state of Connecticut. On the one hand, our state medical society has been lobbying the Connecticut legislature, hard, in favor of medical liability reform. On the other hand, the society has filed lawsuits against several big health insurance companies that doctors believe are not playing fair. After the medical society achieved a favorable result in one of the lawsuits, I spoke to their executive director, suggesting that there might be some irony in their using the courts to advance doctors' interests—while at the same time trying to limit what patients could do in court.

He explained that there is no conflict in the two positions: the medical society's lawsuits involve different issues and different fields of law than medical malpractice. I had to agree that he was correct in technical, legal terms. But to my mind, the society is walking a tightrope. The skilled artisans and craftsmen who formed the American Federation of Labor used to think that they had more in common with businessmen than with the industrial trade unions. They changed their view in the early part of the twentieth century, when the expansion in the scope of manufacturing and construction restricted their independence and control over the workplace. Will doctors follow a similar path in the twenty-first century, when large health plans place greater pressure on health-care providers to control costs and take a more businesslike approach to health care?

Part of the art of politics is keeping supporters focused on the things they agree upon so they don't break up the coalition by fighting about other things. Tort reform is one issue on which doctors, health insurers, and most businesses clearly agree. The medical malpractice myth helps to maintain that alliance, by keeping rank-and-file doctors and the medical societies completely committed to tort reform and grateful to the (mostly Republican) politicians who deliver it.

President Bush's January 2005 speech on medical liability reform in Collinsville, Illinois, shows just how strongly his administration is promoting the medical malpractice myth. As with any major political address by a politician from either party, the visual images, alone, tell a significant story. The White House video of the speech opens with a wide-angle shot of the president walking toward a podium stationed in front of a bleacher full of cheering doctors in white coats, beneath a large banner on which the words "Affordable Healthcare" are framed between two large images of the caduceus—the twined snake and wing symbol of the American medical profession. When the camera pulls in tight for the speech, we see a striking image: President Bush, the presidential seal on the podium below, and doctors in white coats all around.

In advance of the Collinsville address, the White House had announced that the president would be discussing medical liability reform. By linking "affordable health care" with medical liability reform and surrounding the president with cheering doctors, the image conveyed a clear message. Medical malpractice lawsuits are a big reason health care is so expensive. The president supports doctors' efforts to eliminate that cost. And doctors support the president.

The speech itself delivered the same message. "I'm here to talk about how we need to fix a broken medical liability system," the president announced to a roar of applause. He mentioned by name the Illinois Republican politicians attending the speech, explained how they are supporting the cause, and offered special thanks to the Republican legislator who was "leading the medical liability reform effort" in the Illinois state legislature. After running through the top agenda items for his administration and a few other health-care reform ideas designed to control health-care costs, he arrived at his main topic:

> What's happening all across this country is that lawyers are filing base-less suits against hospitals and doctors. That's just a plain fact. And they're doing it for a simple reason. They know the medical liability system is tilted in their favor. Jury awards in medical liability cases have skyrocketed in recent years. That means every claim filed by a personal-injury lawyer brings the chance of a huge payoff or a profitable settlement out of court. That's what that means. Doctors and hospitals realize this. They know it's expensive to fight a lawsuit, even if it doesn't have any merit. And because the system is so unpredictable, there is a constant risk of being hit by a massive jury award. So doctors end up paying tens of thousands, or even hundreds of thousands of dollars to settle claims out of court, even when they know they have done nothing wrong.

From there, the speech proceeded point by point through the medical malpractice myth: the frivolous lawsuits, the courts' bias against doctors, the skyrocketing jury awards, the huge settlements in cases in which doctors did nothing wrong, the direct link between lawsuits and insurance premiums, the doctors leaving the practice of medicine, the patients who cannot find doctors, and the huge waste of money on defensive medicine. "This liability system of ours is," the president said, "what I'm telling you, is out of control."[15] It was an effective, succinct, and powerful statement of the medical malpractice myth.

It would take a book—this book I hope—to set the record straight after a speech like that.

MEDICAL MALPRACTICE LIABILITY:
PRINCIPLES AND RELATIONSHIPS

This is a book about medical malpractice: the events to which we affix the label "medical malpractice," the legal liability that may accompany that label, and the insurance that health-care providers buy to manage that liability. Medical malpractice, itself, is the topic of the next chapter, and I will discuss medical malpractice insurance most directly in chapter 3. Before going further, however, it is worth reviewing some basic features of medical malpractice liability.

Medical malpractice liability is a form of tort liability. In general, a tort occurs when one person injures another while doing something that does not meet the standard of care that the law applies in that situation. For our purposes, we can think of tort liability as resting on three legs: (1) a failure to meet the standard of care (2) that causes (3) damage. Lawyers and judges refer to these three elements of liability as standard of care, causation, and damages.

In thinking about medical malpractice, I find it helpful to compare medical malpractice liability with auto liability. There are many more auto accident claims than medical malpractice claims, so more people have experience with auto liability. Also, most people have an intuitive sense of what auto liability is about.

Consider someone who drives through a red light at an intersection and hits another car. Driving through the red light is the failure to observe the standard of care. The damage is the harm to the other car and the people inside ("damages" is the legal term for the value of that damage in monetary terms). Causation is the link between the failure to observe the standard of care and the damage.

For present purposes, we can regard the legal rules about causation and damages as essentially the same for both auto and medical liability cases. But the application of those rules, particularly causation, can be very different in a medical malpractice case. In an auto case, there is usually good evidence of a crash, so there is not any doubt that running through the red light or reaching down to answer the cell phone caused some damage. In-

stead, the typical causation question concerns only the extent of the injuries. Does the plaintiff's neck really hurt, and, if so, was that because of
the auto accident?

Causation can be much more complicated in a medical malpractice case.
Cars do not usually run over people who are about to die or lose their leg.
If death or dismemberment follows an auto accident, we can be pretty sure
that the accident was the cause. But patients usually go to doctors because
they are sick or injured. So it can be harder to sort out what difference a
mistake by the doctor may have made. The death or disability might well
have occurred whether the doctor acted properly or not.

Disputes about causation in medical malpractice cases almost always
become disputes over the possibilities and limits of medicine. Doctors and
hospitals focus on the limits of medicine, arguing that the patient would
have died or been disabled no matter what they did. Patients focus on the
possibilities of medicine, arguing that an earlier or more skilful interven-
tion, or a better-designed system, would have made all the difference.

This dynamic may help explain some of the psychological discomfort
that the topic of medical malpractice liability produces in doctors. On
the one hand, doctors are only too aware of the limits of medicine. On the
other hand they, perhaps even more than their patients, understand what
it means to believe in the possibilities of medicine. The problem is that the
boundary between the limits and the possibilities is not very clear, and the
limits can seem so much more present than the possibilities. As surgeon
and writer Atul Gawande explains, "We look for medicine to be an orderly
field of knowledge and procedure. But it is not. It is an imperfect science,
an enterprise of constantly changing knowledge, uncertain information,
fallible individuals, and at the same time lives on the line."[16] Anger about
medical malpractice liability is one place doctors direct the anxieties that
this dynamic creates. "Blame displacement," my patient-safety colleagues
call it.

At a more practical level, the defense that the doctor did not cause the
patient's injury matters most when there is some evidence that the doctor
failed in some way to measure up to the standard of care. In that case the
doctor has to argue, "Even if I did make a mistake, the patient would have
died or become disabled anyway." That is a psychologically difficult position to be in.

With standard of care, the legal rules are slightly different in auto and medical liability, in an important way. In both situations the overarching question is the same: "Did the defendant meet the standard of care?" The difference comes in how the standard of care is determined. In an auto case, the standard of care is the degree of care that a reasonable person would exercise in the circumstances. Although that may seem like an impossibly vague standard, most juries or judges do not in practice seem to have trouble applying it, perhaps because everyone has experience riding in a car, and most people have experience driving one. Also, the traffic laws define what is reasonable to an important extent, so that, in practice, questions about standard of care often become questions about whether the defendant went through a red light, ran a stoplight, crossed the yellow line, or did something else that would merit a ticket.[17]

In medical malpractice cases, the standard of care is the degree of care that a reasonable doctor would exercise in the circumstances. Most jurors and judges are not doctors, so they are not ordinarily able to evaluate whether the doctor's conduct met that standard of care without hearing evidence from other doctors. This means that a medical malpractice case almost always requires expert testimony from doctors who explain what doctors expect other doctors to do in this kind of situation.

This reasonable-doctor standard of care means that doctors, as a group, set the boundaries for what kinds of things can lead to liability. Lawyers think that this should give doctors much more comfort than in fact it does. One reason relates, again, to the limits and possibilities of medicine.

To a greater extent than many people are aware, medicine is an art rather than a science. Doctors learn to do what they do by watching and learning from other doctors, often without scientifically acceptable evidence about what works. Atul Gawande described this as well: "Spend almost any time with doctors and patients, and you will find that the larger, starker and more painful difficulty is the still abundant uncertainty that exists over what should be done in many situations. . . . In the absence of algorithms and evidence about what to do, you learn in medicine to make decisions by feel. You count on experience and judgment. And it is hard not to be troubled by this."[18]

If there is no scientifically proven, universally agreed-upon treatment, then there will be other people who would treat any given patient differently. In an actual lawsuit, the lack of certainty and the existence of multiple schools of thought or approaches turn out, perhaps surprisingly, to be very helpful to a doctor—because they make it more likely that what the doctor did was reasonable according to at least some respectable group of doctors. But this lack of certainty does not feel very comforting to a doctor in an examining or operating room. Fear or anger directed at medical malpractice liability is one possible response.

Researchers who studied obstetrical care in British Columbia wrote an evocative account of one such example. A doctor who chose a self-consciously noninterventionist approach to delivering a baby, at the mother's request, became "virtually consumed with fear" about blame and litigation when labor extended beyond the point when other doctors might have intervened.[19]

After delivering a healthy baby, the doctor told the researchers that he knew there was no rational reason for him to be concerned about legal liability. The mother strongly agreed with his approach, there had never been an obstetrical malpractice lawsuit in his community, and he did not think that she would even blame him, let alone sue him, for a bad outcome. But that knowledge did not eliminate his fear. This suggests that what he really feared was his own uncertainty about what was the right thing to do. He also feared he would blame himself if something happened to the baby. But he directed that fear at legal liability. "Fear displacement," perhaps we should call it.

As this example illustrates, medical malpractice liability differs from auto liability, not only in the rules that apply to the standard of care, and not only in the relative importance of disputes about causation, but also in the meaning that the risk of liability has for the people involved. People do not drive around in their cars worrying about auto liability blame and litigation. If there are people who do, that tells us something about them, not something about the "limits and possibilities of the automobile."

On the other hand, doctors do worry about malpractice liability often enough that those worries tell us something beyond the quirks of a few doctors. The reports about fear and anxiety are constant and validated by field research in both Canada and the United States.[20] The doctors' fear and anxiety deserve our attention, even if they are out of proportion to what the research shows about the actual risk of liability.

Another difference between auto and medical malpractice lawsuits concerns the relationship between the people involved. Over the course of a lifetime, each of us is about as likely to be a defendant in an automobile accident lawsuit as a plaintiff. Even careful drivers sometimes become distracted or neglect a traffic regulation. Thankfully, we usually manage to catch ourselves before something goes wrong, but not always. The fact that "it could be me" on the other side of the lawsuit, whichever side I am actually on, helps to dampen extreme emotions in an auto lawsuit—with the notable exception of suits involving drunk driving or other reckless behavior.

Medical malpractice lawsuits are truly different in that regard. Doctors are sometimes patients, but most patients are never doctors. In addition, the doctor and the patient have a relationship that extends beyond the lawsuit, unlike the drivers of two cars that crashed. Significantly, that relationship is hierarchical. The doctor is the expert caregiver, the patient the person in need of care, and in many cases the doctor has higher social status outside their relationship as well.

A malpractice lawsuit turns that relationship upside down. Doctors spend most of their time in institutions in which their time is a precious resource not to be wasted. Anyone who has spent any time as a patient in the hospital, or as the parent or child of a patient, is only too aware of the sense of entering a parallel universe, with the suspension of ordinary time and the expectation that the world outside the hospital will recede into the background. For doctors, however, the hospital represents an orderly flow of purposeful activity, organized to a large extent to accommodate their needs. There are good reasons for this, and the result is that the doctors are used to being in control of their environment.

Lawsuits interrupt that orderly flow of purposeful activity and deprive doctors of that sense of control. The meetings, phone calls, and paper flow of a lawsuit are just as different from doctors' usual environment as the hospital is for patients, and a great deal more hostile. Patients enter the hospital to get better. The most that a doctor can hope from a medical malpractice lawsuit is not to get worse. Interesting recent work by ethicist Lee Taft suggests that a properly managed lawsuit can provide therapeutic "ethical opportunities" for a doctor, but that idea has yet to catch hold, and I do not expect doctors to embrace malpractice lawsuits as a result. (I will discuss this further in chapter 8.)

What rational doctor would not want to reduce the chances of being pulled into a lawsuit, with its upside-down relationships and loss of control? The odds that Doctor X will one day be a patient who wants to sue another doctor are vanishingly small compared to the odds that a patient will sue Doctor X. So, unlike the auto situation, there is no internal check on Doctor X's powerful and understandable drive to restrict medical malpractice liability.

Of course, the fact that the drive is powerful and understandable does not mean that we should give it full rein. But it does help explain why doctors are ready to sign on to a worldview that tells them that this drive is noble and good, and why they are ready to support people who tell them, "Go ahead. I'll help you."

OVERVIEW OF THE BOOK

This is a book with a mission. My goal is reframing the public discussion about medical malpractice lawsuits, just as the public health research reframed the public discussion about medical malpractice itself. I want to shine so much sunlight on the medical malpractice myth that doctors and other people who care about health care cannot help but see what a misleading picture it presents. That way, the people who know a lot about medicine and the people who know a lot about law can start to talk *to* each other, rather than *at* each other, about the role that law can play in improving the quality of health care.

Because of this mission, most of the book follows the pattern of describing both myth and reality. In each chapter I lay out part of the myth, and then I explain what the research tells us about the reality. At the end of the book, I propose a set of evidence-based alternatives to the liability reform ideas that have emerged out of the medical malpractice myth.

Chapter 2 tackles the myth that medical malpractice lawsuits pose a greater threat to the public good than medical malpractice. The reality is that we have an epidemic of medical malpractice. Compared to the amount of medical malpractice, we have very little malpractice litigation. The number of lawsuits is not growing, and the overall size of the lawsuits is tracking the rate of medical inflation.

Chapter 3 addresses the myth that the explosion in medical malpractice

lawsuits and jury verdicts is to blame for the recent medical malpractice insurance crisis. The reality is that there has not been an explosion. The
boom-and-bust cycle in the insurance industry is really to blame. Tort reform will not eliminate that cycle, so we are almost certain to face similar
price increases again at some point in the future. The challenge is to re-
design the malpractice insurance market so that the cycle does not place
so much stress on doctors the next time.

Chapter 4 examines the crucially important parts of the myth laid out
in the excerpt from the president's Collinsville address: that patients sue
at the drop of a hat with no good reason, that juries regularly hand out
huge sums to almost anyone who asks, and, as a result, that doctors, hospitals, and their insurance companies have to pay large ransoms even when
the doctors did nothing wrong. None of this bears even a passing resem-
blance to reality. In fact, the research is so clearly to the contrary that the
most interesting question is why the research has not changed people's
minds.

The fact that so many medical malpractice plaintiffs do not succeed in
their suits fuels the myth, especially for doctors. But that does not make
the lawsuits frivolous. As the *L.A. Times* reported in the editorial about
Jesica and Jeanella, doctors do not have a good track record when it comes
to admitting their mistakes. One important reason people file lawsuits is to
get an answer about what happened to them, or their loved ones, because
doctors and hospitals too often do not tell them. Most people who get solid
proof that there was no mistake drop their suits once they find out.

Chapter 5 takes a break from the myth-and-reality framework to make
the case for malpractice lawsuits. It is one thing to show that malpractice
lawsuits do not have all the bad consequences that the medical malpractice
myth says. It is quite another to show that the lawsuits actually do some
good. This chapter lays out that important evidence. Medical malpractice
lawsuits are the reason we know what we know about the extent of medical
malpractice. Medical malpractice lawsuits improve patient safety. Medical
malpractice lawsuits provide compensation for some patients. And medical malpractice lawsuits promote traditional American values like justice,
responsibility, and freedom from intrusive government control.

Chapter 6 turns to the myth that fear of lawsuits leads to defensive medicine and that defensive medicine is one of the main reasons why health

care is so expensive in this country. The reality is that no one has ever been able to reliably measure defensive medicine at the health-care system level, let alone separate the good parts of defensive medicine from the bad. And even the most exaggerated numbers represent a very small share of our trillion-dollar-plus health-care system. If we are really concerned about the cost of health care, it would be much more productive to focus on all the wasteful procedures and poor-quality care that have nothing to do with fear of lawsuits.

Chapter 7 answers the myth that fear of lawsuits and high insurance prices are depriving Americans of access to health care. The reality is that we have more doctors than even before. There are occasional mismatches between patient populations and doctors. Rural areas have had doctor problems for years, and the supply of doctors in rapidly growing areas does not always keep up with demand. But those problems have almost nothing to do with medical malpractice lawsuits or malpractice insurance prices. Insurance prices may be discouraging some doctors from doing high-risk procedures, especially on a part-time basis. But that trend may actually be good for patients in some instances. The research shows that doctors and hospitals that perform procedures more frequently have better outcomes. In any event, if the concern is access to certain kinds of doctors, such as obstetricians, there are insurance reforms that could easily solve that problem.

Chapter 8 offers a program of research-driven, evidence-based legal reform. In contrast to the myth-based medical liability reforms that the White House and the American Medical Association have presented, evidence-based reform would make it easier for injured patients to bring claims. Even more important, evidence-based reform would allow patients to find out what caused their injuries without having to bring a lawsuit. Evidence-based reform would also encourage doctors and other health-care professionals to take responsibility, learn from their mistakes, and create stronger *systems* that protect patients from the inevitable human errors. Finally, evidence-based reform would provide doctors with a real solution to their liability insurance problems.

2 AN EPIDEMIC OF MEDICAL MALPRACTICE, NOT MALPRACTICE LAWSUITS

The myth that medical malpractice lawsuits pose a greater threat than medical malpractice reminds me of a phoenix. You can explode the myth as often as you want. It always rises from the ashes.

This struck home when I taught my first torts class after the Institute of Medicine of the U.S. National Academy of Sciences released its report, *To Err Is Human* in November 1999.[1] In the report the academy announced that medical errors kill up to 98,000 people in the United States every year. Newspapers across the country ran stories the next day leading with that fact.

It is not every day that a torts story gets front-page coverage in the *New York Times*, so of course I noticed. But, for me this was old news. The main study they cited was nearly ten years old. Law professors had been telling their students for years that medical malpractice kills more people than auto and workplace accidents combined.[2]

So I was surprised at the effect the story had on my students. When I arrived in class the next day there were newspaper clippings on the desk at the front of the room. I could tell that even more students had brought copies of news stories to class.

The room was buzzing. Everyone wanted to talk:

"Do you think there really is that much malpractice?"

"What are doctors and hospitals going to do about it?"

"Is it safe to go to the hospital?"

"No wonder there are so many medical malpractice lawsuits!"

That last comment got my attention. "How many medical malpractice suits do you think there are each year in Connecticut?" I asked.

"I don't know. A couple thousand?" one student ventured.

"Let's do a little math," I said, to a chorus of groans. Law students *hate* math.

"Let's assume that about ninety thousand people in the United States are killed by medical mistakes each year. Connecticut has a population of just under three and a half million, which is a little more than one percent of the U.S. population. So that means that medical mistakes kill about a thousand people each year in Connecticut. How does that fact affect your answer?"

"Well, they probably don't all sue," the student said. "After all, we learned that not even everybody who gets hurt in a car accident sues. So maybe two thousand is too high."

"But if so many people die from medical malpractice," another student offered, "probably a lot more are injured. Our torts book says that something like forty thousand people are killed in auto accidents each year. That's less than half the medical malpractice number. And think about how many auto accident cases there are. So I think you're too low. I'll say five thousand."

If you want to generate a lot of ideas on the basis of very little information, there is nothing quite like a group of bright law students. After a few more students offered their opinions, I turned to the student who guessed five thousand and asked, dramatically, "Ms. Jones, what would you say if I told you that there were fewer than four hundred medical malpractice lawsuits in Connecticut each year?"

"I'd say that's a problem," she replied. "Why aren't there more?"

Indeed. In every year since 1995 there have been over 10,000 automobile accident cases filed in the Connecticut courts and fewer than 400 medical malpractice cases.[3]

As we will soon see, there really is not any question about the epidemic of medical malpractice. Report after report stretching back into the 1970s makes that fact very clear. The reports also make clear that there really are very few medical malpractice lawsuits, especially compared to the amount of medical malpractice. Depending on how we count, there are between seven and twenty-five serious medical malpractice injuries for every one medical malpractice lawsuit. By comparison, almost everyone who gets injured by a negligent driver files an auto lawsuit or claim.

Yet, medical and hospital associations across the country act as if medical malpractice lawsuits threaten the public health even more than medical malpractice. And the tort reform legislation enacted in many states since 2000 suggests that legislators and voters believe them. Patient advocacy groups in each of the states that passed tort reform in the last few years surely knew about this research. So knowing the facts is not enough.

Documenting the extent of medical malpractice is only the beginning. If we want to begin to understand how to motivate people to do something about the epidemic, we need to answer some very different questions.

Why is the medical malpractice epidemic news each time the next report confirms the old reports? Why does the old news never stick in the public's mind? Why were my students surprised in 1999 when the Institute of Medicine report came out? Why are the well-educated and very bright students in my first-year law school torts class *always* surprised about the extent of medical malpractice?

It is not just that people are allergic to statistical information. There is more going on. Part of that "more" is the totally untrue, but firmly believed myth that there is more medical malpractice litigation than medical malpractice. There is enormous power in a simple and widely repeated myth, particularly when the underlying reality it describes is not something that you can see or touch.

But now I am getting ahead of myself. We first need to review the research documenting the high rate of medical malpractice and the low rate of medical malpractice lawsuits.

THE RESEARCH ON THE MEDICAL
MALPRACTICE EPIDEMIC

Experts think that most serious medical mistakes either happen in the hospital or have consequences that put people in the hospital. For this reason, researchers who want to learn about medical malpractice usually look in hospitals. When they do, they use one of two approaches. Either they review a large number hospital records from many hospitals and count the number of mistakes. Or they watch doctors and nurses in one hospital, real time. Both approaches have strengths and weaknesses.

The hospital record approach has two main strengths. Researchers can easily preserve the anonymity of the hospitals. This makes it easier to get hospitals to participate. And the researchers can look at records from many hospitals. This allows them to make a strong claim that the rate of errors they find in their research is the same as the rate of errors in hospitals generally. The hospital record approach also has an obvious weakness. Namely, the researchers look only at the hospital records. Common sense tells us (and the research we will review confirms) that not all mistakes get noted in the record. Also, not all mistakes take place in the hospital.

The strength of the hospital observation approach comes from its very nature. Watching doctors and nurses in the hospital gives researchers a much more complete understanding of what happens. But we can never be sure how the hospital they are studying compares to other hospitals. Overcoming that weakness requires disclosing information about the hospital, making it more likely that we could figure out which hospital it was. Few hospitals today are willing to open themselves up to intense public scrutiny, especially when it is possible that other people could "break the code" and use that information against the hospital.

Over the next few pages I will review the leading hospital records studies and the leading hospital observation study. As we will see, all the studies demonstrate that a surprisingly large amount of medical malpractice takes place in American hospitals.

The California Medical Insurance Feasibility Study

The first important hospital record study was the mid-1970s California study I mentioned in the first chapter. The California Hospital Association and the California Medical Association commissioned this study during the first medical malpractice insurance crisis. They called the study the Medical Insurance Feasibility Study because the goal was to evaluate whether it would be feasible to create a no-fault medical insurance alternative to medical malpractice litigation.[4]

The California study took place so long ago that it is difficult to know for sure, but the California team apparently expected to confirm two aspects of the 1970s version of the medical malpractice myth. The California researchers expected to find that medical malpractice was not as big a problem as lawyers had claimed. And they expected to confirm that the price of a no-fault system would be less than medical malpractice premiums doctors and hospitals were paying.[5]

What they found was very different.

They found that doctors and hospitals injured what must have been to them an almost unbelievably large number of patients: one out of every twenty patients discharged from the hospital. Even more striking, one out of every ten of the injured patients died as a result. This meant that doctors and hospitals injured at least 140,000 hospital patients in California in 1974 and killed nearly 14,000 of them.[6]

The California researchers not only found an epidemic of medical injuries, they also found an epidemic of medical malpractice. They concluded that one out of every six medical injuries resulted from malpractice. This means that doctors and hospitals committed malpractice on 24,000 California patients in 1974. The California researchers also found that the more severe the injury was, the more likely that it was caused by malpractice. As many as 80 percent—four out of every five—of the most seriously injured patients were the victims of medical malpractice.[7]

Thus, the research clearly contradicted the assumption that injured patients and their lawyers were exaggerating the malpractice problem. The research also contradicted the assumption that doctors in California could save money by adopting a no-fault approach to compensating patients with medical injuries. That assumption was based on the belief that medical malpractice was not a widespread problem. Once the researchers discovered how many medical injuries there were, a no-fault approach was almost guaranteed to be more expensive than what they had. Under a no-fault approach, all of the injured patients would qualify for compensation, not just the patients who were injured by negligence.

Although the California researchers did not publish any cost calculations, Wharton professor Patricia Danzon later used their results to show that there is no way that a broad no-fault system would be less expensive that the existing tort system. As she demonstrated, only a very small percentage of injured patients were compensated through medical malpractice claims—somewhere between one in seventy five and one in a hundred of those who were injured. This means that at least seventy-five times more patients would be eligible for no-fault compensation than were then collecting in tort.[8]

If even a quarter of the eligible people actually filed claims, no-fault would be much, much more expensive than tort, almost no matter how meager the benefits or how much the cost savings that resulted from eliminating the tort system's negligence requirement. So it is easy to see why the sponsors of the California study—the California Medical Association and the California Hospital Association—did not immediately start lobbying for a new no-fault medical-injury compensation fund.

Putting all this together, what can we say? We can say that the California study showed that the real medical malpractice problem was medical malpractice, not medical malpractice litigation. It showed that by far the largest share of medical malpractice costs fall on injured patients and their families, not on doctors and hospitals. And we can say that the response of the California Hospital Association and the California Medical Association to the study was disappointing. The associations put the study on the shelf and turned their priorities elsewhere.

The Harvard Medical Practice Study

The next, and most important, hospital record study was the New York study I also mentioned in the first chapter. In the mid-1980s, during the second medical malpractice insurance crisis, the State of New York commissioned a team of doctors, public health researchers, and lawyers from Harvard to study medical injuries in New York and to evaluate approaches to compensating injured patients. Because the Harvard Medical Practice Study has been the most important study for the malpractice policy debates, I will spend more time explaining how they conducted their research.

The Harvard team had the benefit of both the California study and Professor Danzon's analysis. So they knew that they were likely to find a lot of malpractice. They also knew that the conventional wisdom among doctors was that medical malpractice was a very rare event and that there were more medical malpractice lawsuits than cases of medical malpractice. So they knew that they had to put together a bulletproof research design that would produce a credible and very conservative measure of medical malpractice injuries.

The Harvard researchers began by selecting a random sample of 31,000 hospital records from over fifty hospitals. They reviewed the records in two stages. In the first stage nurses reviewed all 31,000 records using a detailed screening form. The form contained a very specific list of conditions that could indicate that the patient was injured from medical treatment. For example, did the patient develop an infection shortly after surgery, or was the patient readmitted to the hospital soon after being sent home? If

the record did not contain any of the evidence that the nurses were looking for, the hospitalization was classified as not involving a medical management injury and the records for that hospitalization did not receive any
further review.

Nearly 8,000 of the 31,000 records—about one in four—contained evidence of a possible medical injury.[9] Each of these 8,000 records advanced
to the second stage of the review process.

For the second stage, the researchers taught doctors how to use hospital records to identify medical management injuries and how to evaluate
whether the injuries resulted from substandard care. Two doctors reviewed each record using a special form prepared to guide the review. The
doctors worked independently, so that no one doctor's conclusions affected any other doctor's conclusions. This is one of the hallmarks of good
research.

Each doctor first confirmed that the nurse who had reviewed the hospital record had accurately identified one of the conditions indicating a
possible medical injury. If not, the research team classified the record as a
"no injury" case, and set the record aside. If the nurse had correctly inter-
preted the record, the doctor gave the hospitalization an "adverse event"
score from one to six indicating the strength of the evidence of a medical
management injury.[10]

If that adverse-event score was two or higher, the doctor filled out a section of the review form titled "Is there evidence for negligence?" The first
step in the negligence section asked the doctor to answer "yes" or "no" to
the following question: "Was this adverse event possibly due to a reasonably avoidable error, or carelessness by either an individual or medical care
system, or both?" If the doctor answered "no," the review was over, and
the team classified the hospitalization as a "no negligence" case. Impor-
tantly, if either doctor answered "no," the research team classified the injury as nonnegligent.

If the answer to the first negligence question was "yes," the doctor answered questions about the circumstances. The questions ended by asking
the doctor to reconsider whether the injury was possibly due to negligence.[11] If the doctor changed his or her mind, the review was over, and the
team classified the hospitalization as a no-negligence case. Otherwise the
doctor gave the hospitalization a negligence score from one to six indicat-

ing the strength of the evidence for negligence (like that for medical management injuries). A score of six meant "virtually certain." A score of one meant "little or no evidence."

A supervisor took the two doctors' forms, checked to be sure that they had looked at the same records, and then calculated the averages of their confidence scores. The supervisor classified the hospitalization as an injury case only if the average of the doctors' confidence scores on that point was more than 3.5. Similarly, the supervisor classified the injury as negligent only if the average of the reviewers' confidence scores on that point was more than 3.5. The practical effect of this 3.5 cutoff is that either doctor could veto the decision of the other. If one doctor classified the case as a no-injury case, that was it. And if one doctor said that the injury did not result from negligence, that also was it.

This was a very conservative approach to identifying negligent medical management injuries, an approach that would be trusted by doctors. Doctors designed and supervised the study. Doctors trained the nurses who carried out the first-stage review. Doctors conducted the second-stage review. And the review process had a variety of safeguards against a mistaken conclusion that there was a medical management injury or negligence (and essentially no safeguards against a mistaken conclusion that there was not negligence).[12] This means that we can be reasonably confident that there is *even more* medical malpractice than the Harvard team reported.

It is important to be clear that I am not criticizing the Harvard team. They knew that their results would be scrutinized and that organized medicine stood ready to attack even the slightest weakness in their data or analysis suggesting that they were exaggerating the extent of medical malpractice. Given that political reality, it was perfectly reasonable to design the study to withstand the anticipated attack. After all, even their very conservative estimates showed that medical malpractice was a much bigger problem than almost anyone had thought.

The results were essentially the same as the earlier California results. The Harvard team found that doctors and hospitals injured about one out of every twenty-five hospital patients and that there was negligence in about one out of every four of those cases.

This means that there were at least 27,000 injuries from medical malpractice in hospitals in New York during 1984. As in the California study, more serious injuries were more likely to be the result of negligence. Ex-trapolating to the United States as a whole, the researchers concluded that there are "over 150,000 iatrogenic fatalities annually, more than half of which are due to negligence."[13]

By comparison, there were only about 3,800 claims filed in New York under malpractice insurance policies covering the year 1984.[14] That means that there were more than seven malpractice injuries for every medical malpractice claim.

The Utah and Colorado Validation Study

During the 1990s two significant research projects found even higher rates of medical management injuries than either the Harvard or the Cal-ifornia studies. One of these projects was a large-scale hospital record study in Australia. The second was an intensive, hospital-based observa-tion study in Illinois.[15] I will discuss these studies shortly. Although the definitions used in the two studies are not exactly the same, a fair reading of their results is that one out of every six hospital patients suffers from some kind of medical management injury, a substantial proportion of which should have been prevented. This was an even more disturbing fig-ure than the already disturbing result from the California and New York studies.

In light of these other studies, the Harvard team decided to conduct a second study to check their earlier results. In order to avoid the objection that their results were unique to New York, they conducted the second study in a different part of the country: Utah and Colorado. This time the study year was 1992.

As before, the team obtained a sample of records from almost every hospital in the region. They put the records through a two-stage review similar to the one in New York. They improved their ability to eliminate "false positives" (mistaken conclusions that there was a medical injury or negligence). And for the first time they took measures to reduce "false negatives" (mistaken conclusions that an injury did not result from neg-ligence).[16]

The Utah and Colorado results were essentially the same as the results from New York and California. The team found a slightly lower rate of medical injuries—3 percent in Utah and Colorado in 1992 as compared to 5 percent in California in 1974 and 4 percent in New York in 1984. But they also found that a larger proportion of the medical injuries resulted from negligence, so that the overall rate of negligent injuries was approximately the same—1 percent.[17]

The slight differences between the results of the two Harvard studies make sense in light of the changes they made in the hospital record review process. The new Utah/Colorado review process did an even better job of eliminating false positives, so it makes sense that they found a lower rate of injuries. But the Utah/Colorado review process also did a better job of reducing the chance that negligence would be overlooked, so it makes sense that they found that more of the injuries resulted from negligence. All in all, the differences in the New York and Colorado/Utah results probably reflect the changes in the review process more than differences in the true rate of injuries or negligence.

Details aside, both studies showed that there is much more medical malpractice than most people think. Imagine if a new drug made one out of a hundred people sick. How long would it last on drugstore shelves? Or if one out of a hundred planes or buses crashed? Or if one out a hundred lawn mowers sent people to the emergency room? Yet the Harvard studies represent the low end of estimates. Other well-regarded studies suggest that there is even more—a lot more—malpractice.

The Quality in Australian Health-Care Study

By all accounts, the Australian health-care system is among the best. As part of a commitment to health quality, the Australian government decided to fund a research project modeled on the Harvard New York study. The goal was to identify ways to improve the quality of health care in Australian hospitals.

After the experience in California and New York, the Australian government surely expected to find some mistakes. But what they found was even worse than they expected. Using what they thought were the same research methods as the Harvard team, the Australians found that doctors and hospitals injured one out of every six hospital patients in Australia and that half of those injuries were preventable.[18] This was four times the rate of injuries found in the Harvard Medical Practice Study. For obvious reasons, these results shocked the Australian medical community and public as well as public health investigators in the United States and elsewhere.

Among public health researchers, the Australian study raised almost as many questions about the American studies as it did about Australian hospitals. Given the similar education, training, and practices of doctors in hospitals in the United States and Australia, it seemed unlikely that the quality of medical care in the two countries would differ so widely. Experts knew that the Harvard estimates were low, but was the real extent of medical management injuries as high as the Australian research suggested?

So, in addition to conducting the Utah/Colorado validation study, the Harvard research team sat down with the Australians and carefully compared their research methods and results. What they found was that the two research teams had not in fact used the same methods to identify medical management injuries.[19] The Australians had trained their nurses to send a higher percentage of cases to the second-stage review. The Australians used a lower threshold on the medical management injury score. The Australian doctors' review process was less heavily weighted toward avoiding false positives. And the Australians counted injuries that happened during the study period but were not discovered until afterward.

The details of these differences do not matter for us. What matters is that the Australians' research design was reasonable, as the members of the Harvard team who compared the studies agreed.[20] This confirms that the Harvard approach to measuring medical injuries produces a low estimate. Analyzing the Australian data using the Harvard approach reduced the rate of injuries in Australian hospitals by 70 percent. And analyzing the Harvard data using the Australian approach would increase the rate of injuries in Colorado and Utah hospitals by 70 percent.[21]

The Australians considered whether the injuries were preventable, rather than whether the injuries resulted from negligence, so the two studies are not completely comparable in that regard. The Australians defined "preventable" to mean "an error in management due to the failure to follow accepted practice at an individual or system level."[22] As noted earlier, the Harvard team defined negligence to mean "a reasonably avoidable error, or carelessness by either an individual or medical care system, or both."

Although these definitions are almost identical, there are negative overtones to the label "negligent" that are not associated with "preventable." For this reason we cannot directly compare the results. The Australian researchers concluded that half of the medical management injuries were preventable, which is nearly twice the proportion of medical management injuries that the Harvard teams concluded were negligent.

For our purposes, the important point is that changing the review process in relatively small ways increases the number of preventable medical management injuries substantially, and that many of these surely result from negligence. Once again, this is not a criticism of the Harvard team. Given the political context in which they were operating, they had to design and carry out a study that counted medical injuries and medical malpractice so conservatively that no one could complain that they were exaggerating the extent of the medical malpractice epidemic.

There is not any question about whether they succeeded in documenting the medical malpractice epidemic. They did. The question is why it is taking so long for people to notice. We will turn to that question after looking at the hospital observation studies.

Hospital Observation Studies

Hospital observation studies take a very different approach. Trained observers watch and listen to what is happening to patients. The researchers are "flies on the wall," recording events as they happen and as doctors and nurses talk about them later. They can take advantage of the information in the hospital record, but they are not limited to that information.

A research team from Chicago universities conducted the most significant hospital observation study at "a large, tertiary care, urban teaching hospital affiliated to a university medical school." As this description of the hospital suggests, hospital administrators are cautious, and understandably so, about opening their hospital up to this kind of study. Based on the identities and affiliations of the researchers, it is not hard to guess about which hospital they were in. So it is hardly surprising that very few studies of this type have been done.

Although experts know that there is a lot of medical malpractice in hospitals, the public and even a surprising number of doctors do not know this. So a very public announcement about the high rate of injuries in a particular hospital could easily lead people to conclude that this hospital is much less safe than other hospitals. Probably only one of the safest hospitals would even consider allowing researchers in the door, but the public might well not understand this.

The Chicago hospital observation study took place over a nine-month period in 1989 and 1990, well after Professor Danzon published her analysis of the California study and while preliminary results of the Harvard Medical Practice Study already were trickling out. In light of all the injuries and errors found in these hospital record studies, the Chicago team was certain to find something in the hospital they were observing. If they could find so many mistakes just by looking in the hospital records, imagine what a fly on the wall could see.

In fact, an early observational study from the 1960s found that 20 percent of hospital patients suffered a medical management injury. A later study found that the number was even higher—36 percent—and many of those were very serious.[23] That is more than twice the rate of injuries that even the Australian hospital record researchers had found. Opening the "large, tertiary, urban teaching hospital affiliated to a university medical school" to the research team was therefore an act of courage, and the hospital administrators deserve our appreciation.

Four experienced and specially trained researchers did the observation. For nine months one of the four observed every organized daytime setting in which nurses and doctors discussed the patients being treated in three units in the hospital. This included the rounds by attending physicians, rounds by residents, nursing shift-change discussions, case conferences and every other scheduled meeting in the units. They also attended relevant section and department meetings, including quality-assurance reviews and morbidity and mortality conferences.

The observers recorded everything that anyone said about adverse events during any of these meetings or discussions. The research team defined "adverse event" for this purpose to mean any "situation in which an inappropriate decision was made when, at the time, an appropriate alternative could have been chosen." This means that adverse events included mistakes that did not cause any harm. And it also means that an adverse event that caused harm would not in all cases be regarded as negligent for purposes of a medical malpractice claim. So we must be careful when using the study to draw conclusions about medical malpractice.

The observers did not make medical judgments. They simply noted who said what about an adverse event, including whether anyone was blamed and whether the patient was harmed as a result. They did not ask questions either, with the result that they sometimes were missing information, for example about the consequences of an event. The research team also reviewed all the records about adverse events, including the patient charts, incident report forms, and documents relating to any complaints that the patients made.

The results of the research were troubling. Mistakes were made on almost half of the patients. The mistakes seriously injured nearly 20 percent of the patients, causing anything from temporary disability to death. The sicker the patient or the longer she was in the hospital, the more likely there was a mistake. And mistakes caused patients to stay in the hospital longer, increasing the chance that there would be another mistake.

For our purposes, the key finding is that 20 percent of the patients suffered a serious injury from an adverse event. Does that mean that 20 percent of the patients in the Chicago study hospital were the victims of medical malpractice?

As I just noted, the Chicago team's definition of "adverse event" does not match up perfectly with the legal standard for medical malpractice. Courts instruct juries to consider whether the medical treatment met the standard of generally accepted medical care. This is not exactly the same as the Chicago team's definition—"an inappropriate decision was made when, at the time, an appropriate alternative could have been chosen."

As with the Australian researcher's "preventable" standard, I think that the Chicago team's "adverse event" standard is functionally very close to the legal standard for negligence. But, as with the Australian research, a conservative approach to interpreting the Chicago research would not count all of their adverse events as medical malpractice. That means that we need to estimate what percentage of the Chicago team's adverse events involved negligence.

One way to do this is by comparing the results in the Harvard and Australian studies and then using that comparison to adjust the Chicago results.

As I pointed out earlier, both the Australian and the Harvard research teams asked reviewers to evaluate whether there was an adverse event, by which they meant an injury that resulted from medical treatment (or lack of treatment). The Australians went on to ask whether the injury was preventable, while the Harvard teams asked whether the injury resulted from negligence.

The labels here can be difficult to keep track of, but it is safe to say that the Australian approach corresponds closely to the Chicago team's approach. In other words, a "preventable" injury in the Australian study is the equivalent of an injury from an "adverse event" in the Chicago study. So we can estimate the rate of negligent errors in the Chicago hospital by comparing the rate at which the Australian research teams decided that medical management injuries were preventable with the rate at which the Harvard team decided that medical management injuries were negligent.

The Australian researchers were twice as likely to conclude that an injury was preventable as the Harvard researchers were to conclude that an injury was negligent. This gives us a good reason to believe that at least one half of all *preventable* medical management injuries are *negligent*. And that gives us a good reason to believe that nearly 10 percent of the patients in the Chicago study suffered from a negligent medical management injury.

This is larger than the rate of preventable injuries in the Australian study and five times the rate of negligent injuries in the Harvard study. While of course it is possible that the Chicago study hospital was a particularly unsafe hospital, the fact that the hospital opened the hospital to the researchers suggests that the hospital's administrators did not think so. Although it is impossible to be absolutely sure that the "large, tertiary, urban teaching hospital affiliated to a university medical school" is representative of hospitals generally, other hospital observation studies reach very similar results.[24] The more likely explanation for the large difference between the Chicago and the Harvard results is that a "fly on the wall" sees and hears much more than someone who only gets to look in the medical record. Toward that end, it is important to note that the Chicago researchers observed only regularly scheduled, daytime meetings. As a result, they concluded that there almost certainly were even more preventable medical injuries than they had found.

Putting all this together, both the Australian hospital record research and the Chicago hospital study provide good evidence that the Harvard team's estimate was low and that the medical malpractice epidemic is even worse than they reported.

THE RESEARCH ON MALPRACTICE LAWSUITS

I will review much of the research on medical malpractice law-suits in chapter 4. For now, I will simply report what the research says about the number and size of malpractice lawsuits in order to demonstrate that there is no epidemic.

Each of the major hospital record review studies showed that there were many more cases of medical malpractice than medical malpractice law-suits. As Professor Danzon explained, the California study showed that there were ten serious injuries from medical malpractice for every medical malpractice lawsuit filed in the 1970s. The Harvard research showed that there were at least seven serious injuries from medical malpractice for every medical malpractice lawsuit filed in New York in the late 1980s and at least six serious injuries from medical malpractice for every medical malpractice lawsuit filed in Utah and Colorado in the early 1990s.[25] And, as I will discuss further in chapter 4, the Harvard researchers and the Chicago researchers each found that only one out of every twenty-five pa-tients with a negligent or preventable medical injury brought a medical malpractice claim.

This is hardly a picture of medical malpractice lawsuits running amok. Nevertheless, the careful reader will notice that those studies are getting old and wonder whether more patients have started bringing malpractice claims in recent years.

They have not. The three states for which we have the best information are Texas, Florida, and Missouri. These states require insurance compa-nies to file detailed reports about medical malpractice claims. The reports show that the rate of claims has held steady or even declined in relation to population and economic growth over the last fifteen years.

The results from Texas and Florida are particularly important. Texas is the second most populous state in the country. Florida is the fourth. The American Medical Association listed both as states with a "medical lia-bility crisis" in 2003.[26] Both were "plaintiff-friendly" jurisdictions at this time. If in fact there were any states with an epidemic of medical malprac-tice lawsuits, Texas and Florida would surely have been among them.

Texas requires insurers to report all malpractice claims when they are closed, whether there is a payment or not. A team led by University of

Texas researchers has analyzed the Texas claim records for the 1988–2002 period. The title of their report is telling: "Stability, Not Crisis: Medical Malpractice Outcomes in Texas, 1988–2002." The number of claims increased during this period, but so did the population and the number of doctors in Texas. Adjusting for population growth, the number of claims was stable; adjusting for the growth in the number of doctors, the number of claims declined. The size of claims increased as well, but the researchers concluded that all of the increase is due to medical inflation and a shift toward more severe-injury claims.[27]

Florida also requires insurers to report medical malpractice claims when they are closed, but Florida stopped requiring insurers to report claims closed without a payment in 1997. This means that we do not have a measure of the total number of claims closed for years after 1998. Nevertheless, the information that we do have strongly suggests that claiming has remained stable for over ten years. A Duke research team analyzing the Florida records reports there is trend toward an increase in the number of paid claims, but the trend is comparable to the rate of population growth in Florida. The total number of claims closed each year between 1990 and 1997 (the last year insurers reported claims closed with no payment) fluctuated from year to year, but there was no consistent increasing trend. The size of claims did increase over the period, but this increase appears to result largely from inflation and an increase in the severity of injuries.[28]

Missouri requires insurance companies and self-insured hospitals and groups to report each medical malpractice claim they receive and each claim that they close. Figures from the Missouri Department of Insurance show that the number of new medical malpractice claims filed each year has declined from 1988 to 2002. So, too, the number of claims closed. For example, the average of the number of closed claims per year declined from 1894 per year during the 1988–1991 period to 1572 per year during the 1999–2002 period. With regard to the size of claims, Missouri reports that "wage inflation (for patients' lost income), medical inflation and increasing injury severity continue to account for *all* the increase in awards since 1990."[29]

WHY AREN'T MORE PEOPLE MORE UPSET
ABOUT THE MALPRACTICE EPIDEMIC?

As I pointed out at the beginning of the chapter, the medical malpractice epidemic is not exactly news. Although the California associations did not publicize their results, Professor Danzon did. Her book came out in 1985. The Harvard team published two books in the early 1990s, and other books about malpractice came out at about the same time.[30]

Yet, common experience suggests—and opinion polls confirm—that most people still do not think medical mistakes are a serious public health problem. One highly regarded academic research team surveyed doctors and the public in 2002 asking whether they or a member of their family had personally experienced medical malpractice in their own health care. The survey also asked people to state in their own words the two most important problems with health care and medicine.[31]

The survey team found that an enormous number of people had personal experience with medical errors. Among doctors the rate was 35 percent, and among the public the rate was 42 percent. Half of those with personal experience said that the health consequences of the mistakes were serious. Also, nearly one-third of all the doctors said that they had seen a mistake in their professional capacity during the last year.

But neither the doctors nor the general public said that medical errors were one of the most significant health-care problems. Doctors most often said that the cost of malpractice insurance and lawsuits was a serious problem, followed by the cost of health care. Ordinary people most often said that the cost of health care was a serious problem, followed by the cost of prescription drugs. Only 5 percent of the doctors and only 6 percent of the general public said that anything to do with medical mistakes was one of the most serious problems—except of course the doctors, who complained about the liability and insurance consequences of the mistakes, but not the mistakes themselves.

A very recent poll by the same research team suggests that people might be starting to realize we have a problem. About half of the general public said that improving the quality of medical care and reducing errors should be a top priority for the president and Congress this year.[32] But they continued to regard the cost of health care as the most significant problem. And well over half said that medical malpractice lawsuits were a very important factor in that high cost.

Why has it taken so long for the doctors and the public to focus on medical mistakes? And why are they so wrong about the impact that medical malpractice lawsuits have on health-care costs? The best research shows that the price tag for medical malpractice insurance, medical malpractice lawsuits, and the associated expenses is somewhere between 1 and 2 percent of health-care expenses,[33] so malpractice lawsuits in fact are *not* an important factor in the high cost of health care. (Some readers surely are wondering about defensive medicine at this point. I discuss defensive medicine in chapter 6. The short answer is that there is a lot of talk about defensive medicine, but little proof.)

With regard to doctors, I do not have a better answer to these questions than their self-interest and the influence of organized medicine. No one believes that all doctors have consciously put their heads in the sand. There were doctors on all the teams that documented the medical malpractice epidemic. And no one is working harder than public health doctors to do something about that epidemic.

But ordinary doctors working sixty or more hours a week, seeing patients, dealing with health insurance, and trying to keep up with the medical literature, do not have time to do a careful review of the health-care policy literature. They develop their understandings about health system problems through a diffuse and hard-to-pin-down process that involves lots of talking with other doctors and, at best, a quick look at a short abstract describing the results of the research. Organized medicine overwhelms that process with horror stories about medical malpractice litigation and insurance, to the point where ordinary doctors can almost be forgiven for still believing that medical malpractice litigation is a more serious problem than medical malpractice.

What psychologists call the "self-serving bias" helps explain how doctors process information about medical mistakes and medical malpractice lawsuits. As psychologists explain, "People attempt to construct a rational justification for conclusions that they want to draw. To that end they search through memory for relevant information, but the search is biased in favor of information that is consistent with the desired conclusions."[34]

This bias is nearly universal and does not reflect any kind of character flaw on the part of doctors. But it does means that stories about unfair lawsuits literally count more than the occasional references to research on medical mistakes, despite the fact that the research is a far better guide to medical malpractice and medical malpractice lawsuits.

Perhaps ironically, the evenhandedness of most of the research on medical malpractice lawsuits reduces the likelihood that the research will persuade busy doctors. As we will see in chapter 4, careful research on medical malpractice lawsuits always reports that plaintiffs sometimes are paid in situations in which the doctor did nothing wrong and that even larger numbers of, ultimately unsuccessful, lawsuits are brought in such situations. When seen through the lens of the self-serving bias, these parts of the research appear to be consistent with the medical malpractice myth, despite the fact that the research shows that the legal system does a good job weeding out weaker claims.

Experts at the AMA and the other organizations that represent doctors' interests certainly have the capacity to pull together the research as I have done in this book and reeducate their members about medical malpractice and medical malpractice lawsuits, but the results would not serve the short-term financial and political interests of their members.

The theologian Reinhold Niebuhr explored how organized self-interest overcomes good intentions in the aptly named book *Moral Man and Immoral Society*. As he explained, individuals "may be moral, in the sense that they are able to consider interests other than their own" and "they are capable, on occasion, of preferring the advantages of others to their own." But it is nearly impossible for groups to be moral in this sense: "In every human group there is less reason to guide and to check impulse, less capacity for self-transcendence, less ability to comprehend the needs of others and therefore more unrestrained egoism than the individuals, who comprise the group, reveal in their personal relationships."[35] Niebuhr would hardly have been surprised at the political behavior of organized medicine.

With regard to the public, my answer turns on the politics of risk perception. The politics of risk perception affect doctors and other health-care workers, too, but professional self-interest provides such a strong explanation for their behavior that we hardly need consider anything else.

Self-interest cannot explain the behavior of the general public, however, so we need to look deeper.

_____

MEDICAL MALPRACTICE AND THE
POLITICS OF RISK PERCEPTION

No one wakes up in the morning, boots up his brain, and then runs a risk calculation program that spits out the things to worry about that day. Instead, we worry about what our coworkers, friends and family say to us, what is reported in the newspaper, what we listen to while driving to work in the morning, or what we see on television.

Even then, we do not count up the references to different problems, weight them according to the degree of confidence we have in the source, and then test the results against our past experience. Most of us, most of the time, process whatever information we receive about important public policy issues in an unconscious fashion that no one fully understands.

How this works is a hot topic in any number of departments in universities all over the world today. Psychologists, economists, anthropologists, political scientists, and even people in humanities departments like English and philosophy are trying to figure out why we notice what we notice and how we come to have the view of the world that we do. I have only dabbled in this area,[36] but I am confident that the answer at this point is largely "Who knows?" Nevertheless, there are a few things to report that might help answer the question before us.

First, researchers in a variety of fields report what we probably all learned long ago, the hard way: it is very hard to change people's minds. People are so attached to their views of the world that they notice things that fit with how they think the world works, and they do not notice things that conflict with how they think the world works. This does not mean that people never notice contrary information, just that they tend not to.

So if I do not think that medical malpractice is a big problem, it is going to take more than a few newspaper articles about complicated research projects to get me to change my mind, especially if I basically like and trust my doctors. Similarly, if I think that medical malpractice lawsuits are a big problem, it is going to be very difficult to change my mind because I will notice every news story and other report about medical malpractice lawsuits, while I will be much less likely to notice reports that compare the rate of medical malpractice with the rate of malpractice litigation. As the *Wall Street Journal* headline writers put it, "People Believe a 'Fact' That Fits Their Views Even If It's Clearly False."[37]

Second, although our brains have capacities that outstrip even the most advanced computers, we are not very good at estimating how often something happens, and we are even worse at estimating whether one thing happens more often than another. If we decide to be worried about a very low-frequency event—for example an explosion at a nuclear power plant—we tend to imagine that the chances of this happening are much higher than they really are. On the other hand, we often act as if there were absolutely no chance that some really horrific things could happen when the chances are well above zero.[38] The World Trade Center disaster comes to mind.

We are not much better at evaluating the frequency of things that are much more likely to happen. As psychologists report, our ideas about how often something happens depend on many things that have little or nothing to do with how often they actually happen. Something that confirms our view of the world counts more than something that conflicts with our view of the world. Something that happens to someone we know counts more than something that happens to someone we don't know. Something that we hear about often counts more that something we hear about less often.

When it comes to politically charged things like medical malpractice and medical malpractice litigation, we do not hear about a randomly selected set of events. We hear more—much more—about events that organized interests tell us about, either directly or through public relations campaigns aimed at the media and public opinion leaders. And when it comes to medical malpractice, the organized interests who want to downplay the impact of malpractice and exaggerate the impact of lawsuits have outhustled, outspent, and just plain beat the other team in mobilizing public opinion.[39] The AMA and their tort reform allies have a clear, simple story that fits into the larger story about the litigation explosion. As a result, every news story about a lawsuit scores a hit on the information receptors in the litigation-myth sector of the brain. Research showing that malpractice lawsuits are not the big problem people think, probably will not even make the news. But if it does make the news, it makes the news just once—hardly enough to overcome the information-processing bias that keeps people wedded to their views.

If you are reading this book, you have decided to give considerably more attention to this issue. I urge you to keep reading, especially if you are inclined to disagree with me. The next chapter will explain how we could have a malpractice insurance crisis despite the fact that the malpractice lawsuit situation was stable. After that, I will review the research showing that malpractice lawsuits generally have more merit than the AMA would have you believe and that the legal system does a reasonably good job weeding out the weaker claims.

3 AN INSURANCE CRISIS, NOT A TORT CRISIS

I don't like to hear insurance-company executives
say it's the tort system—it's self inflicted.
—Donald J. Zuk, chief executive of SCPIE Holdings,
a leading medical malpractice insurer.

Anyone who reads the paper or watches the news knows that medical malpractice insurance premiums have gone up over the last few years—and that doctors, hospitals, and insurance companies blame lawyers, judges, and juries for this situation. The AMA's refrain is "The tort system is out of control." The TV or newspaper image that anchors that refrain in the public mind is a throng of doctors in white coats massed on the steps of the state capital demanding tort reform.

It is not crazy to think that malpractice lawsuits are the reason for the insurance premium hikes. Few people really understand how insurance companies work, but most people do know this: Over the long run, an insurance company works something like a bank. The amount of money going in has to equal the amount of money going out. So it is not crazy for doctors to think that big increases in the amount of money coming in the front door—the malpractice insurance premiums—must reflect a big increase in the amount of money going out the back door—payments for medical malpractice cases.

Not crazy, but not right either. As we will see, the insurance industry goes through a boom-and-bust cycle that creates medical malpractice insurance crises like this past one. Lawyers, judges, and juries have little or nothing to do with it.

For much of the 1990s, malpractice insurance companies (and the reinsurance companies that they work with) got locked into an increasingly cutthroat competitive cycle. At the end, the biggest player in the game was practically bankrupt, and others were close to bust.

Thanks in part to the bursting of the stock market bubble, a downturn in interest rates at about the same time, and then the September 11 attacks, insurance companies reached the bottom of the cycle at the end of 2001. Premiums shot up across the whole property and casualty insurance business, not just medical malpractice.

How much did this have to do with medical malpractice lawsuits? Not much. In the long run, the amount of money coming in to a malpractice insurance company does in fact have to equal the amount of money going out. But the long run is very long. As we will see, insurance accounting practices give malpractice insurance companies more than enough rope to hang themselves. And hang themselves they did.

In this chapter, I will explain the insurance business cycle and why it has such a dramatic effect on medical malpractice insurance prices. I will also address the trial lawyers' claim that insurance company mismanagement and declining investment returns were the true causes of the crisis. As we will see, this story does not explain the insurance crisis any better than the lawsuit explosion story. The real story is more complicated and less convenient than both sides in the highly partisan debate over medical malpractice reform would like.

After explaining the cycle, I will consider the public policy consequences. As we will see, the real problem is not the total cost of medical malpractice insurance premiums. Instead, the real problem is the disruptive effect of rapid price increases, and the related unfairness of asking a few, hospital-based specialty groups, such as obstetricians, to bear the brunt of those increases. These are insurance problems, not tort problems, and they need insurance solutions. An insurance reform that I call "enterprise insurance" could protect doctors from the worst effects of the insurance cycle in the future. The full description of enterprise insurance appears in chapter 8.

INSURANCE: MONEY FOR A PROMISE

What do you get when you buy insurance? You get a promise that the insurance company will do something for you at some point in the future. With life insurance, the company promises to pay money when you die. With property insurance, the company promises to pay to replace your kitchen after a fire. With health insurance, the company promises to pay your medical expenses.

In each case, you pay money *today* in return for the insurance company's promise to pay money *in the future*, if the right conditions are met. This money-for-promise situation creates complications for the "money in the front door" and "money out the back door" metaphor I used earlier. The size of these complications depends on how much time passes between the time that you pay the money and the time that they have to come through on the promise.

For medical malpractice insurance, insurance companies get the premiums long before they finish paying out the claims. For the moment we do not need to understand precisely why. (One reason is that it takes a long time to resolve malpractice cases.) Instead, we need only to focus on the consequences.

There are two important ones. The first follows from the fact that the insurance company does not put doctors' money in a vault in the basement. Instead, it invests that money, along with most of the other premiums it collects, in government bonds, the stock market, real estate, and just about any other place that capital goes in search of a return. For an insurance company, time is money. So money comes into the insurance company not just through the front door, but also through side doors—in the form of investment income. The longer the time between the payment of the premium and the payment of the claim, the more important investment income is to the insurance company.

Investment income really matters for medical malpractice insurance— much more than for auto or homeowners or health insurance, for example. With auto or homeowners or health insurance, an insurance company can be pretty sure that by the end of 2006 it will pay almost all the money that it will ever have to pay for the policies that cover accidents that happen in 2005. But for medical malpractice, an insurance company will hardly even have begun paying by then. It can take three or four years after the year of the insurance policy to get to the halfway point, and several years longer to get to the point where the insurance company will pay out 80 or 90 percent of the money.

By now, the second important consequence of the timing complication may be obvious. A malpractice insurance premium represents a guess about the future, a guess that can be wrong. A malpractice insurance company not only has to guess what will happen to medical malpractice litigation over the next five or more years, it also has to guess about what will happen to the investment market.

All insurance involves some kind of guess about the future. On average, guesses about what will happen next year are more accurate than guesses about what will happen the year after that. Also, guesses about slowly changing aspects of life are generally more accurate than guesses about rapidly changing aspects. As we will see, medical malpractice insurance falls on the less accurate side on both counts, and the resulting uncertainty explains why the boom-and-bust cycle is especially severe for medical malpractice insurance.

INSURANCE ACCOUNTING 101

To understand the dynamics of the boom-and-bust cycle, we need some basic insurance accounting concepts. For our purposes, the key concepts are "loss expenses" and "reserves."

Like other businesses, insurance companies keep track of how they are doing by figuring out their profits. "Profit" is one of those words that people think they understand, until they have to define it precisely. In simplest terms, we can think about profit as what is left over after we subtract a company's expenses from revenues and adjust for changes in the value of the company's assets and liabilities.

But what counts as revenue, what counts as an expense, and, above all, *when* it counts can be almost metaphysical questions in any business. For example, do I count the sale of a steel beam as revenue in the month that I get a strong indication of interest from the customer, the month that the customer places an order for the steel beam, the month that I ship it out, or the month that the customer pays me? Similarly, do I count the cost of the iron used to make the steel as an expense in the month that I order the iron, the month that it arrives at my plant, the month that I pay for it, or the month that I sell the steel made from the iron? (And of course there are choices about which month counts as the month of the sale.)

Like other businesses, the insurance industry has developed rules for what counts as revenue and expense and when to count it. Insurance premiums count as revenue, but only once they are "earned," meaning that the customer can no longer ask for a refund. By law you can ask for a partial refund of your premiums at any time until your insurance policy has expired. This means that your insurance company "earns" your premium on a day-by-day basis over the entire insured period, not all at once when you pay the premium up front.

Money for paying insurance claims counts as an expense as soon as it is incurred, meaning as soon as it is recorded as a liability on the insurance company's books. These "loss expenses" include the money paid or to be paid to claimants, along with all the associated expenses involved in handling the claim (the insurance adjuster, the rent for the adjuster's office, the insurance defense lawyer, and so on). By law, insurance companies have to record the cost of paying future claims as soon as they sell the insurance promising to pay the claims.

This means that the insurance company incurs losses under your policy on a day-by-day basis over the insured period, not when it actually has to pay the claims much later. The expenses incurred for future losses are called "reserves," and insurance companies are supposed to set aside assets to match those reserves. Those assets are the source of the investment income I talked about earlier.

This earned-premium and incurred-loss approach to insurance company accounting represents a conservative approach to measuring profits, and appropriately so. Because of the boom-and-bust cycle (among other reasons), unregulated insurance companies are extraordinarily vulnerable to running out of money. So the better insurance companies have always been very conservative in counting revenues and expenses. Back in the nineteenth century, the better companies got together and persuaded government regulators to make all insurance companies count their profits this way.

So to review the two key points, first, insurance companies record future loss expenses as reserves as soon as they sell their insurance policies; and, second, those reserves count as an immediate expense. This means that the companies' predictions about the future have an immediate effect on their profits today.

Our last Insurance Accounting 101 topic looks at what happens when an insurance company changes its predictions about the future. Suppose the company decides in 2004 that it has overreserved its 2003 policies, meaning that it will not have to pay as much money for claims under those policies as predicted. Or suppose that the company decides in 2004 that it has underreserved its 2003 policies, meaning it will have to pay more than predicted. What effect do these reserve corrections have on the insurance company's profits?

Like almost anything else to do with accounting, there are any number of possible answers to this question. But there is only one answer that satisfies legal requirements. If the insurance company decides that its reserves are too high, it is supposed to correct that situation. And it must treat the reserves that it "releases" when it makes that correction as immediate revenue. These reserve releases make insurance company profits look good.

Similarly, if the insurance company decides that its reserves are too low, it is supposed to correct that situation. And it must treat the money used to "strengthen" the reserves as an expense in the year that it makes that correction. This reserve strengthening makes insurance company profits look bad.

The main idea here is that an insurance company's reserves are supposed to reflect the best current estimate of what it needs for paying future claims. Changes in the reserves lead either to immediate revenue or to immediate expenses, both of which affect profit today.

As we will see next, a medical malpractice insurance crisis happens when insurers are too optimistic about future losses for too long. As a result, they do not charge enough for their policies. When the gap between hope and reality gets too wide, they have to strengthen their reserves dramatically.

Remember, a medical malpractice insurance company barely even starts paying out money for claims until at least a year or two after the policy period is over, and it keeps paying out money for up to ten years. When the gap between hope and reality gets too wide, companies may have to correct their reserves on *all* their open policies. That could be a majority of the policies that the companies sold in the last three or four years, and a substantial portion of the policies that they sold for the last ten. When that happens, profits fall off a cliff, and insurers cut back on the amount of insurance that they are willing or able to sell.[1]

MEDICAL MALPRACTICE AND THE
INSURANCE UNDERWRITING CYCLE

The insurance industry term for the boom-and-bust cycle we are discussing is the "underwriting cycle." Underwriters are the people in insurance companies who decide whether to sell a policy and at what price. In the earliest days of the marine insurance business, brokers would write the name of the ship and the captain on a slip of paper, along with a description of the cargo, the destination, and the route. People who were willing to share in the risk of loss would write their names on the slip of paper under the description, indicating their share of the risk and the premium. "Writing under" became "underwriter," and, so, a new profession was named.

When insurance industry people talk about the underwriting cycle, they do not talk about booms and busts. Insurance is supposed to be a safe, stable business; talk about booms and busts would only upset customers and investors. Instead, they talk about hard markets and soft markets. Those terms mean just what they sound like.

In a hard market, prices are high and insurers can be choosy about whom they are willing to insure and for what. In a soft market, prices decline and insurance is much easier to get. There is no straightforward way to say exactly when a hard market shifts into a soft market, but there is no mistaking the shift from a soft market to a hard market. Profits take a dive as insurers strengthen their reserves, and prices go up almost as fast.

Historians have traced the underwriting cycle back to the nineteenth century, and I am willing to bet they could trace it back to Lloyd's famous coffeehouse in seventeenth-century London, if not further.[2] There are many ideas about what causes the underwriting cycle, but there is no disagreement about the fact that the cycle exists and that there is nothing that any insurance company can do to prevent it.

As I explain in detail in a recent, more technical, article,[3] the medical malpractice insurance crises of the mid-1980s and the early 2000s did not reflect a sudden or dramatic change in either litigation behavior or malpractice payments. What changed, instead, were insurance market conditions and the investment and loss predictions built into medical malpractice insurance premiums. Insurers that offered low prices based on optimistic predictions in the soft markets of 1981 and 1997 switched to high prices based on pessimistic predictions in the hard markets of 1986 and 2002.

Chart 1 shows a picture of the medical liability insurance underwriting cycle from 1980 to 2003. The three lines on the chart show the results for all medical malpractice insurance sold in the United States during that period using three important insurance accounting measures.[4]

The first measure, "operating profit," is represented by the solid line. Operating profit has a technical definition,[5] but the basic idea is that years with positive numbers are profitable years for insurers and years with negative numbers are unprofitable years.

Operating profit is measured in percentage terms, so the operating profit line in the chart should be read using the percentage numbers on the left side. The exact numbers do not matter for our purposes. What matters is the basic shape and timing of the profit cycle. The operating profit line shows the well-known features of the underwriting cycle: a profit "valley" in the beginning of the hard markets of both the 1980s and the 2000s, followed soon after by significant improvements.

The second insurance accounting measure, shown in chart 1 by the dotted line, is "predicted losses." (The official insurance industry term is "initial incurred loss.")The predicted losses line shows the total amount of medical malpractice losses that the insurance industry predicted it would pay on policies, at the time it sold those policies. For example, the number shown on the chart for the year 1991 is the amount that the insurance industry predicted in 1991 that it would have to pay in the future on all of the policies that it sold in 1991.

As my label reflects, these are predictions; they are not dollars actually paid out to claimants or lawyers or insurance company employees handling the claims. The predicted loss line should be read using the dollar figures on the right side of the chart. Again, the exact numbers do not matter. What matters is the shape of the line and its relationship to the other lines, as I will explain.

The dashed line on chart 1 shows the last insurance accounting measure, which is actual losses ("developed losses," in industry parlance). The actual losses line shows the total amount of losses that the insurance industry had paid, or expected to pay, for policies sold in the indicated year, as those losses were known ten years later.

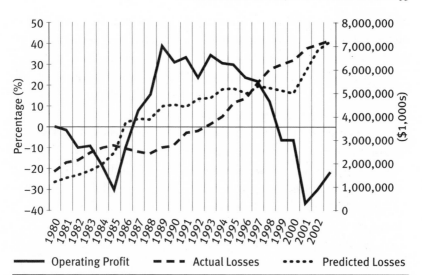

CHART 1. Operating Profit and Losses, U.S.
Medical Malpractice Market, 1980 to 2003.

In other words, the actual loss number in chart 1 for the year 1982 is a
number that could not be known until the end of 1991, and the actual loss
number for the year 1994 is a number that could not be known until the end
of 2003. Well over 90 percent of medical malpractice claim payments are
made within ten years after the policies are sold, so the figures for the years
1994 and earlier come very close to the total losses that will be paid under
policies sold in each of those years. For policies sold since 1995, the actual
loss numbers come from industry figures prepared in 2004. This means
that the "actual loss" figures in my chart involve an increasingly larger
share of predictions and an increasingly smaller proportion of actual claim
payments the closer that line gets to 2003.

As with the predicted losses line, the actual losses line should be read
using the dollar figures on the right side of the chart. And as with both of
the other lines, the exact dollar or percentage amounts do not matter. What
matters is the relationship between the lines.

As I will explain in just a moment, this relationship confirms the finding of the Texas and Florida closed-claim research: that the two most
recent medical liability insurance crises did not result from sudden or dramatic increases in medical malpractice settlements or jury verdicts. Instead, this relationship shows that the crises resulted from dramatic in-

creases in the amount of money that the insurance industry put in reserve for claims. Those reserve increases were so big because the insurance industry systematically underreserved in the years leading up to the crisis.

Unless you are used to reading charts like this, those facts are not likely to jump out at you. So I will explain how you can draw such significant conclusions from the three lines on the chart.

The first thing to do is to compare how fast the predicted loss line (the dotted line) changes in comparison to the actual loss line (the dashed line) in chart 1. Notice how the *actual* loss line shows a slow but steady increase in the amount of claim payments and related expenses that the insurance companies actually paid (except for a relatively flat period from 1986 to 1989, reflecting a decline in the amount of insurance sold during the mid-1980s insurance crisis, as well as the effects of the 1980s tort reforms). Now notice how the *predicted* loss line jumps dramatically at the low point in the profit cycle and grows very slowly at all other times. This tells us that *predicted* losses increase dramatically at the beginning of a hard market, not *actual* losses. (Chart 2 will make this point even more clear.)

The next thing to do is to look at the relationship between the predicted loss line and the actual loss line. Notice how the predicted loss line is *below* the actual loss line toward the end of each of the soft market periods shown in the chart (1980–1984 and 1987–2001). This means that the insurance industry *under*predicted its actual losses during those years.

Now notice how the predicted losses rose *above* the actual loss line following the onset of the hard market in 1985. This later relationship means that the insurance industry *over* predicted losses during the mid-1980s hard market and following years (1986–1995). We know from earlier reports that the same thing happened in the mid-1970s hard market,[6] and my sense is that the same thing is happening now because of recent news reports about high profits in the property casualty insurance industry.

Chart 2 shows the effect of the underwriting cycle on insurers' loss predictions in a slightly different way. As with chart 1, the solid line in chart 2 shows the operating profit and the dotted line shows the predicted losses. But this time, the dotted line does not show the dollar amount of predicted losses. Instead, it shows the rate of change in predicted losses, adjusting for medical inflation.[7] When the predicted losses line is at zero, predicted losses increased at exactly the rate of medical inflation. When the dotted

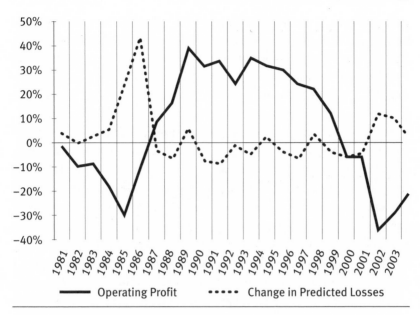

CHART 2. Change in Predicted Losses, U.S.
Medical Malpractice Market, 1980 to 2003.

line is above zero, predicted losses increased faster than medical inflation. And when the dotted line is below zero, predicted losses increased more slowly than medical inflation.

I adjusted for medical inflation for two reasons. First, medical expenses are the biggest and most predictable part of the damages in the high-severity cases that drive medical malpractice litigation. As a result, we would expect medical malpractice payments in individual cases to increase at a rate that is closer to the rate of medical inflation than to the rate of inflation in the other areas. Second, the health-care sector of the economy is growing more rapidly than the economy as a whole. Malpractice payments can be expected to grow at about the same rate as the size of the health-care sector of the economy and as fast as medical prices. This is in fact what the researchers studying the Texas closed-claim database have found.[8] Adjusting for medical inflation helps prevent us from mistaking normal growth for excessive growth.

Medical inflation is not the perfect tool for this purpose. Normal growth in medical malpractice payments is probably a bit higher than medical inflation because growth in the health-care sector hits medical malpractice losses three ways: increasing the price for medical expenses, increasing the number of things that can be done to help injured people recover, and increasing the number of medical care "events" that could possibly go wrong and therefore produce a medical malpractice claim. So I probably have not adjusted the loss expenses quite enough to factor out normal growth in loss expenses, but you can still see my basic point.

With this explanation, chart 2 presents quite a dramatic picture of the relationship between predicted losses and the underwriting cycle. Predicted losses increased more than medical inflation only during the initial hard market years. At all other times, predicted losses increased at a rate that on average was less than medical inflation. As a result, the reserves failed to keep up. This set the stage for the dramatic reserve increases that launched the medical malpractice insurance crisis.

Insurance industry executives probably do not change their real understanding of future losses in quite as dramatically cyclical a fashion as these charts suggest. There is lot of room for judgment in predicting losses, and the research in this area shows that there is some "income smoothing" going on.[9] In other words, insurance industry executives to at least some degree make optimistic predictions when prices are low because they do not want their profits to be too low in those years, and they make pessimistic predictions when prices are high because they do not want their profits to be too high in those years.

Also, it is important to remember that insurance companies are organizations, not individuals. There are different kinds of people with different roles and different interests in each company. When prices in the insurance market are low, people in sales pressure the company actuaries to keep their loss predictions low. Otherwise, the company would have to raise its prices above the competition, customers would go elsewhere for their business, and the sales department would not meet its goals.

When the tide finally turns, the people in the claims department and the unhappy actuaries get to say, "I told you so" to the sales reps, and the power of the company's pessimists goes up. While the pessimists are in charge, they pile on the reserves, in part to build a margin of safety to protect the company the next time the sales department gets the upper hand.[10]

There is nothing nefarious about this. No single insurance company gets to set the price for medical malpractice insurance. All that any company can do is respond to the market conditions it faces. Even an insurance company that dominates the market in one state has to deal with national and even international conditions, because local malpractice insurance companies almost always have to buy reinsurance.

Reinsurance is insurance for insurance companies, and it is especially important in the area of medical malpractice. Think of the local medical malpractice insurance company as the retailer and the reinsurance company as the wholesaler. The reinsurance market is a very competitive, international market, just like the wholesale market in other kinds of businesses in which the local market may not be quite as competitive.

This means that a competitive national and international market sets the prices for medical malpractice insurance. About all that any one insurance company can decide is whether or not to offer the insurance at the going price, and how to account for its own future losses. Accounting for future losses involves a great deal of judgment. We cannot expect insurers to ignore the market when they make those judgments. The practice of underpredicting losses at the end of the soft market and overpredicting losses at the start of a hard market allows insurers to manage their bottom line and preserve their capital.

With that said, we should not overstate the role of conscious income smoothing. There are real changes in perceptions over the course of the cycle. It is hard to make accurate predictions about future medical malpractice losses. The competitive dynamics of the insurance market cannot help but affect those predictions. When prices are low and everyone is competing for market share, there will be an inevitable and very human tendency to become more optimistic about the future in order to allow the company to compete in the market. And, when profits have crashed, and people are scared about their careers, there will be an inevitable and very human tendency to become more pessimistic in those guesses.

Part of what is going on here is simple herd behavior. Watching premiums flow to other, lower-pricing insurers would lead any underwriter to wonder what it is that the other companies know that she does not and to reexamine her pricing assumptions. No one would be surprised when she decides that those assumptions were too pessimistic and revises her prices so that they are more in line with those being offered elsewhere in the market.

Herd behavior is a rational response to many kinds of decisions under conditions of uncertainty.[11] "If I'm wrong, at least I won't be alone." Given that there is no absolute measure of success in the insurance business, a decision that involves a substantial risk of being just as wrong as everyone else exposes an executive to much less career risk than a decision that involves even a small risk of being wildly more wrong than others. (And if the safer decision also produces the bigger bonus, all the better.)

Another explanation comes from the idea of the "winner's curse" economists have studied in auction markets. When buyers choose among insurance companies based on price, companies that offer the lower price will sell more insurance. So, even if insurance underwriters on average are accurate in their predictions of the future, the market selects against pessimistic underwriters in favor of optimistic underwriters.[12]

The "winners" in the competition for market share are the optimistic, low-pricing insurers. The "curse" is the logical result of this process: in the end, premiums are too low to pay the claims. The insurers offering a lower price are not necessarily behaving irrationally; they may simply make more optimistic guesses based on uncertain information.

COMPARING AUTO AND MEDICAL
MALPRACTICE INSURANCE

Comparing the auto accident and medical malpractice situations can help us see why medical malpractice insurance pricing is particularly hard to get right.

As I mentioned earlier, an auto insurance company can be very sure that, by the end of 2006, it will pay out most of the money that it will ever have to pay for auto policies that cover accidents that occur in 2005. There are many reasons for this. People usually file claims right after an auto accident. Most auto claims are small. And it is fairly easy to tell how much an auto claim is worth, especially for damage to cars.

Serious-injury cases can be different.[13] But thanks to improvements in auto safety, serious-injury cases represent only a tiny fraction of auto claims. Also, many people do not buy enough auto insurance, so the amount of insurance is much less than the victim's damages. If that happens, the insurance company pays out the full limits right away. This means that even serious auto injury cases often get resolved very quickly.

In addition, an auto insurance company can be very sure that, at least with respect to auto insurance claims, the world that exists a year or two later will be very similar to the world that exists when it sells a policy. Road design and construction cannot change in that time. Car technology will not change much, if at all. And people's willingness to claim will not change much either. Just about everyone who is eligible to bring an auto claim already does, so there is not much room for growth.[14]

For auto insurance companies, the most significant unknowns probably are the price of gas and the price of medical care. The price of gas matters because it affects how much, and possibly how fast, people drive, both of which affect the rate of auto accidents. The price of medical care matters because it affects the cost of bodily injury claims. But the insurance company has to predict the price of gas only until the end of the year of the policy, and it has to worry about the price of medical care only for another year. Yes, some serious-injury claims will involve health-care costs far into the future, but serious-injury claims thankfully represent only a small share of the auto insurance business.

The medical malpractice situation is very different. The health-care industry and health-care technology are changing much faster than the auto industry and auto technology, so insurance companies cannot be as sure that the number and kinds of injuries will be the same next year as this year. Also, as we saw in the last chapter, many eligible people do not bring medical malpractice claims. For that reason, insurers have to be worried about claims growth, especially in an era of the managed-care backlash. People's willingness to bring medical malpractice claims has been stable so far, but that easily could change.

Most significant of all, however, serious-injury claims dominate the medical malpractice insurance business, and doctors usually have million- or multimillion-dollar insurance policies available to pay those claims. Because hospitals and malpractice insurance companies—and earlier tort reforms—have made it so hard and so expensive to bring a medical malpractice case, almost no lawyer will take a small one. According to the National Practitioner Data Bank, the median settlement in medical malpractice cases against physicians in 2002 was $275,000, and more than half of all the money paid out was for settlements larger than $500,000.[15] (The "median" is the midpoint. Half of all the settlements will be smaller and half will be larger than the median amount.) Hospitals and other organizations do not have to report their malpractice payments to the national data bank, but anecdotal evidence suggests that those payments can be larger than physician payments.

A serious-injury case takes longer to resolve, and any resolution usually involves paying for future medical and rehabilitation expenses. This means that medical malpractice insurance companies have to predict health-care costs and technology far into the future. There is lots of room to go wrong in making that guess.

BAD INVESTMENTS AND MISMANAGEMENT DID NOT CAUSE THE CRISIS

Before discussing what, if anything, we might do in response to the medical malpractice insurance underwriting cycle, I should clear up one myth being promoted by the trial lawyers' side of the medical malpractice debates. This is the myth that the *real* reasons for the medical malpractice insurance crisis were bad investments and mismanagement by insurance companies. It is probably already clear that I do not think that is right, but I want to respond directly.

My first response to this myth is simple common sense. Do we really think that every medical malpractice insurance company and every reinsurance company is incompetent? Surely some are better than others, yet all of them went through the same underwriting cycle.

Reinsurance companies do not have to file the same kinds of reports with state insurance departments as ordinary, retail insurance companies. So we cannot be as sure about them. But my informed judgment is that they all had a similar experience. Some farsighted reinsurance underwriters may have realized sooner than others that medical malpractice insurance prices were too low, and therefore shifted out of medical malpractice into another line of insurance. But the end of the soft market appears to have produced serious reserve deficiencies in all lines of property casualty insurance, so shifting out of medical malpractice into some other part of the business would not have helped them much.

In retrospect, the smartest thing for a reinsurance company to have done during the last few years of the soft market would have been to close up the shop and send the underwriters out to play golf. But not even the "sage of Omaha," Warren Buffett, had his underwriters do that. Berkshire Hathaway's big reinsurance company, General Re, suffered through the cycle just like the others.[16]

My second response is that bad investments cannot possibly add up to a number that is even remotely large enough to explain the crisis. The trial lawyers are right that investment income did go down at the start of the hard market. In fact, insurance companies were hit with a double punch: the stock market bubble burst and interest rates declined at about the same time.

I am persuaded that these two things probably played a role in starting the hard market, much like the straw that broke the proverbial camel's back. *But* neither the bursting of the stock market bubble nor the decline in interest rates can explain the reserve shortages that built up during the end of the soft market or the full extent of the premium increases during the hard market. The stock market certainly cannot be the explanation, because U.S. liability insurance companies put most of their assets into bonds. And the decline in interest rates only gradually affects insurance companies' income because they tend to hold their bonds to maturity. Also, the short-term effect of a decline in interest rates is to increase the value of the higher-interest bonds that the company holds.[17]

Pointing fingers at bumbling insurance company executives is simple and convenient, but it is no more accurate than pointing fingers at lawyers, judges, and juries. The real story is more complicated and less convenient. We have had insurance crises in the past. We will have insurance crises in the future. Second-guessing insurance company investment and management decisions will not do any more to stop the insurance underwriting cycle than enacting restrictive tort reforms.

WHAT, EXACTLY, IS THE PROBLEM WITH
A MALPRACTICE INSURANCE CRISIS?

Before rushing to do something about an insurance crisis, we need to be clear about what problem we are trying to fix. The upshot of the discussion of the medical malpractice epidemic in the last chapter is that the problem cannot be the absolute size of malpractice premiums. Medical malpractice premiums actually are quite low compared to the costs that the epidemic imposes on patients. That may be a surprising statement, I know. I will defend it in a moment.

If there is a problem, it is more likely to be a combination of one or more of the following. First, some doctors may find it hard to get malpractice insurance in an insurance crisis, at any price. Second, doctors in some specialties and in some locations pay what seems to them and to at least some others a disproportionate share of malpractice insurance premiums. Third, rapid and unpredictable price increases are disruptive, particularly for small medical offices.

I will call the first of these problems the "access" problem, the second the "unequal burden" problem, and the third the "volatility" problem. These problems are insurance problems, not lawsuit problems. If we want to do something about them, the place to focus is on malpractice insurance, not malpractice lawsuits.

Before discussing these real problems and what we might do about them, I will explain why we should not worry that, in the aggregate, medical malpractice insurance premiums are too high.

MEDICAL MALPRACTICE INSURANCE PREMIUMS ARE NOT TOO HIGH

Reducing total medical liability insurance premiums is not a worthy policy goal. This may seem like a shocking statement in light of all the attention given to the recent malpractice insurance crisis. I assure you that I do not say this lightly.

My reasoning is simple. Medical malpractice insurance is the way that medical providers share the costs of medical malpractice. Whether we understand insurance premiums as the way that health-care providers take responsibility for injuries caused by their profession or as an incentive to avoid injuries, the premiums are too high in an absolute sense only if they exceed the costs of medical malpractice.

The costs of medical malpractice include medical and rehabilitation expenses for medical injuries, earnings lost as a result of those injuries, and a myriad of additional expenses borne by injured patients' families, as well as very substantial losses that do not produce an easily measured out-of-pocket expense. Only if the price of malpractice insurance (and alternative forms of malpractice protection) exceeds the total of all these costs could we say that it is too expensive. In fact, the research shows that the total price of medical malpractice insurance and related forms of protection are much less than the costs of medical malpractice. If anything, the price is much too low, either to satisfy health-care providers' moral obligation to take responsibility for consequences of their mistakes or to provide an adequate incentive to avoid mistakes.

Professor Danzon's analysis of the California study showed that tort lawsuits compensate only one out of every twenty-five people injured by medical malpractice. As we will see in the next chapter, the Harvard and Chicago studies reached the same conclusion. Even if we knew nothing else about the costs of medical malpractice and the price that hospitals and doctors were paying for medical malpractice protection, this fact alone would tell us that the price that doctors and hospitals are paying is much less than the cost of the medical injuries that they cause.[18]

But we do know more. We know that the price for medical malpractice protection is much less than the price for workers' compensation insurance or for automobile liability insurance, despite the fact that medical malpractice kills far more people each year than workplace accidents and automobile accidents combined. In 2003 the premiums paid for medical malpractice insurance in the United States totaled $11.3 billion, while the premiums for workers' compensation insurance and automobile liability insurance were $56.9 billion and $142.4 billion. In other words, the price of insurance for medical malpractice is only about 5 percent of the price of insurance for workplace and automobile accidents.[19]

None of this is to say that we should stop trying to find more efficient and effective ways of compensating injured patients. What it does say, however, is that we should use any resulting cost savings to increase the number of people who are compensated, not to reduce the bill that doctors and hospitals are paying.

In addition, the fact that the total price is not too high does not mean that everything else about our medical malpractice insurance arrangements is fine. As we will see, there are several legitimate reasons to be concerned about the effects of the insurance underwriting cycle.

THE ACCESS PROBLEM

Medical malpractice insurance is a necessity for doctors, not a luxury. Some states, and many hospitals and other health-care institutions, require doctors to get insurance. In addition, medical providers as a group have assets that make medical liability insurance a practical necessity even when it is not otherwise required.

What is more, we want doctors to have malpractice insurance. Without insurance, they will not be able to meet their legal obligations and they may make socially unproductive choices to reduce their exposure. They may hide their assets. They may abandon high-risk locations. And they may abandon high-risk medical specialties. As I will show in chapter 7, the evidence seems fairly clear that, at least so far, doctors in fact have not abandoned high-risk locations or specialties, at least not in sufficient numbers to reduce patient access to care. But concerns that they might are legitimate.

THE UNEQUAL BURDEN PROBLEM

There are two reasons to think that the burden of paying medical malpractice insurance premiums falls too heavily on at least some doctors. First, doctors have to pay a larger share of malpractice insurance premiums than their share of health-care revenues. Doctors bear most of the costs of medical liability despite the fact that they receive less than 15 percent of health-care revenues. As Columbia law professor William Sage, M.D., reports, "The medical profession is insufficiently capitalized to fund insurance for such a multiple of earnings, particularly when the burden falls mainly on a few specialties."[20]

Second, doctors in high-risk specialties and high-risk locations pay large premiums that may be out of proportion to their ability to prevent medical injuries. Preventable mistakes are to some degree inevitable in complicated, high-risk medical systems. It is fair to compensate the injured patient. And we want to provide an incentive for the doctor to be careful. But the mistake really results from the health-care system, of which the doctor is only a part.[21]

In a perfectly competitive market we would not worry about either of these problems. If doctors' share of the premiums was out of proportion to their share of health-care revenues, they could raise their prices in response. So, too, with physicians in high-risk specialties or locations. But the medical market lies very far from the world of perfect competition. Large government and private financing organizations set prices, and consumers only rarely pay any attention to prices for specific medical procedures. Health-care providers are not entirely pawns in this process, but we appear to be in a period of gradual reduction in physician income relative to other professionals. As a result, physicians have little or no ability to raise prices in response to increased costs.

When a malpractice insurance crisis hits, the burden falls disproportionately on physicians in high-risk specialties and locations, who cannot raise their prices in response. This, too, raises legitimate concerns—both about the impact of a medical malpractice insurance crisis, specifically, and about the way that we fund the malpractice liability system more generally.

THE VOLATILITY PROBLEM

One way to think about medical liability insurance is as a special-purpose group savings plan for doctors and other medical providers. Doctors contribute to the "savings" plan today so that they have money to pay claims in the future. The crux of the volatility problem is this: What rational savings plan would dramatically increase contribution requirements at random intervals that bear no connection to the income of the people making the contributions?

As we have already seen, there are some real benefits to occasional medical malpractice insurance crises. High premiums are one of the few ways to get the medical establishment to focus on medical malpractice. Without the crisis of the 1970s, the California Hospital and Medical Associations would never have commissioned their study. Without the crisis of the 1980s, the State of New York would never have commissioned the Harvard study. In addition, I think that the recent crisis helped keep the Institute of Medicine's 1999 report about medical injuries in the limelight. As I showed in my article on the underwriting cycle, the number of articles about medical malpractice in both medical journals and the general-interest press fluctuates with the underwriting cycle. The number goes up during insurance crises and then comes back down after.

But the fact that the financial burden falls on doctors who are not well equipped to deal with it diverts public attention in unproductive ways. Doctors are very busy. They are afraid of lawyers and lawsuits. They are in a financial bind. So an insurance crisis presents a perfect opportunity to turn them into very appealing front men for otherwise very unappealing business interests. For that reason alone, we need to protect doctors from the consequences of the boom-and-bust insurance cycle.

SUMMARY

A one-minute version of what I have covered in this chapter would go something like this. Liability insurance goes through a boom-and-bust cycle. In the early years of the cycle, insurance companies take a pessimistic view of future losses and set aside more reserves than they need. Toward the end of the cycle, they take an increasingly optimistic view of future losses and do not set aside enough reserves. As a result, they begin charging prices that are too low in relation to the risk. Because medical malpractice claims take so long to resolve and contain such a high percentage of high-value claims, the shortfalls in the reserves to pay medical malpractice claims accumulate over a number of years. When the insurance climate shifts back toward a pessimistic view of future losses, insurance companies need to increase their reserves, sometimes quite dramatically, to make up for the underreserving of the past, and prices rise accordingly. This means that the swings of the insurance cycle are more dramatic for medical malpractice insurance than for most other kinds of insurance.

The public policy problem here is not the overall size of malpractice premiums. Premiums are low in relation to the total social cost of medical malpractice. Because the vast majority of injured patients do not bring claims, they and their families and health insurers bear most of those costs. As I said in chapter 1, the average premium for doctors in the United States is about $12,000. While $12,000 is not an insignificant amount of money, it is not an unaffordable business expense for doctors who generally earn good six-figure incomes, after they pay for medical malpractice insurance. Even if that number were doubled to take into account the fact that some doctors are not practicing and that many doctors are covered by hospitals or other large organizations that do not purchase traditional medical malpractice insurance, the cost per doctor is not as high as most people think.

The real public policy problem stems from the way that insurance companies divide up the premiums among doctors. Most doctors pay relatively affordable premiums. But some specialists, such as obstetricians, pay very high premiums, and they are not equipped to deal all by themselves with the ups and downs of the insurance cycle.

PREPARING FOR THE NEXT MEDICAL
MALPRACTICE INSURANCE CRISIS

If lawyers, judges, and juries are not the problem, restrictive tort reform will not prevent the next medical malpractice insurance crisis. And if investment mistakes and mismanagement are not the problem, intrusive insurance regulation will not prevent the next crisis, either. Can we prevent a crisis?

The short answer is that we cannot eliminate the insurance underwriting cycle, but we can make sure that doctors do not bear the brunt of the next hard market. An insurance market reform idea I call "enterprise insurance" provides a way to do just that. The basic idea is that doctors who work or perform procedures in hospitals or other organizations should get their liability insurance coverage from that organization. The doctors who suffer most during a malpractice insurance crisis face their biggest risks in the hospital. Hospitals and other large health-care organizations are better positioned than doctors to manage their liability insurance problems and to negotiate with Medicare, Medicaid, and private insurers.

This and other evidence-based medical malpractice reforms are the topic of chapter 8. Between here and there, I will let you in on the malpractice insurance companies' secret, explain why we need medical malpractice lawsuits, and then address the remaining parts of the medical malpractice myth.

4 THE MALPRACTICE INSURANCE COMPANIES' SECRET

The malpractice insurance companies' secret is that their own claim files show that the medical malpractice myth is not true. According to the myth, people sue at the drop of a hat with no good reason, juries regularly hand out huge sums to almost anyone who asks, and, as a result, doctors, hospitals, and their insurance companies have to pay large ransoms to escape from the clutches of the tort system even when the doctors did nothing wrong.

The research shows—overwhelmingly—that this is simply not true. And since the most important research comes out of the insurance companies' own files, we cannot dismiss it as the product of hyperactive imagination.

The reality is most people do not sue. Juries do not favor plaintiffs in medical malpractice cases. Malpractice insurance companies fight weak claims, and strong claims, too. When the companies do pay to settle a questionable case, they pay much less than for a clear case. Finally, claimants and their lawyers usually make reasonable decisions based on what they can know at the time. Patients are not experts, and doctors and hospitals are not known for publicly admitting their mistakes, so denying that there was a mistake does not count for much. When patients get credible and conclusive evidence that there was no mistake, most drop their claims.

MOST PEOPLE DO NOT SUE

Patients sue their doctors at the drop of a hat, right? That is what the nurses and doctors in my law school classes tell me, and what doctors tell each other at medical society meetings. Indeed, the litigious patient is such a well-known feature of the U.S. tort system that I have heard about it at meetings in China, France, Israel, Switzerland, Germany, Canada, and the UK. And I expect to hear it in other places too, because it is one of the facts about the United States that the foreign lawyers who come to study at my law school know before they arrive.

Yet they could not be more wrong. On this point all the research agrees. As we have already seen, there are far more cases of medical malpractice than medical malpractice litigation. Professor Danzon reported that there were ten incidents of medical malpractice for every one malpractice claim in the United States. The Harvard group found a seven-to-one ratio in New York and Colorado and a five-to-one ratio in Utah.[1] Because hospital record reviews miss so much medical malpractice, the real multiple is much higher.

One way to get a handle on the actual ratio between malpractice and claims is to look at the claims that the Harvard researchers matched with the records they studied. The results show that only a very small fraction of the eligible patients filed a claim. As you may recall from chapter 2, the Harvard team looked at about 30,000 hospital records in New York and found conclusive evidence of a serious injury from medical malpractice in the records of 280 patients. How many of those 280 patients brought a claim? Eight. That is less than 3 percent.

In Utah and Colorado the team looked at about 15,000 hospital records and found conclusive evidence of a serious injury from medical malpractice in the records of 161 patients. How many of those 161 patients brought a claim? Four.[2] That is also less than 3 percent.

We can make a similar calculation using the Chicago hospital observation research. The Chicago research team observed a total of 1,047 patients and found that 185 of them suffered a serious, preventable medical injury. How many of those 185 patients brought a claim? Thirteen asked for compensation and only six pressed their claims to the point of bringing a lawsuit. Researchers report, and malpractice lawyers agree, that insurance companies rarely pay a medical malpractice claim without a lawsuit, so only those six were serious claims. That is less than 4 percent.[3]

As we discussed in chapter 2, the number of medical malpractice claims today is about the same as in the 1990s, when the Harvard team studied Utah and Colorado and the Chicago team studied the "large, tertiary care, urban teaching hospital affiliated to a university medical school."

I have said it before, and I will say it again: We have an epidemic of malpractice, not an epidemic of malpractice litigation. The vast majority of eligible patients do not sue.

The idea that Americans are suit-happy, litigation-crazy, and ready to rumble in the courts is one of the more amazing myths of our time. It grows stronger with each piece of the by now overwhelming research showing that it is simply not true.[4]

Yes, our courts occupy an unusually large space in the public imagination. Remember O. J. Simpson and the Menendez brothers in court in California? Paula Jones in court in Arkansas, and Michael Eisner and the rest of Disney on trial in Delaware? And, yes, our courts—especially the Supreme Court—play an unusually prominent, maybe even unique, role in debates over public values.

But the prominence of law and litigation in the public imagination does not mean that ordinary citizens are filing tort actions left and right. Reader, when was the last time that you filed a tort lawsuit? Yet, unless you are a personal-injury lawyer, a law professor or a tort claim researcher, I am prepared to bet that you believe that there really is something to the idea that Americans are an especially litigious crowd.

I do not expect to wean you entirely from that belief, but I hope you will reexamine it for medical malpractice at least.

IF ANYTHING, JURIES FAVOR DEFENDANTS
IN MEDICAL MALPRACTICE CASES

When it comes to juries in tort cases, there is no denying that the United States is special. Most of the world does not use juries at all. Countries that do use juries usually follow the British example and reserve them for criminal cases, so that judges decide medical malpractice and other tort cases.

The medical malpractice myth says that juries favor plaintiffs in medical malpractice cases and that overly generous juries are driving malpractice insurance costs through the roof.[5] On these points the research also clearly contradicts the myth.

Researchers use many different approaches to study juries. Some use court records to track verdicts over time. Some use quasi-official records called jury verdict reporters, which contain more information about the cases. Others use mock juries to conduct experiments on jury decisions. Some research teams study malpractice insurance company claim files. Others study the claim reports that insurance companies in some states file with the department of insurance. As with all research, there are benefits and weaknesses to each approach.

Using court records allows researchers to compare lots of verdicts in many different times and places. But court records contain so little information about the cases that it is hard for researchers to know whether they are comparing apples to apples or apples to oranges.

As any malpractice lawyer can report, not all medical malpractice cases are the same.[6] A sponge left in the stomach after surgery provides very clear evidence of negligence, but the damages will not be large because the patient will recover. On the other hand, a baby with brain damage due to a possible lack of oxygen during delivery could produce enormous damages, but there would be more questions about negligence than in the sponge case. A shift in the mix from sponge in the stomach cases to brain-damaged baby cases would result in a decline in the plaintiff success rate, but a dramatic increase in the damages when plaintiffs do win.

Jury verdict reporters usually provide enough information about the injury and the case to address the problem of comparing apples to oranges. But the jury verdict reports are notoriously incomplete. Many researchers believe that the reports tend to leave out cases that the plaintiffs lose. As a result, the reports may make it appear that juries are more generous than they really are. Also, unless the researchers carefully examine the composition of cases over time, they may reach inappropriate conclusions.[7] For example, an increase in jury verdicts over time would show that juries are becoming more generous only if the average severity of the cases stayed the same.

Using mock juries allows researchers to control what they are studying. The researchers decide what facts the mock jury hears, so they can adjust those facts to test their theories. And they can videotape the deliberations so that they can see exactly how the juries decide and what makes a difference in their decisions. But mock juries are not real juries. They do not decide real cases, with doctors and patients whose lives will be changed as a result. So we cannot be entirely sure that mock juries behave the same as real juries. (Though the fact that real lawyers use mock juries to help them decide whether to settle a case and for how much suggests that mock juries have some real-world value.)

Insurance company claim records provide detailed information about the nature and severity of the injury, the strength of the evidence about liability, and the final resolution of the claim. But it turns out that taking a medical malpractice case all the way to a jury is so rare that it is hard to find enough cases within the files of a single insurance company in order to carefully compare apples to apples, especially over time. And insurance companies tend to maintain their records in different ways, so it is difficult to combine records from different companies to get a larger group of cases.

Finally, using the claim reports filed with state insurance departments has the potential to overcome the problem of incompatible insurance company records. Typically, the state requires all the insurance companies to file their reports in the same form, so that the reports from different companies can be compared. But it turns out that many of the reports are incomplete and that there are systematic differences in the ways that different companies and different people within companies fill out the forms.[8]

But these imperfections do not mean that we should throw up our hands and fall back on the conventional wisdom. Instead, they mean that we have to study medical malpractice juries from many different angles. The results from any single study cannot tell us how juries decide cases or whether the results have changed over time. But if the same picture emerges from a variety of approaches, we can be pretty sure that we are seeing something real.

A consistent picture does emerge from the research on juries and medical malpractice. We see conscientious jurors who take their responsibilities seriously, pay attention to their instructions, and, if anything, give doctors the benefit of the doubt. While no one would say that juries always make the right decision, no judge or expert panel would always get it right, either.

Jury verdicts do seem to be getting larger over time, but the increase is not out of line with the underlying costs. Because of advances in medical technology, the costs of injuries are increasing.[9] Medical miracles mean that we can do more for injured people, but that "more" is not free. Also, juries are deciding more and more severe cases. These developments help explain the increase in jury verdicts. But whatever the explanation, the evidence does not support the dramatic claims about jury verdict inflation that accompanied the onset of the insurance crisis in 2002.

There is so much research on juries in tort litigation that I cannot begin to describe it all. I will provide a selective review that illustrates the different kinds of research. Readers who want to learn more should start with the excellent book by a law and psychology professor from Duke, Neil Vidmar (*Medical Malpractice and the American Jury*), and they should be on the lookout for new research growing out of the very recent insurance crisis, particularly by Professor Vidmar's team studying cases in Florida and the Texas team I mentioned in chapter 2.

The court record research. University of Cornell researchers have conducted what may well be the most significant research using court records. They used federal court records to compare the results of jury trials in tort cases with the results of cases tried before a judge, without a jury. Their results are subject to the apples-to-oranges problem, meaning that cases tried to a jury may be different from cases tried to a judge. Nevertheless, taken along with all the other research, the results are informative. The Cornell research team found that judges decide in favor of plaintiffs more often than juries do, and that the damages awarded are similar. The Cornell results are consistent with studies reporting that judges usually agree with jury decisions in tort cases.[10]

In a very clever follow-up study, the Cornell researchers looked at what happens to the jury and judge trial verdicts on appeal. They found that federal appellate courts reverse plaintiffs' jury verdicts in tort cases more often than they reverse plaintiffs' jury verdicts in contract cases, more often than they reverse defendants' jury verdicts in tort or contract cases, and more often than they reverse judge trial verdicts of any kind. As they concluded, this suggests that appellate judges believe that juries favor plaintiffs in tort cases and that the judges try to counter the effects of that bias. Since the earlier Cornell research suggests that juries in fact are not biased in favor of plaintiffs, this could mean that federal courts actually favor defendants in tort cases. A colleague and I have found a similar pattern in Connecticut state court appeals, suggesting that this result may be true in state courts as well.[11]

The jury verdict research. Many researchers have used jury verdict reporters to study what juries do with tort cases. Two of the more significant
studies are a RAND study tracking forty years of jury verdicts in San
Francisco and Cook County (Chicago) and an American Bar Foundation
study of jury verdicts in sixteen states.[12] The RAND research tells a simple
story about juries in tort cases at a very high level of generality. The American Bar Foundation research tells a more complicated story. Both contra-
dict the medical malpractice myth.

In their study, the RAND researchers looked at the change in jury
awards from 1960 to 1999, controlling for only three simple variables: case
characteristic (e.g., auto vs. medical vs. products liability), the amount of
claimed medical loss, and the amount of claimed nonmedical economic
loss. The researchers concluded, "Our results are striking. Not only do we
show that real average awards have grown by less than real income over the
40 years in our sample, we also find that essentially all of this growth can
be explained by changes in observable case characteristics and claimed
economic losses (particularly claimed medical costs)."[13]

Increased medical losses accounted for over half of the growth in jury
awards. Changes in the case mix over time (fewer auto, more medical malpractice cases) and increases in wages and other measurable losses explained most of the rest. What this means is clear. Larger jury verdicts reflect increases in the costs of injury, not jury generosity.

In their study the American Bar Foundation researchers examined all
the jury verdicts reported in a wide variety of locations over a three-year
period at the end of the 1980s. The Chamber of Commerce, the American
Medical Association, and other special interest groups were saying the
same things about juries during the mid-1980s insurance crisis that they
are saying today. The American Bar Foundation wanted to see whether
they were right. They were not.

The Bar Foundation research team found that juries were not indis-
criminately handing out money to plaintiffs and that plaintiffs were particularly unsuccessful in medical malpractice cases, losing 70 percent of
the time. Nevertheless, the researchers cautioned against sweeping gener-
alizations about jury verdicts. They explained that claiming patterns and
jury results in medical malpractice cases varied depending on the severity
of the injury, the medical setting in which the patient was injured, and the
kind of mistake the patient claimed the doctor made.

For some of the courts they studied, the Bar Foundation researchers found reliable reports of medical malpractice jury verdicts from the early 1970s. They compared those with verdicts from the late 1980s and found, like the RAND researchers, that verdicts had increased at a modest pace. They also found that the mix of cases that juries were deciding had shifted toward the kind that produce higher damage awards. Plaintiffs were younger, the errors involved more general medical management problems, and the injuries became more severe. Like the RAND results, this suggests that the increased cost of injury, and not increased generosity, explains the higher verdicts.[14]

One observation of the Bar Foundation researchers bears quoting at length:

> Because they play a critical role in the civil justice system, juries have an important symbolic place in the rhetoric of reform. The rhetoric, we have seen, overstates and misrepresents that role. . . . Underlying this characterization of the jury's role is an image of a system out of balance or run amok with jury verdicts at the heart of it all—increasingly high plaintiff win rates and skyrocketing awards in a system that is no longer predictable, consistent or fair. This is an image politically created and marketed in order to affect the public agenda. It is not part of a candid debate on the goals of the justice system geared toward constructing solutions in the light of good evidence and then empirically evaluating the effects of reforms.[15]

I could not have put this better. Whatever connection there is between the tort reformers' rhetoric about juries and the reality is almost purely coincidental (and then exploited to maximum and misleading effect in popular articles and books unconstrained by the standards of serious research).

The mock jury research. Mock jury research helps us learn how different factors affect jury decisions. Researchers from Duke led by Professor Neil Vidmar have conducted some of the most significant research on how juries decide medical malpractice cases. One of their best-known experiments tested the "deep pockets hypothesis"—the idea that juries are more generous when they think defendants have more money.[16] This matters in the medical malpractice context because doctors and hospitals usually have multimillion-dollar insurance policies and other assets as well.

The Duke researchers created six scenarios to test this hypothesis. In each scenario the plaintiff received the same injury, but from a different kind of accident or defendant. They created malpractice scenarios with individual doctor defendants and hospital defendants, and they created auto accident scenarios with individual defendants and corporate defendants. In each scenario, the defendant was liable and the parties had agreed on the amount of medical expenses, lost wages, and other easily calculable damages. The only question left for the jury to decide was the amount of damages the plaintiff should receive for pain and suffering.

People waiting to serve on real juries in North Carolina agreed to participate in the research. The research team randomly assigned each juror to a single scenario and analyzed the results. Significantly, the juries valued the pain and suffering the same in all six scenarios, regardless of who the defendant was. There was "no support for the deep pocket hypothesis." Of course, mock jury experiments can take us only so far. But these results are consistent with the jury verdict reporter research. Juries do what they are told. They assess damages based on the plaintiffs' injuries, not the size of the defendants' pocketbook.

The closed-claim record research. The research using insurance company claims files is so important that I will discuss it at length. For the moment, however, I will simply leave you with the observation that the results of the closed-claim file research suggests that juries follow their instructions. Juries decide cases based on the merits and they award damages based on the actual injuries to the plaintiff.[17]

The insurance department record research. As I explained in chapter 2, insurance companies doing business in Florida, Texas, and Missouri are required to file a report on every medical malpractice claim that they handle in those states. In the report they are supposed to describe the injury, the alleged negligence, the plaintiff, and the defendant. They also are supposed to itemize the damages and defense costs that they paid. The obvious objective is to create a reliable and consistent information base to inform public policy in this area. While the reports are not as complete and consistent as we would like, researchers have managed to use the Florida and Texas reports to good effect.

The Duke and Texas research teams are in the middle of exhaustive studies of the Florida and Texas records.[18] What they are finding strongly confirms the pattern that I have described. Although jury verdicts in Florida are increasing slowly over time, there is no explosion, and the increase appears to be explained by the increasing severity of the injuries in the cases that go to the jury. In Texas, jury verdicts are not rising. Moreover the Texas claim reports show that the amounts actually paid in jury verdict cases are much less than the jury verdicts would suggest, and that the "discount" is increasing over time. This means that the amounts that are actually paid because of jury verdicts are going down in medical malpractice cases.

INSURERS DO FIGHT WEAK CLAIMS,
AND STRONG ONES, TOO.

The medical malpractice myth says that insurance companies are pushovers and that they regularly hand out large sums of money to settle malpractice cases that doctors should win. Not so.

The research shows that doctors, hospitals, and their insurance companies put up a strong fight even when they know that the patient should win. And they rarely pay anything when they are sure that the doctor did nothing wrong. When they do pay in that situation, which is not often, they settle the case at a deep discount relative to the injuries.

Whatever you might think about frivolous litigation (we will talk about that next), there clearly are not a lot of frivolous settlements. The best evidence on this point comes directly from insurance company files.

Here is what a team of doctors reported after examining eight thousand claim files at the home office of the largest medical malpractice insurance company in New Jersey: "Further efforts to clarify the frequency of unjustified payments are needed, but our data suggest that such payments are uncommon."[19] "Further efforts to clarify" is academese for "we know that you are not going to like this, so we do not want to stick our necks out too far." And "our data suggest that such payments are uncommon" is academese for "almost everyone who got paid really was injured by medical malpractice."

Good closed-claim file research is very time-consuming and expensive, and it requires persuading medical malpractice insurance companies to open up their files when they do not have to. Such persuasion takes cooperation from doctors and hospitals, because medical malpractice insurance companies do not want to do anything that will alienate their customer base. So this kind of research almost always takes place with the strong support of a medical society or a medical school—hardly the sort of organizations that are going to be eager to combat the medical malpractice myth.

This last point is important. I cannot stop people from discounting what many of the jury researchers say, based on the fact that they teach in law schools. Not so for the closed-claim file researchers. With only two exceptions, doctors headed all the closed-claim file research teams. And those two exceptions were very focused, individual hospital studies strongly supported by the hospitals in question.

Now, to the research.

The New Jersey closed-claim study. This is the study I just mentioned. A team led by faculty from a New Jersey medical school analyzed over eight thousand claims from the leading New Jersey medical malpractice insurer. For each claim, they recorded the severity of the injury, the amount of any payment to the claimant, whether the payment was made before or after trial, and whether the insurance company had classified each of the claims as "defensible," "indefensible," or "unclear." The researchers compared the outcome of each case according to the insurer's classification and found that there was a very close relationship. The insurer paid 91 percent of indefensible cases, 59 percent of the unclear cases, and 21 percent of the defensible cases.

The New Jersey review team emphasized that payments made in defensible cases were not necessarily unjustified. In fact, as noted above, they concluded that unjustified payments were uncommon. Their reasoning was as follows. First, "the determination about physician care was made very early after a claim was generated and may have been inaccurate as more information became available." Second, "a physician-based review process may be biased toward assessing physician performance in the physician's favor." Finally, "the insurance company may err toward an initial determination of physician care as defensible to avoid unnecessary payments."[20] The careful, measured, and conditional nature of these statements reflects the fact that the article appeared in a prestigious medical journal. In plain English, their bottom line was this: the insurer only very rarely paid weak claims.

The American Society of Anesthesiologists' closed-claim study. Beginning in the mid-1980s the American Society of Anesthesiologists began studying the records of all malpractice claims for anesthesia-related injuries in order to teach their members how to avoid injuring patients and being sued. Trained members of the society review every file. They evaluate whether the care met "the standard of care for a prudent anesthesiologist practicing anywhere in the United States at the time of the event," and they record a variety of information relating to the risk management goals of the study.

This effort has paid off impressively. Anesthesiologists used to pay more for medical malpractice insurance than almost any other medical specialty. As a result of the closed-claim study, they have improved their safety record. Now their malpractice insurance premiums are lower than those of surgeons.[21]

In 1989 the society published the results of their analysis of the first 1,175 claims that they collected.[22] They reported that plaintiffs were twice as likely to be paid in inappropriate-care cases than in appropriate-care cases (82 percent vs. 42 percent). Thus, as in the New Jersey research, the merits matter. Although payments were made in what seems to be a disturbingly high percentage of appropriate-care cases, there is good reason to discount this result.

Most significantly, when I carefully studied the tables and figures in the published article, I discovered that two-thirds of the appropriate-care cases that the insurance companies paid were cases that involved minor injuries and tiny payments.[23] The fact that the article did not emphasize this point makes me suspicious that the authors were eager to discredit the tort system.

We know from the hospital record research that reviewers more often disagree about whether there was negligence in minor-injury cases than in serious-injury cases. For example, most of the differences between the Australian and American research results I discussed in chapter 2 came in how the two teams classified minor-injury cases.[24] Different researchers might well reach a different conclusion about whether appropriate care was in fact provided in the anesthesiologists' minor-injury cases. This seems especially likely when we consider that a professional society conducted the research. As the New Jersey researchers noted, peer review processes tend to be biased in favor of the doctor.

The median payment in the anesthesiologists' minor-injury cases was less than $15,000, so in addition to reaching a different conclusion in some of those cases about whether there was negligence, the insurance companies may well have decided that it was not worth fighting over who was right. All these cases date back to a time before physicians and insurance companies were required to report all medical malpractice payments on behalf of doctors. Since the U.S. Congress enacted that requirement, nuisance payments have become much less common, so we would not expect to find so many paid appropriate-care cases today.[25]

Although payments were made in a few appropriate-care cases involving serious injuries or death,[26] the amounts were much less than in similar cases involving inappropriate care. For permanent-disability cases, the median payment in the paid appropriate-care cases was only one-fifth the size of the median payment in the much larger number of paid inappropriate-care cases. For death cases the median payment in the paid appropriate-care cases was only about one half the size of the median payment in the much larger number of paid inappropriate-care cases. This suggests that the insurers made a business decision to settle a small number of questionable cases, as is common in all kinds of litigation, not just tort cases.

Florida closed-claim studies. Research teams led by Vanderbilt University professor Frank Sloan conducted two closed-claim studies using Florida Department of Insurance records supplemented by physician reviews. Their published reports do not provide exact figures, so I cannot do a very detailed analysis. The first study concluded that "cases involving a higher appearance of fault were more likely to be paid" and that the amount of the payment was positively correlated with the severity of the injury. The second study reached a similar conclusion. Nonnegligent cases were far more likely to be voluntarily dropped without payment. Negligent cases were far more likely to be settled with a payment to the claimant. And the cases that were "uncertain" were more mixed.[27]

The economists' closed-claim studies. Two different teams of economists made detailed studies of claims at two large hospitals. The first study, by Henry Farber and Michelle White, studied claims from incidents between 1977 and 1989 at a hospital in an unnamed state that had not enacted tort reform. The second study, by Stephen Spurr and Sandra Howze, studied claims closed between 1987 and 1995 brought against a hospital in Michigan. In each case they had access to all the records of both the hospital and the hospital's insurance company and they had good cooperation from the hospital. The teams closely examined each case and recorded the amount and timing of payments, as well as the quality of the care. As in the New Jersey study, they assigned quality-of-care ratings based on what the hospital or insurance company had decided.

Their results were similar to the New Jersey results. Claimants were paid in the vast majority of the inappropriate-care case, much less often in the appropriate-care cases, and somewhere in the middle in the difficult-to-classify cases. Significantly, among the appropriate-care cases there was no difference in the settlement rate between cases involving serious injuries and cases involving minor injuries. This means that the insurers were not giving in on the severe-injury cases because they were afraid of what juries would do.

Consistent with the New Jersey research, the teams emphasized that the payments made in the appropriate-care cases were not necessarily unjustified. In addition, their research showed that malpractice insurance companies and hospitals vigorously fight strong claims as well as weak claims.[28]

Smaller studies. Several other smaller studies reinforce the conclusions of the larger studies. A team from the University of Washington reviewed all the birth-related claims from a physician-sponsored insurance company in the 1980s. The senior doctor on the team reviewed all the cases put into suit and found that there were no unjustified payments. The team concluded, "For those cases in which payments were made, there was general consensus among insurance company staff, medical experts, defense attorneys and the physician defendants that some lapse in standard of care contributed to the observed outcome."[29]

A team from the University of Minnesota reviewed all the birth-related claims in the files of the St. Paul Insurance Company that were closed in the early 1980s.[30] They carefully studied cases in which babies died or received serious injuries and concluded that the families received payment in 90 percent of the cases involving clearly substandard care and an unspecified, but much smaller, percentage of cases with good or uncertain care.

Finally, a team from Duke University recently analyzed the claim files of North Carolina medical malpractice cases that were sent to court-ordered mediation. They found an even stronger relationship between the insurer's judgment about the quality of the care and the outcome of the case. Ninety percent of the substandard-care cases were paid—but only after the insurer put up a strong fight. Fifteen percent of the good-care cases were paid. And 35 percent of the uncertain-care cases were paid.[31]

The Harvard Medical Practice Follow-up Study. The only study that reached a different conclusion was a follow-up study of a small number of malpractice claims that the Harvard team matched to their New York hospital records. I have written a somewhat technical article explaining all the reasons to disregard this study.[32] For our purposes it is sufficient to note the following four points.

First, the follow-up study looked at only forty-six cases. The very thorough and high-quality nature of the hospital record review study should not mislead people into thinking that the follow-up malpractice claim study was just as strong. It was not.

Second, the insurance companies handling these forty-six cases knew the claims were being studied, raising the potential for troubling "observer effects." The insurance companies knew that the results of the study could be significant for political decisions, and they knew that the dollar value of these few claims was nothing compared to the financial consequences of the political decisions that could be affected. It is not hard to speculate how they could have manipulated these claims to "prove" that the tort litigation process is erratic.

Third, the researchers' classification of a large percentage of the forty-six claims is open to question, and the statistical analysis is so weak that changing the classification of only a few claims could dramatically change the results. Finally, their conclusions conflict with all the other research.

MALPRACTICE CLAIMS GENERALLY HAVE
SOME BASIS; IF NOT, MOST GO AWAY

As I have just explained, the research clearly refutes the myth that the wrong people generally get paid in medical malpractice cases. No one can deny that the wrong people sometimes do get paid. But the research shows that that does not happen often. In the real world there is no such thing as a perfectly accurate liability system.

But, what about the fact that doctors win well over half of all medical malpractice trials, and that even more plaintiffs drop their claims before trial? That proves that there are many frivolous claims, right?

I will admit that there is a surface plausibility to this argument. But the plausibility disappears on close examination. In fact, the research shows that most malpractice claims are reasonable in light of what plaintiffs and their lawyers can find out at the time.

The Farber and White study. The study that most directly refutes the frivolous-claims myth is one of the economists' closed-claim studies I described a few pages back. Henry Farber, then from MIT and now at Princeton, and Michelle White, then from University of Michigan (where she was director of their economics PhD program) and now at the University of California in San Diego, studied all the medical malpractice claims brought against a hospital during a long period that ended in 1993. Although they looked at only one hospital, their analysis is consistent with all of the other closed-claim studies. Economists and other social scientists who study the tort system regard their study as one of the best in the field. To the best of my knowledge, no one has ever contradicted their analysis, and certainly not in a peer-reviewed journal.

Professors Farber and White answered the frivolous-claim argument by showing that most malpractice lawsuits are reasonable based on what the plaintiff could know at the time. As they explain, "In the medical malpractice arena, potential plaintiffs considering filing a lawsuit do not know whether the hospital was negligent or not." All that an injured patient can know for sure is that she is injured. The research shows that many hospital injuries, especially more serious injuries, result from negligence. The only way that the plaintiff can get access to all the information needed to find out whether her injuries are among the negligent ones is to "file a lawsuit and proceed with the discovery process."[33]

They presented two particularly strong pieces of evidence in support of their conclusion. First, they showed that cases with clear evidence about the quality of care, whether good or bad, are dropped or settled sooner than cases in which the evidence was ambiguous. If the quality of care was clearly good, plaintiffs tend to drop the cases early, and if the quality of care was clearly bad, the insurance company tends to settle the case early. The cases that take longer to resolve tend to be cases in which the evidence about negligence is unclear.

This shows that patients use litigation to find out whether the hospital was negligent. If they get good evidence that the hospital was not negligent, they tend to drop the case. As Professors Farber and White explained, in most cases the decision to file a medical malpractice lawsuit is reasonable based on what the plaintiff could know at the time. A later decision to drop the lawsuit does not mean that the lawsuit was frivolous.

The second piece of evidence came from their very clever decision to look at how participation in the hospital's voluntary complaint process affected the outcome of malpractice lawsuits. They found that patients who brought a suit after going through the voluntary complaint process were much more likely to be paid than patients who brought a suit without going through the process.

Was this because patients with stronger claims chose to go through the process? No. The percentage of good, bad, and ambiguous care was the same among the patients who started their claims with the complaint process and patients who skipped the complaint process and just filed a lawsuit.

The lawsuits filed after the patient went through the complaint process were stronger for a very different reason. Those lawsuits were stronger because patients with weak claims tended to drop their claims after going through the complaint process. Apparently, that process gave patients information about the quality of the care that they otherwise could get only through litigation. So the patients learned something about whether there really had been a mistake in the course of their treatment. If the answer was clearly "no," they chose not to file a lawsuit.[34]

It is important to point out that this does not mean that it was irresponsible for patients to file lawsuits without going through the complaint process. Skipping the complaint process probably seemed reasonable to most patients and lawyers because the hospital very rarely paid even the most deserving patients during the process. When they did, they paid much less than comparable patients received through litigation. As Professors Farber and White discovered, "The hospital uses the informal dispute resolution process to learn about the litigiousness of specific patients" and "it uses the filing of lawsuits as a hurdle that patients must overcome in order to convince the hospital that they are sufficiently litigious to justify a high settlement."[35]

In fact the complaint process was valuable for patients, but it took the economists' research to figure that out. The process was valuable for patients because it provided them with good information about their treatment. If we really want to increase the accuracy of medical malpractice claims (and not just reduce the frequency), there is much to learn from the Farber and White study. I'll return to this point at the end of this chapter and also in chapter 8.

The Harvard Medical Practice Study. The Harvard Medical Practice Study also shows that medical malpractice claims generally have some basis in fact. Along with measuring the extent of medical management injuries and medical malpractice, the team also collected information on all of the malpractice claims filed in New York in the 1980s arising out of the 1984 hospitalizations that they studied. They matched those claims with the patients whose records they studied and found forty-seven claims that involved hospital records that they had reviewed.[36] When we look at the results of their review process for the matched records, we can see that there was some basis in fact for nearly all of the claims.

As I explained in chapter 2, the Harvard researchers put the hospital records through a two-stage review process. In the first stage nurses looked at the record to see whether it contained an indication of a possible medical management injury. If so, they passed the record on to the second stage. In the second stage, two doctors independently reviewed each record to make a final judgment about whether there was a medical management injury and, if so, whether the injury resulted from negligence. According to the rules for the study, the team classified an injury as resulting from medical management only if both doctors agreed. Likewise for negligence.

Out of the forty-seven malpractice claims that the Harvard team matched to their records, all but twelve matched records that the nurses had referred to the doctors for the second-stage review. Of the twelve that had not made it to the second-stage review, nearly half involved treatment in an outpatient facility, not the hospital. As the Harvard researchers explained to the State of New York, the nurses could easily have missed medical management injuries that took place outside the hospital, as long as the treatment in the hospital did not cause any additional injury.[37] This means that we can conclude that 90 percent of the claims either involved potential medical management injuries or involved injuries that were particularly difficult to evaluate on the basis of the hospital records alone.

In twenty-one of the thirty-five cases that went to the second-stage review, both of the doctors concluded that there was evidence of a medical management injury. In four more, one of the doctors concluded that there was evidence. Because the researchers reached a decision about negligence only if both doctors decided that there was a medical management injury, we have information about negligence for only twenty-one of the cases. Out of those twenty-one, the two doctors agreed that there was negligence in eight, reached a split decision in seven, and agreed that there was not negligence in six.

Putting all this together, we can say that *the hospital records alone* provided some basis in fact for three-quarters of the claims, good evidence of negligence in three-quarters of the cases for which that determination was made, and very strong evidence of negligence in over one-third of those cases.[38]

Indeed, given that claimants usually have to file suit in order to get the information that they need to evaluate negligence, the proportion of claims with good evidence of negligence in the hospital record is higher than I would expect. As the research shows, doctors and hospitals typically do not disclose that they caused an injury, let alone that they made a mistake.[39]

Using the figures provided in the Harvard study, I calculated how the strength of the evidence of malpractice in the hospital record affected the chance that a patient would file a claim. What I found contradicts the myth of patients running amok. A patient whose hospital record provided the strongest evidence of medical malpractice was twenty-two times more likely to make a claim than the average patient, eight times more likely to make a claim than all other patients whose records reached the second stage of the review, and two and a half times more likely to make a claim than all the other patients the doctors agreed had suffered a medical management injury.[40]

The Chicago hospital observation study. The Chicago hospital observation study provides even stronger evidence that most medical malpractice claims have a good basis in fact. Because they actually watched and listened to the doctors and nurses, the Chicago researchers had a much more complete picture of the patients' quality of care. This means that their conclusions about the validity of medical malpractice claims are even stronger than those of the Harvard hospital record reviews.

Like the Harvard team, the Chicago researchers matched the patients they studied to medical malpractice claims. Because they studied a smaller number of hospital cases, they matched a smaller number of claims: thirteen. Even though the number is small, the pattern is very clear. There had been a preventable medical mistake during the treatment of eleven out of the thirteen patients who brought a claim. And for one of the remaining two cases, a nurse had filed an occurrence report with the hospital's legal department—a strong indication that there was some basis for that claim as well.[41]

What is the bottom line? The research clearly rejects the claim that most medical malpractice lawsuits are frivolous.

TONY SABIA'S CASE

Sabia v. Norwalk Hospital was a Connecticut medical malpractice case brought on behalf of Tony Sabia, Jr., who nearly died shortly before he was born. Tony's twin brother Michael did die, and Michael's death starved Tony's brain of oxygen long enough to cause profound damage. The defendants in the case were Maryellen Humes, the doctor who delivered Tony and Michael, and Norwalk Hospital, the hospital where Tony was born and that ran the maternity clinic that treated Tony's mother.

The case settled shortly before trial and would have been lost to history except for a series of fortuitous events. Most important, the talented science writer Barry Werth was following the case in the hope of writing a book about the trial. Almost equally important, Tony's parents were so upset about the course of the negotiations that they refused to agree to any settlement that limited in any way their freedom to talk about the case. Finally, Barry Werth did not give up on the case once it settled. He realized that a case that settled was actually the best kind of case for a science writer, at least for one who wants to write about real life. As a result, he immortalized the case in a book that I cannot recommend strongly enough: *Damages*.[42]

As Werth's *Damages* makes clear, no one disputed that Tony suffered a terrible harm. What was in dispute, however, was almost every other aspect of a medical malpractice lawsuit. What was the standard of care that Dr. Humes was to have followed at the time of delivery and did she breach it? What was the standard of care the maternity clinic was to have followed in the months leading up to the birth, and did the clinic breach it? Even if there was negligence, did that negligence cause Tony's harm? And, what is the proper measure of that harm?

The claim against Dr. Humes turned on the legal significance of the fact that, because she did no fetal monitoring and never checked the babies' heartbeats during the delivery, she did not know that Tony's twin was dead until he was born. The claim against the hospital turned on the conduct of the nurses in the delivery room (one of whom did check for heartbeats but did not tell anyone that all she heard was one) and, more important, on the fact that the maternity clinic had not done two prenatal tests that might have revealed that Michael was in distress the week before the delivery. The causation dispute turned on whether any of this made any difference to Tony's condition, and the damages dispute turned on how long Tony would live.

Tony Sabia's case and Barry Werth's book are so important because they show that the yes/no, on/off classifications of the medical malpractice research projects glide over the complexities of medical malpractice.

Based on the exhaustive discussion in Werth's book, I have little doubt that researchers looking only at Tony Sabia's hospital records would have concluded that there was no medical management injury in Tony's case. His twin brother Michael died in utero, before Tony's mother got to the delivery room. Even Tony's experts agreed that most of the harm to Tony happened shortly after Michael died. And the hospital's experts hotly contested whether the outpatient clinic could have done anything to prevent that harm.

Under the Harvard research protocol, a decision that there was no medical management injury would have ended the matter. No one would have considered whether the nurses or the doctors should have known that Michael was dead. And I doubt whether anyone would have aggressively researched whether the outpatient clinic should have done the tests that Tony Sabia's expert testified should have been done.

Does that make Tony Sabia's case frivolous? Does that mean that the case was a paid "appropriate care" or "defensible" case in the terms of the closed-claim research?

Dr. Humes came to talk to my torts class, and it was clear to me that she felt vindicated by Barry Werth's book. Tony's lawyers also came to my class, on a different day, and it was just as clear to me that they felt that Barry Werth understood the case from their perspective and that he had presented facts that showed, conclusively, that Dr. Humes had been negligent.

Two of my students challenged Tony's lawyers. "How could you do that to Dr. Humes?" one asked. "It wasn't her fault," said another.

"You think Maryellen Humes wasn't responsible because that was *our* case, when it was us against the hospital," Tony's lawyer responded. "We all worked together on that—Maryellen's lawyers, us, even the hospital's lawyers. We couldn't ignore the delivery, but we never had to look at it too hard. *It was never in anyone's interest to prove Maryellen Humes caused the harm.* Certainly not in her interest, and not in ours. Even the hospital had to stay away from it because their nurses were in the delivery room, too. Believe me, *if we had to prove she caused the harm, we could have.* Getting shoved through the birth canal is a punishing process for even a healthy baby, and Tony was practically dead. You'll never persuade me that didn't hurt Tony. She should have done an emergency C section as soon as she got in the room. Did that cause five percent of Tony's disability or ten percent? More? Less? Who knows? Who cares? All we had to do is prove that she caused *some* of the harm."[43]

My students certainly were persuaded. Would a jury have been? And, if so, does that mean that juries should not be entrusted with these decisions?

Barry Werth's *Damages* cannot help us decide what to think about that question, because Tony's case never made it to a jury. But I believe the book can help us appreciate how hard it can be to decide the most basic elements of a medical malpractice case: whether the treatment was appropriate and whether the harm resulted from the treatment.

The malpractice cases that most people talk about make things look too easy. Tort reform advocates have a stock of ridiculous cases. Trial lawyer associations have a stock of cases involving outrageous mistakes. And the medical malpractice researchers write up their studies as if there were a clear line between patients who suffered medical management injuries and patients who did not, and as if there were a clear line between medical management injuries that resulted from negligence and those that did not.[44] Some times there is and some times there is not.

This complicated reality has important consequences, not only for how we interpret the research on medical malpractice, but also for how we think about taking care of people with bad medical outcomes. We will return to this topic in chapter 8.

A PLEA FOR COMMON SENSE

As we have seen in this chapter, most injured patients do not sue, and there is far more medical malpractice than medical malpractice litigation. Also, juries largely do what they are supposed to do and, if they are biased, that bias is in favor of doctors.

In a backhanded acknowledgment of that reality, tort reform advocates build their strongest attack on medical malpractice lawsuits on those facts. They combine the fact that doctors win most jury trials with the fact that many plaintiffs drop their claims before trial and conclude that most medical malpractice claims are frivolous. They then use that conclusion to support their political agenda of making it harder for people to sue.

That appears to be a strong argument. But appearances can be misleading.

The research shows that the patients who file claims in fact are sick or injured, almost always as a result of their treatment. That means that the real question in most cases is whether that treatment was proper. Tony's case provides one example.

The patients did not provide the treatment, so we cannot expect them to know whether it was proper. They are not experts. They did not get to hear what the doctors and nurses said to each other. And common experience as well as research tells us that, first, doctors and nurses usually do not tell patients about their mistakes and, second, that mistakes often do not appear in the medical record. So patients and their lawyers often have to file a lawsuit in order to find out whether the treatment was proper. When they do, that is not a frivolous lawsuit, even if they decide to drop the lawsuit after finding out for sure that the doctor either did not cause the injuries or did not make a mistake.

Sometimes patients and their lawyers can make this decision after getting the patient's records from the hospital, without filing a lawsuit. In fact, there are many situations in which a lawyer requests a patient's records but never files a lawsuit. Significantly, a request for patient records counts as a "claim" for most insurance companies. Insurance companies usually require doctors and hospitals to report those kinds of requests to the company. And insurance companies also usually require doctors and hospitals to report a particularly bad outcome that might result in a claim, even before the patient does anything. In either case, insurance companies open a claim file as soon as they receive the report.

If the patient does not bring a lawsuit—which is often the case—the insurance company will eventually close the file. That closed file becomes part of the larger mass of claims closed without a payment, despite the fact that, from the patient's perspective, there never was a claim of any kind. Most of the closed-claim research has not carefully separated these kinds of claims closed without payment from the real claims in which lawsuits were filed. In the hands of the tort reform advocates, all claims closed without payment—whether real or not—get lumped together into a large mass of frivolous claims.

A related reason to discount the statistics about the number of claims closed without a payment comes from the fact that patients often have to file a lawsuit against all of the doctors involved in their care, as well as the hospital, in order to get to the bottom of the case. If it becomes clear that one of the doctors did not contribute to the injury, the patient will dismiss the suit against that doctor. That becomes another claim closed without payment, even if another doctor or the hospital eventually agrees to settle the case or loses at trial. If the same insurance company covers both doctors, the company may treat them as a single claim, but there is no guarantee that the company will do so. If different insurance companies cover the doctors, or if different insurance companies cover the hospital and the doctors, the single lawsuit will almost definitely be counted as multiple claims for purposes of the closed-claim statistics.

Even if we ignore these counting problems, it is remarkable that such a high proportion of medical malpractice claims do have merit. Making it harder to sue probably would reduce the number of suits against doctors and hospitals who did not make a mistake. But it would also reduce the number of suits against doctors and hospitals who did make mistakes. And it will not increase the accuracy of real medical malpractice claims. That is because the accuracy problem stems from the fact that many patients today have no way short of litigation to know for certain what happened.

If we really want to solve the accuracy problem (rather than use the accuracy problem to support an ideological agenda), we should be supporting a very different legal reform. We should be pushing to require doctors and hospitals to tell us all that they know when something bad happens. I discuss this reform further in chapter 8. For the moment I will end with this observation.

We make bakeries tell us the fat content of our cookies. We make credit card companies tell us when they make a mistake in our monthly statements. We make car companies tell us when they find out about even a very minor problem with their cars. In terms of what really matters in our lives, these are small things compared to what happens to us in the hospital. Why not require doctors and hospitals to tell us what we need to know?

We go to doctors and hospitals for their expert knowledge. They have a moral obligation to provide us with *all* the benefits of that knowledge. When there is an "adverse event," they clearly have a moral and professional obligation to tell us all that they know about what happened. The fact that they do not tell us shows that moral and professional obligations are not enough.

5 WHY WE NEED MEDICAL MALPRACTICE LAWSUITS

So far, we have seen that there is an epidemic of medical malpractice, not malpractice lawsuits. We have seen that the boom-and-bust cycle in the liability insurance industry, not malpractice lawsuits, caused the recent rise in malpractice insurance premiums. We have seen that most victims of medical malpractice do not sue. And we have seen that insurance companies' own files show that the legal system works: the litigation process weeds out most of the weaker malpractice claims and even the weaker claims generally are not frivolous.

We still have two more parts of the medical malpractice myth to address—the claim that lawsuits cause wasteful defensive medicine and the claim that lawsuits reduce access to medical care. Those are the topics of chapters 6 and 7.

But first we should put malpractice lawsuits to the test. It is one thing to show that malpractice lawsuits do not have all the bad consequences that organized medicine says. It is quite another to show that they actually do some good. What is the evidence of that?

In this chapter I will present four kinds of evidence. First, I will show that medical malpractice lawsuits are the reason that we know what we know about the extent of medical mistakes and injuries. People who say that fear of lawsuits drives information about medical mistakes underground have the story exactly backward.

Second, I will show that medical malpractice lawsuits improve patient safety. My strongest case is anesthesiology. More than any other group of doctors, anesthesiologists have been willing to learn what lawsuits can teach them about their mistakes. As we will see, the results are impressive. Anesthesiology has become safer, and anesthesiologists now pay less for malpractice insurance than most of their hospital-based colleagues.

Third, I will show that medical malpractice lawsuits help injured patients by providing them compensation that they need. Whether lawsuits are the best way to compensate people with medical injuries is debatable. And lawsuits clearly do not compensate enough people. But until we provide a better compensation program, lawsuits are what we have.

Finally, I will show that malpractice lawsuits promote traditional American values like justice, responsibility, and freedom from intrusive government control. When we consider other ways to compensate people with medical injuries, we need to stay true to these values.

MALPRACTICE LAWSUITS BROUGHT THE MALPRACTICE EPIDEMIC TO LIGHT

With few exceptions, all the research documenting the medical malpractice epidemic came in response to medical malpractice lawsuits. At first, the research grew out of doctors' efforts to prove that injured patients and their lawyers were in the wrong, and that the real problem was malpractice lawsuits. More recently, the research has grown out of concerns that medical malpractice lawsuits do not do enough to prevent injuries or compensate patients.

I discussed the origins of the mid-1970s California study and the mid-1980s Harvard study in chapter 2. Both studies came in response to medical malpractice insurance crises. Although the timing of insurance crises has little connection to lawsuits, insurance companies are in the medical malpractice business only because of lawsuits. So lawsuits get the credit for both of these important studies.

The California study sponsors expected that their study would help rescue the medical profession from a siege of frivolous lawsuits, and the researchers themselves may well have expected that result. The Harvard research came nearly ten years later, so the researchers could not have been surprised at what they found. But we can be confident that the doctors, hospitals, and associations that supported the Harvard study expected vindication.

I lived through the 1980s insurance crisis surrounded by doctors, and I can report that they thought malpractice lawsuits were a bigger problem than medical malpractice. In fact, doctors still think that *today*, as the survey I discussed in chapter 2 showed. When asked to list the two most important problems with health care and medicine today, nearly one-third of U.S. doctors listed medical malpractice lawsuits and insurance, while only 5 percent listed medical mistakes, injuries, or related topics.[1]

After the California and Harvard studies no serious researcher would ever claim that medical malpractice lawsuits are a bigger problem than medical injuries. Nevertheless lawsuits remain one of the driving forces behind the research on medical injuries. What has changed is simply the nature of the concern. It used to be that too many patients were bringing lawsuits, leading doctors to engage in too much unproductive, defensive medicine. Now the concern is that too few patients get compensated and lawsuits get in the way of patient safety.[2]

Patient compensation and patient safety are legitimate concerns. But those are the goals of malpractice lawsuits, not a reason to make them harder to bring or less effective. Certainly there is room for improvement on both fronts. But there also is great irony in the complaint that medical malpractice lawsuits do not do enough.[3]

The medical establishment used to say that injured patients and their lawyers were making up the medical malpractice problem. Now they say that patients and their lawyers are not doing enough to fix that problem:[4] "Get out of the way and let the medical professionals do the job."

MALPRACTICE LAWSUITS DO NOT DRIVE MEDICAL MISTAKES UNDERGROUND

Dr. David Hyman, a professor at both the law and medical schools at the University of Illinois, and Charles Silver, a professor at University of Texas Law School, recently took a careful look at what they call the "conventional wisdom" that the fear of lawsuits drives medical mistakes underground.[5]

They began by checking that this is in fact the conventional wisdom. It is. As Hyman and Silver report, the Institute of Medicine says that "the threat of medical malpractice . . . discourages the disclosure of errors." Harvard researchers say malpractice liability "may well stifle efforts to reduce error" because doctors worry about "reporting events that may leave them open to accusations of negligence" and "the specter of litigation currently stands as a major barrier to the free flow of information about medical errors." Australian researchers say "Blaming and punishing . . . drives the problem of iatrogenic harm underground." The American Medical Association says liability prevents the creation of "a climate where reporting of errors will occur."[6]

Prominent doctors and nurses agree. "The deeper problem with medical malpractice lawsuits is that by demonizing errors they prevent doctors from acknowledging and discussing them publicly." And, "The threat of medical malpractice litigation is one of the most obvious barriers to the improvement of safety." Medical school professors agree. Public health researchers agree. Even law and medicine professors agree. In fact, it seems that almost everybody who is anybody in the medical establishment agrees. As Hyman and Silver conclude, "The best evidence of acceptance of the conventional wisdom may be the dearth of commentary disputing it."

They then looked at all these recitations of the conventional wisdom in search of supporting studies and evidence. This is what they found: "Although commentators routinely invoke the conventional wisdom, they *never* offer any evidence or empirical research supporting their position."

That is right. Never. Not the Institute of Medicine. Not the Harvard researchers. Not the Australian researchers. Not the American Medical Association. Not the prominent doctors and nurses or the medical school professors or the public health researchers or the law and medicine professors.

My own look at the literature confirms their conclusion. People often refer to articles that support the conventional wisdom, but when you actually read those articles, what you find is a naked assertion or, at best, testimony. What you do not find is research or empirical evidence.

As even the most casual glance through this book shows, there has been an explosion in research about medical injuries. (In contrast to the mythical explosion in medical malpractice lawsuits.) My research assistants and I have put together boxes of binders filled with studies and reports. We have binders on the accuracy of medical claiming, the incidence of medical injury, the frequency of malpractice claims and the severity of the injuries involved, risk management studies of medical injuries and malpractice claims, the anesthesiologists' malpractice experience, the jury research, attempts to measure defensive medicine, the claim that doctors are leaving medicine, the insurance underwriting cycle, literature reviews, and ideas for alternative compensation approaches. We also have stacks of books and reports.

In this mountain of paper there is no research testing the conventional wisdom that medical malpractice lawsuits drive medical mistakes underground. Could it be that the conventional wisdom is wrong?

Based on the research I have already described, we can say for sure that this wisdom is wrong at the macro level. We know more today than we have ever known about medical mistakes, thanks to the studies prompted by medical malpractice lawsuits.

But maybe fear of lawsuits does drive information about mistakes underground at the micro level—the nurse who chooses not to put something in the patient record, the surgeon who does not tell the family about the adverse event during surgery, the ER doc who is afraid to talk to his colleagues. Do those kinds of decisions happen often, and is fear of lawsuits the reason?

Hyman and Silver think not. They agree that information is left out of the record and that medical providers too often do not talk about their mistakes—either to each other or to patients. But they conclude that fear of lawsuits is not the reason: "The case for the conventional wisdom has not been made and the best available evidence actually undermines the conventional wisdom."[7]

As they point out, to prove that lawsuits drive medical mistakes underground, you first have to prove that mistakes would be out in the open if there were no medical malpractice lawsuits. That is clearly not the case. Here is just some of their evidence.

They compared disclosure practices in the United States today with disclosure practices in the United States before the rise of medical malpractice litigation in the 1960s and 1970s. If the conventional wisdom were right, there would have been more disclosure earlier. Yet, there was less, not more.

They compared disclosure practices in the United States today with disclosure practices in the UK, which has a similar culture but less malpractice litigation. If the conventional wisdom were right, doctors in the UK would be more likely to disclose their mistakes. Yet, they are not more likely to disclose. If anything, doctors in the UK are less likely to disclose, and error reporting and health-quality information systems are far more developed in the United States than in the UK.

They compared whether doctors disclose more information about minor injuries or "near miss" mistakes. If fear of lawsuits really is the explanation for silence, doctors should provide more information about mistakes that cause less harm. But the research they review shows that the opposite is true.

Finally, they compared whether Veterans Hospital Administration doctors are more likely to disclose mistakes than other doctors in the United States. By law, VHA doctors cannot be sued for medical malpractice, setting up the perfect comparison case. If the conventional wisdom were right, VHA doctors would be more likely to disclose and VHA hospitals would be safer. Yet, if anything, VHA doctors were less likely to disclose and VHA hospitals less safe, until Congress and the Veterans Administration forced them to pay more attention to patient safety. But, even now, a strong "shame and blame" culture and a dysfunctional reporting system still exists. As they conclude, "The existence and persistence of this culture *in the absence* of personal legal liability for mistakes is inconsistent with the conventional wisdom's assertion that malpractice lawsuits poison a well that otherwise would be pure."

In short, medical malpractice lawsuits do not drive mistakes underground. If anything, lawsuits bring mistakes to light. Of course we need to do more to encourage doctors, nurses, and hospitals to disclose medical mistakes, but restrictive tort reforms will not accomplish that goal. A far better approach would be to require them to disclose their mistakes and to use a combination of carrot and stick to make that happen. In chapter 8 I will describe one such approach.

MALPRACTICE LAWSUITS PROMOTE PATIENT SAFETY

Malpractice lawsuits promote patient safety both through visible public policy efforts and through less visible changes in hospitals and other health-care organizations. In the realm of public policy, malpractice lawsuits and the research they spawned have turned patient safety into a public health concern. It is much too soon to tell whether the patient-safety movement will make hospitals as safe as safety advocates would like.

Nevertheless, we already can declare that the patient-safety movement represents a significant success for medical malpractice lawsuits. The movement demonstrates that important groups within organized medicine have accepted the fact that we have a patient-safety problem.

Malpractice lawsuits also promote patient safety through less visible changes in health-care organizations. Lawsuits identify dangerous conditions and risky practices, providing the opportunity to improve those conditions and practices and, sometimes, energizing government agencies to discipline doctors or order hospitals to take corrective action.

Malpractice lawsuits also provide an incentive for doctors and hospitals to avoid injuries. No one would argue that the incentive is perfect. Because so few patients sue, lawsuits almost certainly do not provide as strong an incentive as might be needed, but they provide enough of an incentive that doctors complain about having to practice defensive medicine. As we will see in chapter 7, claims about defensive medicine are part of the medical malpractice myth. Nevertheless there is good evidence that malpractice lawsuits and malpractice insurance premiums do motivate health-care providers to improve their safety record.

Malpractice Lawsuits Identify Dangerous Conditions

There has been no systematic research on the role of medical malpractice lawsuits in identifying dangerous conditions and dangerous doctors. What we have instead are case studies. The best-developed example comes from the American Society of Anesthesiologists' effort to learn from medical malpractice lawsuits, which I will discuss separately.

In addition, any diligent researcher can use newspaper archives and public records to find malpractice cases that led to specific and significant patient-safety improvements. I selected Connecticut cases to discuss here because I live and teach in Connecticut. But, as you will see, there is nothing about these cases that is peculiar to Connecticut. Similar examples surely can be found in any state.

Although there are unique features to each of these cases, they share a common, well-known pattern. In each case, there was an unsafe condition that health-care professionals knew about but did not correct. In each case, it took a serious injury and a malpractice lawsuit to bring the unsafe condition (and the previous failure to act) to light. And in each case, the lawsuit prompted corrective action that we can be fairly confident would not otherwise have occurred, at least not until someone else got injured and brought a lawsuit.

Bridgeport Hospital's staph infections. In July 2002 the *Chicago Tribune* ran a major story about an epidemic of hospital-borne infection that kills tens of thousands of patients a year in the United States. The *Tribune* story featured a detailed account of an outbreak of infections in Bridgeport Hospital in Bridgeport, Connecticut, including photos of one woman who died and another who was disabled as a result. As the *Tribune* reported, a malpractice lawsuit played a crucial role in forcing the hospital to clean up its operating rooms and in bringing the outbreak to light.[8]

The *Tribune* reporter got most of his information about the Bridgeport outbreak from the malpractice lawsuit that the families of the women in the photos brought against the hospital. Based on records from the lawsuit, the *Tribune* reported that a hidden camera showed that half of the doctors using one operating room in the hospital did not wash their hands. Also, doctors wore "germ-laden clothes from home into the operating room," and doctors and nurses came into one operating room during surgery "to make personal calls on a phone mounted on the wall."

Apparently the hospital had known about these and other unsanitary conditions long before the lawsuit, but had not taken necessary corrective action. The *Tribune* reported, "In 1995, hospital officials hired a respected nursing organization to survey the facility after a dozen patient infections were linked to unsanitary conditions." "Many recommendations were ignored," and the "$20,000 repair price" for the most expensive recommendation "was deemed too costly at the time, hospital records show." As the *Tribune* reported, "The case, which involves four patients who contracted infections inside Bridgeport Hospital, also exposes how the bottom line influences decisions that allow germs to flourish in what are supposed to be the most sterile quarters in the hospital."

After a series of deaths and injuries in the fall of 1996 and early 1997 and the resulting lawsuit, the hospital finally improved the operating rooms. The *Tribune* reported that the improvements included "updating air filtration systems in operating rooms; more patient isolation rooms; motion-sensitive sinks with timed release of water to encourage proper hand scrubbing; and waterless soap dispensers for cleaning hands quickly." The results were impressive: "Infection rates that once soared to 22 percent of cardiac surgery patients have been brought down to nearly zero during most months."

The *Chicago Tribune* story achieved considerable notoriety in Connecticut, and not only because it featured Bridgeport Hospital. Just a few days after publication, Bridgeport Hospital sued three of the family members who brought the malpractice lawsuit and their lawyer, claiming that they had violated a confidentiality agreement by talking to the *Tribune* reporter. The suit caused such an outcry that the hospital dropped it immediately. As the *New York Times* reported, "Quick withdrawal of the suit suggested that legal action intended to relieve a public relations headache had created a public relations nightmare instead."[9] Indeed.

Lost in the public relations nightmare was an important public policy lesson about the role of medical malpractice lawsuits. Like almost any other organization, hospitals resist making expensive changes.[10] Malpractice lawsuits can force them to improve patient safety, especially when combined with public health department action. The fear of similar malpractice lawsuits also can encourage others to make improvements. Today, the *Chicago Tribune* story can be found on the Web site of the Public Health Research Institute, where it serves as a cautionary tale for hospital administrators.[11]

Norwalk Hospital's impaired anesthesiologist. In June 2004 the *Hartford Courant* ran a chilling story about a Norwalk Hospital anesthesiologist. The doctor had a long history of substance abuse, but he was investigated by the Connecticut Department of Public Health only as a result of two malpractice cases. The *Courant* reported that in each case, the plaintiff went into Norwalk Hospital for routine surgery and "fell into an irreversible coma after anesthesiologist Jay Angeluzzi failed to notice there wasn't enough oxygen getting to her brain."[12]

The families of the victims brought malpractice lawsuits and asked the Public Health Department to investigate. As the *Courant* reported, the investigators looking into the second case "found that Angeluzzi had disconnected the noisy electronic alarms meant to warn of just such a problem. They also found that he could not account for powerful narcotics he signed for before the procedure." Public Health records about the first case were sealed, but the *Courant* was able to find out that it involved "a frighteningly similar set of circumstances." In both cases, "there was a disconnected monitor, and there were missing narcotics." In both cases, too, other people, not Dr. Angeluzzi, discovered the lack of oxygen. In the first case, orderlies moving the patient from the operating table to a stretcher noticed that she was not breathing. In the second case, an obstetrician noticed that the patient and her baby were turning blue.

As the *Courant* reported, the first case put the hospital and the Department of Public Health on notice of the problem with Dr. Angeluzzi, but it took the second case to get them to move beyond investigation: "This time Angeluzzi lost his hospital privileges immediately, and, facing health department charges, he surrendered his Connecticut medical license." Not surprisingly, Norwalk Hospital and Dr. Angeluzzi also promptly settled the first malpractice case, which was still pending, for an enormous sum: $12 million. (The amount was so large because of the very high costs of caring for someone likely to remain for many years in a coma.) The second lawsuit has yet to be resolved (as of June 2005), but in my view the real question is how much the defendants will pay, not whether they will pay. As the research we examined in the last chapter suggests, cases with clear liability and severe injuries almost never go to trial.

Dr. Angeluzzi's case also teaches us an important public policy lesson about the role of medical malpractice lawsuits. Lawsuits are one of the few ways to get rid of problem doctors. As writer and surgeon Atul Gawande explains, "Even good doctors can go bad, and when they do, colleagues tend to be almost entirely unequipped to do anything about them." Most valid lawsuits no doubt result from momentary mistakes by otherwise effective doctors. Patient-safety advocates would say these kinds of injuries really result from the failure of systems to anticipate and prevent the mistakes (as with the organ transplant mistakes that killed Jesica and Jeanella). But sometimes, as Dr. Angeluzzi demonstrates, there are doctors who should not be practicing, at least not without treatment and close supervision. As many as 5 percent of physicians in practice may be "actually unfit to see patients," Gawande reports.[13] A medical malpractice lawsuit can and should be an opportunity for hospitals to consider whether a doctor is among that 5 percent.

The CVS pharmacist's fatal mistake. In February 2002 the *Hartford Courant* ran a series of stories about Donna Marie Altieri, a fifty-one-year-old woman who died in early 2001 because she was given the wrong drug. Her doctor had prescribed "opium tincture—camphorated," commonly known as paregoric, but the pharmacist gave her "opium tincture," commonly known as laudanum. Despite the very similar medical names, laudanum contains twenty-five times the amount of morphine as paregoric. This means that taking a paregoric-size dose of laudanum can be fatal. As the *Courant* reported, the risk of confusing opium tincture and camphorated opium tincture was well known and there were software programs available to warn pharmacists about drugs with similar names.[14]

Told that their mother had died of a heart attack, Donna Marie Altieri's grown children asked for an autopsy. When the results showed that she had died from morphine intoxication, they asked for an investigation. Their mother's doctor learned of the mistake and told the pharmacy, CVS, but CVS did not tell the family. CVS investigated the death and prepared a report that says, "Updated computer software should recognize dosage and warn of similar name usage." The Altieri family received this report and related information only after retaining a lawyer to consider a medical malpractice lawsuit.

The Altieri children went public about their mother's death at the start of the 2002 session of the Connecticut legislature. They filed a lawsuit and recruited their state senator to introduce legislation requiring pharmacies to report prescription mistakes. The *Hartford Courant* endorsed their efforts, opining, "The state should do the obvious by requiring that pharmacies report all prescription errors," and the state should "require that all pharmacies use already available software to alert druggists to common mistakes." A compromise version of the legislation passed later that year. Among other provisions, the legislation directed the state "to adopt regulations requiring pharmacies to establish programs aimed at reducing errors."

Once again, the public policy lesson is clear. Medical malpractice lawsuits identify dangerous conditions and prompt hospitals and government agencies to act.

Saint Raphael's tragic nitrous oxide hookup. In January 2002 a Connecticut hospital took the unusual step of publicly announcing a serious medical mistake and what the hospital had done to prevent it from happening again. For this reason, the case does not fit the pattern of a malpractice lawsuit leading to corrective action. But it does illustrate the cost-benefit aspect of patient safety and, therefore, the role that lawsuits can play in encouraging hospitals to give appropriate weight to patient safety. This case serves as a transition between our discussion of how lawsuits identify dangerous conditions and how they provide an incentive for patient safety.

The case involved two women, Doris Herdman and Joan Cannon, who died in the Hospital of Saint Raphael in New Haven on January 11 and 15 after receiving nitrous oxide through a breathing tube that was supposed to carry oxygen. As the *Hartford Courant* reported, "Hospital staff noticed the faulty hookup after they had spent minutes trying to revive Cannon with even more 'oxygen' that was, in fact, the deadly nitrous gas." According to the *Courant*, this kind of mix-up had been thought to be "part of medical history—something that occurred decades ago, but was considered extremely unlikely today."[15]

Both women had been in the hospital's cardiac catheterization lab, wearing ventilators to provide them with oxygen. A safety pin on the connector for the oxygen line had snapped off, allowing the oxygen connector to be plugged into a nitrous oxide port that was located next to the oxygen port in the lab. A Department of Public Health inspection revealed that the ports were located under a table where they were hard to see and reach; the respiratory therapy staff and most of the nursing staff assigned to the lab did not know that there was nitrous oxide piped into the lab; and the ventilators in the lab did not have readily available oxygen analyzer alarms.[16] The *Courant* reported, "It was always assumed that the safety prong would prevent any mix-ups."

The *Courant* reported that some doctors questioned why nitrous oxide was even available in the lab: "Cardiologists say that oxygen is not usually administered in routine cardiac catheterizations and that such 'cath' labs do not usually stock gases such as nitrous oxide." The *Courant* reported that the "'cath' lab was originally designed 14 years ago to handle various procedures. Outlets for nitrous oxide, a common anesthetic, were included for that reason and kept as live connections for potential future use."

As the hospital admitted, "Access to nitrous oxide should and could have been removed from the lab."[17] After the deaths, the hospital disconnected the nitrous oxide line and capped the port in the catheterization lab and also adopted a rule requiring that that oxygen equipment and connections be checked before every procedure throughout the hospital. The cost-benefit analysis here is not difficult. Whatever cost might be involved in having to restore the nitrous oxide line in the future was not enough to justify exposing catheterization lab patients to this risk.

The enormity of the mistake and the publicity may well have been enough to prod the hospital to take corrective action. But the threat of liability cannot have been far from hospital officials' minds. The *Courant*'s first report on the incident included a comment from a leading medical malpractice attorney. Later reports made clear that the two families in fact did bring lawsuits. The lawsuits cannot undo the harm, but they provide an incentive for hospitals to remove unnecessary gas lines and other potentially dangerous equipment when they are not needed.

Malpractice Lawsuits Provide an Incentive for Patient Safety

Researchers have tried to measure the effect of medical malpractice lawsuits on patient safety, but that turns out to be difficult to do. The problem comes in sorting out the cause-and-effect relationship between malpractice claims and medical mistakes, as Harvard public health researchers recently reported. For example, suppose we find that there are lots of errors in a hospital with lots of lawsuits. That could mean that all those lawsuits are not doing a very good job of encouraging the hospital to prevent injuries. Or it could mean that more people file lawsuits because there are so many injuries. Or it could mean something else altogether. Maybe we are looking at an underfunded, stressed hospital in a city with an unusually large number of medical malpractice lawyers.

Notwithstanding this problem, the Harvard researchers reported that their research suggests that increasing the risk of medical malpractice lawsuits improves hospitals' safety record. But they concluded that the evidence was "limited" and, furthermore, that statistical research of this sort would be unlikely to provide stronger evidence that malpractice lawsuits prevent medical injuries.[18]

The Harvard researchers reached this conclusion not only because of how hard it is to sort out cause and effect, but also because of what their earlier research showed about the frequency of medical malpractice lawsuits. As you may remember from chapter 2, this research showed that there are too few malpractice lawsuits. As a result, safety too often does not pay.

A hospital that adds up the cost of patient safety and then compares those costs with what it will save from fewer medical malpractice lawsuits will find that in many, perhaps most, cases the costs are bigger than the savings. Although tragic accidents involving obvious errors like those at Saint Raphael's may be likely to result in a lawsuit, most injured patients do not sue. That means it takes a truly massive change in the patient injury rate to pay off, reliably, in terms of fewer lawsuits.

For this reason, people who take a cost-benefit approach to the world are often surprised that malpractice lawsuits have any effect on patient safety. There are a number of reasons that lawsuits do have this effect, however, some of which we have already explored.

One reason is that malpractice insurance crises and tort reform scare tactics make malpractice lawsuits seem much more likely than in fact they are. Another reason is that human beings seem to be predisposed to be more worried about unpredictable events—like medical malpractice lawsuits—than more predictable events.[19] Also, the involvement of government regulators can magnify the error correction effect of malpractice lawsuits, as we just saw in some of the Connecticut case studies. Finally, I think that doctors and other health professionals really do care about their patients, so it is not only a question of whether safety pays. Even a little incentive can go a long way. Malpractice lawsuits improve patient safety by making medical mistakes more visible and by making patient safety a higher priority than it might otherwise be.

Easy to say. What is the evidence?

We have just seen that malpractice lawsuits bring specific unsafe practices to light and lead hospitals and other institutions to take corrective action.

The anesthesiologist case study I will discuss next shows how one professional organization used malpractice lawsuits to mobilize their members to improve patient safety. They used malpractice claim files to identify unsafe practices; they developed new equipment and clear procedures to reduce the risk of injury; and they used professional guidelines and the fear of lawsuits to encourage their members to use the new equipment and procedures.

Recent history also shows that medical malpractice lawsuits have changed the way that hospitals and other large health-care organizations respond to and attempt to prevent patient injuries. The evidence is an entirely new health-care profession—the health-care risk manager—and a new department in most large health-care organizations—the risk management department.[20]

Risk managers and risk management departments keep track of patient complaints, manage malpractice claims, provide feedback to senior administrators on unsafe practices revealed by the complaints and claims, and serve as a clearinghouse for patient-safety information. Do risk management departments do all that they might do to improve patient safety? No. Do they do some good? Yes. If nothing else, they provide hospital administrators a window into patient safety that would not otherwise exist.

In addition, the recent round of malpractice insurance price increases has sped up two potentially very important patient-safety trends: the trend toward sending more patients to doctors and hospitals that specialize in a specific operation or procedure and the related trend toward having "hospitalists"—doctors who work only in hospitals—treating more patients in hospitals. As we will see in chapter 7, the medical establishment has used these trends to try to scare patients and lawmakers into thinking that the malpractice insurance crisis has reduced access to medical care. It is true that some doctors have eliminated some of the more risky parts of their practices, but the best evidence is that patients are safer as a result.[21]

Finally, medical malpractice lawsuits have put liability insurance companies into the medical injury-prevention business, especially for their hospital and institutional customers. Malpractice insurance companies do two main things to promote patient safety. First, they provide patient-safety training to their customers. Second, they look into hospitals' patient-safety practices when they decide whether to offer insurance, and at what price. They consider the hospital's claim records, whether the hospital has a risk management department, what kinds of safety training are provided to hospital workers, and whether the hospital has adopted all the safety measures that hospital accreditation organizations recommend. Knowing that insurance companies care about these things provides an added incentive for hospitals to do them.

Of course these efforts actually improve patient safety only if the insurance companies' information about patient safety is accurate and if the hospitals act on that information. Finding out what actually improves patient safety is no simple matter. Nor is getting hospitals to act. But there are several reasons to believe that insurance companies have an advantage in both.[22]

The first advantage comes from the insurance companies' experience with malpractice lawsuits. No matter how much experience a hospital has, an insurance company will have more, especially compared to smaller hospitals. This is not to say that malpractice insurance companies are the only kind of organization that can see the injury-prevention "big picture" more clearly than individual hospitals (health insurers are another), simply that they are one.

The second advantage is psychological. An insurance company employee does not have the same emotional stake in any particular way of providing health care that a surgeon or nurse has. Information that calls into question the safety of one way of providing health care is not as threatening to insurance company personnel as it may be for a nurse or doctor who has been practicing that way for the last ten years. As a result, insurance people sometimes have an advantage over doctors and nurses in recognizing when a patient injury means that it is time for a change.

The third advantage comes from the relative weakness of administrators in hospitals dominated by high-prestige doctors. The explanation "because the insurance company says we have to" is easier for a highly paid, mobile surgeon to accept from a hospital administrator than "because I'm in charge and I say so" and probably easier to accept from a hospital risk manager than "because I'm an expert and I say so."

The fourth advantage comes from the fact that liability insurers, unlike most other injury-prevention advisors, have their own money at stake. "Because the insurance company says we have to" is a satisfactory explanation because the insurance company is a credible source of information. This credibility comes not only from the other advantages just discussed, but also from the fact that the insurance company's money is on the line if a patient sues.

Malpractice Lawsuits Taught Anesthesiologists How to
Avoid Injuries and Gave Them an Incentive to Do So

"If you can't beat them, join them." In effect, that is what the American Society of Anesthesiologists (ASA) decided at the height of the mid-1980s medical malpractice insurance crisis. They faced up to the unpleas-

ant view of their world offered by medical malpractice lawsuits and decided to learn from those lawsuits.[23] Their experience teaches a valuable
lesson. Doctors and hospitals can use malpractice lawsuits to improve patient safety.

The medical malpractice insurance crisis provided the crucial spark of
emotional energy for the society's leadership and also for the necessary
follow-through at the grass roots level. The chairman of the committee that
supervised the project later explained, "The relationship of patient safety
to malpractice insurance premiums was easy to predict. If patients were
not injured, they would not sue, and if the payout for anesthesia-related
patient injury could be reduced, then insurance rates should follow."[24]

The anesthesiologists launched a closed-claim project that attempted
to find every medical malpractice claim that had ever been filed in connection with anesthesia. By 1989 they had collected and analyzed well over
one thousand claims. By 1999 that number had grown to over four thousand.[25] What they found was disturbing. But rather than hide from the
facts, they faced them.

For example, the anesthesiologists learned early on that over one-third
of the claims came from what they called "adverse respiratory events."
They also learned that those events were both more damaging to patients
and—here is the important point—more preventable than other anesthesia injuries. In response, the ASA backed the development of better anesthesia equipment and new practice guidelines and then worked hard to get
anesthesiologists to use them.[26]

As a result of these and similar efforts, anesthesiology today is "the only
health sector to achieve 'six sigma' quality, or fewer than 4 deaths per 1 million exposures, the same maximum rate of defects routinely achieved by
such corporations as General Electric and Motorola." Medical malpractice insurance premiums for anesthesiologists are way down as a result.
For anesthesiologists "the 2002 average premium was $18,000—about the
same as in 1985 and much lower than for other specialties."[27]

What motivated anesthesiologists? Medical malpractice lawsuits and
the resulting high insurance prices. How did they identify areas that
needed improvement? Medical malpractice claims files. How have they
demonstrated that their efforts paid off? Lower medical malpractice insurance premiums. What is the lesson of the anesthesiologists' experience?

When doctors are prepared to listen, medical malpractice lawsuits have a lot to teach them.

As the anesthesiologists learned, malpractice claimants (and their lawyers) are not the bad news; they are messengers bearing the bad news. As we all know, shooting the messenger is no way to solve a problem.

MALPRACTICE LAWSUITS PROVIDE
NEEDED COMPENSATION

Along with preventing injuries, medical malpractice lawsuits also compensate injured patients. As we saw in chapter 4, the research tells us that the people who bring successful malpractice claims generally deserve compensation. Of course, malpractice lawsuits are not 100 percent accurate. No medical injury compensation system ever could be. As the research shows, there is no perfectly reliable way to tell the difference between normal complications and medically caused injuries; drawing the line between negligent and nonnegligent injuries is even more difficult. Given how hard these decisions are to make, the legal system does a remarkably good job at weeding out weaker claims.

The research also shows that injured patients do not receive too much money. For nearly fifty years, research on tort claims has consistently shown that people with serious injuries receive far less money than they need even to cover their medical expenses and to replace their lost income. Research on medical malpractice lawsuits shows the same thing.[28]

In fact, the special caps on malpractice damages imposed by tort reform efforts in California and other states have made the undercompensation problem even worse in serious medical malpractice cases, because patients use the money they get for pain and suffering to pay their lawyers. In our legal system, the lawyer representing the plaintiff in a medical malpractice lawsuit generally does not get paid unless the patient gets paid. When the patient gets paid, the lawyer gets a share. Recovery for pain and suffering gives patients the means to pay the lawyer's share and still have enough money left to do what they can to put their lives in order.[29]

In addition, patients who win or settle a medical malpractice lawsuit typically have to repay their health insurer for the costs of the treatment for their injuries. By federal law all Medicare and Medicaid expenses related to the injury have to be repaid, and most employee benefit plans also require people to repay the plan out of the proceeds of a lawsuit.[30] Because most people get their health insurance either through an employee benefit plan or from Medicare or Medicaid, these arrangements make taxpayers and employee benefit plans "silent plaintiffs" in medical malpractice lawsuits. The vast majority of injured patients do not bring lawsuits, so the total recoveries are not a significant source of revenue to employment benefit plans or to Medicare or Medicaid. Nevertheless, the recoveries are significant for patients who do bring lawsuits. Paying back the health plan or the government is the fair thing to do, but that reduces the amount of money that the injured patient receives, making damages for pain and suffering even more essential.[31]

On the other hand, as we know from chapters 2 and 3, the research also shows that medical malpractice lawsuits do not help enough people. In addition, lawsuits are an expensive way to provide compensation; only about one out of every three dollars spent in malpractice lawsuits goes to patients. Do those facts support damage caps and other restrictive tort reforms?

No. It is true that malpractice lawsuits do not compensate enough injured patients. But this does not mean we should make it *harder* to bring lawsuits. Instead, it means we should be looking for easier and cheaper ways to help injured patients. I will describe two ways in chapter 8. For the time being, however, malpractice lawsuits are the compensation tool that we have. It would be a terrible mistake to make that tool harder to use without giving people something better in its place.

MALPRACTICE LAWSUITS PROMOTE
TRADITIONAL AMERICAN VALUES

Talking to certain people, I could be forgiven for concluding that there must be something distinctly un-American about lawsuits in general and, these days, medical malpractice lawsuits in particular. I even had the "C" and "S" words thrown at me in long-ago conversations about lawyers and lawsuits. Communism and socialism are yesterday's enemies, so I have not heard that in a while. But I have heard some people starting to use the "T" word—terrorism—in recent conversations about lawsuits.

As I have said each time, that comparison is over the line. And not be-cause, as a late-night comic might say, the comparison is unfair to terror-ists. Lawsuits share nothing of any consequence with terrorism. The joke is funny precisely for that reason, and also because it is the latest twist in a long tradition of poking fun at lawyers. Putting opposites together in new, but familiar ways is a standard of the comedy writer's trade.

I have no problem with poking fun at lawyers, as long as everyone knows that is what we are doing. But as I learned in high school after being hauled down to the principal's office for what I thought was *obviously* a satirical riff in the student newspaper, not everyone recognizes when you are kidding. So I am not surprised to find out that some people actually believe the law-yer jokes and the tort reformers' tall tales.

We should be clear. A lawsuit is the opposite of taking matters into your own hands and blowing up a building. Lawsuits channel the very human but very dangerous desire for revenge into a quest for justice.[32] Lawsuits make people work *through* the system, not against it. Lawsuits take place in the open. Lawsuits provide procedural protections for everyone in-volved. To win a lawsuit you have to be right. It is not enough to be angry.[33]

Most important, lawsuits provide a space in which reason, diligence, and justice can sometimes prevail against even the richest and most pow-erful organizations. Lawsuits provide one of the few such spaces in Amer-ica today, maybe even the only one. And that, of course, is why business interests are supporting the doctors' request for restrictive tort reform. "Hiding behind the doctor's white coat," I call it.

For a good example of what I mean, watch the lobbyists from the phar-maceutical industry and the medical device manufacturers circling around the med mal tort reform circus in Washington, D.C. They are working hard to get the audience to focus on the doctors shouting for change in the center ring, so they can slip in unobserved.[34] They want their clients pro-tected from tort litigation along with the doctors, and it is going to be very hard to stop them if Congress gets into the malpractice tort reform game.

Congress should stay out of that game, and not only because tort law has traditionally been the province of the states. When we look at U.S. his-tory, and when we compare the United States to most other countries, we find that court, lawsuits, and lawyers have played a major part in shaping some of what is best about America.

I will start with the Constitution. The Constitution made our courts a third branch of government to protect us from both the tyranny of an unchecked executive and the mob justice of an unchecked legislature. Also, the Constitution guarantees trial by jury, injecting democracy right into the courthouse. People who bash juries forget just how important the right to trial by jury was to the founders of our country.[35]

Despite their faith in courts, the founders placed checks on courts as well. They limited courts to deciding what the Constitution calls "cases and controversies." This means that courts can decide only matters that the people or the other branches of government bring to them. Our courts cannot become roving inquisitors. How do people bring matters to the courts? By filing a lawsuit. Lawsuits lie right at the democratic heart of our checks-and-balances system of government.

Consider as well the importance of personal responsibility to our national character. Our screens, our stages, and the pages of our popular fiction are filled with heroes who take responsibility, villains who shirk responsibility, and ordinary people who struggle to define their relationship to responsibility.

Responsibility lies at the heart of tort law. A tort lawsuit is a public statement that a defendant has not accepted responsibility, coupled with a demand to do so. Malpractice lawsuits ask doctors and hospitals to take responsibility for their mistakes, not just to prevent future mistakes or to compensate the patient, but also because taking responsibility is the morally proper thing to do.

Once an injury happens, someone bears the responsibility. No matter what we do, the injured patient will be responsible for living with the injury. If the patient dies, the surviving family members will be responsible for going on with life. That fact cannot be wished away. The question is whether anyone else will have to share the responsibility.

A moral accounting for medical injury easily could go so far as to say that whoever contributed in any way to the injury should share the responsibility. Otherwise the patient and the family, alone, are responsible for living with the consequences of an injury that they did not cause and could not have prevented.

Tort law does not go that far, however. Tort law absolves the doctor who could not have prevented the injury. Tort law even absolves the doctor who could have prevented the injury but nevertheless acted reasonably in the circumstances. Instead, tort law holds responsible only the doctor or hospital who made a mistake, who failed to do what should have been done in the circumstances.

Between the patient who has to live with the consequences of a medical mistake and the doctor or hospital who made the mistake—no matter how inadvertently—there is a moral imbalance. A lawsuit corrects that moral imbalance.

The research on why people bring malpractice lawsuits confirms the central role of responsibility. Doctors who explain all the risks, who are honest when things go wrong, who show their patients that they care are less likely to be sued.[36] And the lawyers I spoke to during my field research on personal-injury litigation believe that juries are more forgiving of doctors who accept moral responsibility, even if the doctors dispute the extent of their legal obligation.

Autonomy—freedom from restrictive regulation—is yet another traditional American value fostered by medical malpractice lawsuits. Consider the alternative to using lawsuits to require doctors and hospitals to take responsibility. The alternative is not unfettered freedom for doctors and hospitals. The alternative is intrusive government control—maybe not today, but certainly tomorrow. Now that we know about the extent of medical mistakes and patient injuries (thanks to malpractice lawsuits), we are not going to give up on patient safety, and we are not going to be satisfied with a closed-door, doctor-knows-best approach.

A malpractice lawsuit does not tell the doctor or the hospital how to do their job. A malpractice lawsuit says, "It is your responsibility to make sure that you provide good-quality care," but it does not dictate how. A malpractice lawsuit gives the doctor or the hospital the freedom to figure out how best to provide that good-quality care. Lawsuits represent a free-market, bottom-up approach to safety that fits well with our national character.[37]

Putting all this together, what can we say? Medical malpractice lawsuits promote traditional American values like access to justice, personal responsibility, and freedom from intrusive government regulation.

LEARNING FROM CHINA

In the fall of 2004 I had the opportunity to give a series of lectures in China to people connected in various ways to China's growing insurance industry—underwriters, brokers, lawyers, government regulators, and university teachers. China had just adopted a mandatory automobile liability insurance law, and they wanted to hear about the American experience with tort law and liability insurance, particularly for automobile accidents.

I was pleased to be asked to come over as the American expert. But I was certain that I was going to learn at least as much as I would teach. Explaining what we do to intelligent and informed listeners could not help but improve my own understanding. Also, hearing their questions and learning about their approach would lead me to examine my own assumptions.

The China trip did not disappoint. I arrived ready to explain why the U.S. approach to automobile accidents had been an expensive mistake and why China should adopt a no-fault approach (in which people buy insurance that covers their own injuries or damage in an accident, regardless of who was at fault). In response, I received a series of polite but insistent explanations about the importance of liability based on fault in building a legal system. In other words, I came to teach about the limits of tort law and received, instead, an important reminder about the possibilities of tort law.

The Chinese government officials did not want to hear about how they could replace their new tort and liability insurance approach with a no-fault approach. They explained that they had carefully considered how other countries handle automobile accident compensation. They chose to go with tort law and liability insurance for auto accidents, and they did not make that choice lightly. What they wanted to hear from me was how to make the tort approach work—how to build up a cadre of accident lawyers, how to handle claims, and above all how to manage the day-to-day problems with liability insurance.

They chose a tort law approach because they wanted to build respect for traffic laws, to hold drivers accountable, and, above all, to withdraw the government from the automobile accident compensation arena. The choice that China faces for automobile accidents is not the same choice that we face in America. We long ago made the decision not to use the government to compensate auto accident victims. So we face a choice between competing private insurance approaches: the tort law and liability insurance approach that we now have and the no-fault approach that many law professors think would be better.

China still faces a choice between a government and a private insurance approach. Despite government leaders' wish to make the government less paternalistic, there is still very strong popular support for government programs. The officials explained to me that, if they were going to *require* people to buy a new and expensive kind of insurance for automobile accidents, they wanted that insurance to be liability insurance. Mandatory liability insurance makes sure that other people have insurance that covers injuries that they cause to you. In other words, mandatory liability insurance makes sure that other people can be financially responsible.

China is changing at breakneck speed, and government officials are attempting to channel that change so that it causes the least disruption with traditional Chinese values. Accepting responsibility for harm that you cause to others is a traditional Chinese value as well as a traditional American value.

WITH LIBERTY AND JUSTICE FOR ALL

In this chapter I have set out what my law students would recognize as the classic three justifications for tort liability. We hold doctors accountable to encourage them to avoid injuring their patients. We hold doctors accountable to provide compensation for the patients they injure. And we hold doctors accountable because of traditional moral values like justice and responsibility.

Policy analysts and empirical researchers tend to focus on the first two of these. They ask, "Do medical malpractice lawsuits really prevent injuries?" And, "Are medical malpractice lawsuits the most efficient approach to patient compensation?" On this score, I hope I have made clear that prevention provides a much stronger justification for malpractice lawsuits than compensation. We all benefit from the prevention effect of malpractice lawsuits, but very few people receive compensation. For that reason, I will propose an alternative approach to patient compensation in chapter 8. This approach is similar in many ways to that recommended by other policy analysts.

Where I differ is in the relative importance I give to values like justice and responsibility. I believe that these values, not the social-engineering goals of prevention and compensation, best explain why we do what we do. In America we want to hold people accountable. And we do not want only the government to do that for us.

For people all across our political spectrum, the closing words in the Pledge of Allegiance, "with liberty and justice for all," are guiding principles. Liberty is of course a much bigger idea than autonomy. But, like autonomy, liberty comes only with responsibility. Justice, too, is a much bigger idea than I can possibly address in one short book. And justice certainly includes things that are even more important than tort law. But along with those other things, justice surely includes holding people responsible for medical mistakes. That is why we need medical malpractice lawsuits.

Can we do better? Of course. But that requires legal reforms aimed at improving medical malpractice lawsuits, not legal reforms aimed at undercutting the prevention, compensation, and corrective justice role of medical malpractice lawsuits. I propose a series of such reforms in chapter 8.

6 THE GOODS ON DEFENSIVE MEDICINE

A new poll suggests that doctors, instead of focusing on the best medical judgment, worry more about protecting themselves from potential lawsuits. Legal fear drives them to prescribe medicines and order tests, even invasive procedures, that they feel are unnecessary. Reputable studies estimate that this "defensive medicine" squanders $50 billion a year, enough to provide medical care to millions of uninsured Americans.
— *McGovern and Simpson 2002*

Blaming defensive medicine on the legal system is likely to continue. It provides physicians with a convenient excuse for certain, often self-serving, clinical practice behavior, as well as providing organized medicine with what has been termed a rhetorical tool to resist an intrusion on clinical care by tort law.
—*Bassett et al. 2000*

Of all the parts of the medical malpractice myth, claims about defensive medicine are the most difficult to pin down. Part of the problem lies in defining "defensive medicine." As the quote from former senators George McGovern and Alan Simpson suggests, most people understand defensive medicine as unnecessary tests and procedures that squander time and money. Defensive medicine is not good medicine.

Yet malpractice lawsuits are supposed to influence doctors and other health-care providers to behave differently because they are concerned about lawsuits. As we saw in the last chapter, motivating health-care providers to avoid patient injuries is one of the main goals of tort law.

If defensive medicine always is bad medicine, then measuring the extent of defensive medicine requires distinguishing between the good, injury-prevention effects of malpractice lawsuits and the bad, wasteful effects. Drawing that line turns out to be very difficult. In fact, it is so difficult that when the U.S. Congress asked the Office of Technology Assessment to measure the amount of defensive medicine in the early 1990s, office researchers said they could not distinguish in any quantitative way between the good and bad effects of medical malpractice lawsuits.

The only way that they could report to Congress about the extent of defensive medicine was to define that term to mean something that they would have a better chance of being able to measure. So they redefined "defensive medicine" to mean tests and procedures used "primarily as a protection against potential medical malpractice claims," even if those tests and procedures benefit patients. Even with this broader definition, however, they still were not able to estimate the extent of defensive medicine reliably. And they refrained from providing a best guess because they knew that such a number would be misused to exaggerate the benefits of medical malpractice reform.

As the researchers explain, "Even if tort reforms reduced compensation and administration costs by one-half—a highly unlikely scenario— the impact on health-care costs would still be miniscule. Where, then, are the savings from malpractice reform to come from? Increasingly, the political answer is a reduction in defensive medicine; that is, a reduction in physicians' use of tests and procedures primarily as a protection against potential medical malpractice claims."[1]

With two exceptions that I will discuss in this chapter, none of the researchers who have studied defensive medicine have claimed that they are able to separate the bad, wasteful effects of malpractice lawsuits from the good, injury-prevention effects. Instead they have used the Office of Technology Assessment's definition of defensive medicine or they have used an even broader definition in which defensive medicine means *any* change in health-care practices because of medical malpractice lawsuits. In this broader definition, improvements in medical record keeping and spending more time with patients—obviously good things—are two of the leading examples of "defensive medicine."[2]

The result is a profound disconnect between the research on defensive medicine and the public's understanding of the problem. The public and most doctors understand the term "defensive medicine" to refer to something that is always and everywhere bad. Yet researchers define the term to include an indefinable but undoubtedly large proportion of activities that benefit patients.

As with the mythical litigation explosion, we will see that the really interesting question is not the one that the researchers are attempting to answer. The really interesting question is why there is such a large gap between the research and the public understanding. The results of the research are very clear: while there may be some defensive medicine in the pejorative sense, the impact on health-care costs is small. Yet doctors and the public seem confident that defensive medicine—as they understand it—has a large impact on the costs of health care in the United States. What explains this gap between myth and reality?

Getting there will take some work, but the answer to this question turns out to implicate the relationship between art and science in medicine. Understanding that connection requires that we first review the research on defensive medicine. I will spend the most time explaining why the "reputable studies" that former senators McGovern and Simpson cite do not in fact establish that defensive medicine squanders $50 billion a year. Once I have laid out the research, we will be in a position to examine the gap between myth and reality, and to consider how it came about and why it persists.

THE RESEARCH ON DEFENSIVE MEDICINE

As we will see, there is no simple, straightforward way to measure defensive medicine, however that term is defined. Researchers have taken a variety of approaches, all of which have strengths and weaknesses.

Opinion Surveys

The easiest and earliest approach to measuring defensive medicine is to survey doctors. For example, since 1983 the American Medical Association has included questions about defensive medicine in some of its quarterly surveys of doctors. The strength of this approach is that it is easy and relatively inexpensive. The weaknesses are legion. Backward-looking surveys are a notoriously unreliable way to find out what people actually do (as opposed to what they think they do). The questions may prompt doctors to exaggerate the effect that fear of lawsuits has on their practice. The surveys cannot tell us whether the effects of malpractice are wasteful or beneficial. Doctors who are most upset about medical malpractice lawsuits may be the most likely to respond, biasing the results. And many of the surveys are conducted in the highly politicized environment of a medical malpractice insurance crisis. As a result, most researchers have concluded that opinion surveys do not provide much useful information about the nature or extent of defensive medicine.[3]

With that said, the survey research does confirm that doctors believe that malpractice liability affects how they practice medicine. The most common effects that they mention are maintaining more detailed patient records, spending more time with patients, referring more cases to specialists for consultation, increasing the number of diagnostic tests, and, in earlier surveys, increasing their fees.[4]

Whether these effects are good, bad, or indifferent is impossible to tell from a survey. I would be very pleased to have my family's doctors do a better job maintaining our records and spend more time with us when we have health problems. Also, getting a second opinion can be very valuable, as can a diagnostic test. So it seems quite likely that a substantial portion of this defensive medicine in fact is beneficial.

But my judgments about this are pure speculation, as are the judgments of anyone else who attempts to draw conclusions based on these surveys. As all the independent researchers who have studied defensive medicine agree, we cannot draw any conclusions based on these surveys about the extent of any wasteful consequences of medical malpractice lawsuits.

Medical school professors Laurence Tancredi and Jeremiah Barondess made a related, but larger, point about defensive medicine back in the 1970s. As they wrote in *Science* magazine, "The point is that one cannot handle accurately the issues involved in defensive medicine without first having established epidemiologically the soundness of medical procedures as they relate to specific outcomes in patients." In other words, "The question of whether defensive practices are beneficial for patients, or, instead, result in nonproductive medical activities that are both costly and potentially harmful . . . cannot be resolved until standards of care are established for each specialty and for specific medical diagnoses and treatments."[5]

Put another way, separating the good, beneficial aspects of defensive medicine from the bad, wasteful aspects requires knowing more precisely than we do what works and what does not. It requires medical practices that are grounded in evidence, not in oral traditions.

Clinical Scenario Surveys

Clinical scenario surveys present doctors with a medical problem and ask what they would do in response and why, probing for the role that concern about medical malpractice liability plays. This approach provides a somewhat more concrete measure of what doctors do and how they think medical malpractice liability affects their behavior in specific situations. But these surveys are otherwise subject to many of the same weaknesses as the opinion surveys, and they cannot tell us what doctors do in situations that differ from the scenarios.

With that said, the clinical scenario research provides a useful corrective to some of the more exaggerated claims about defensive medicine. The Office of Technology Assessment of the U.S. Congress sponsored a series of clinical scenario surveys in the early 1990s. They worked with the leaders of three medical specialty groups—cardiologists, surgeons, and obstetricians and gynecologists—to prepare scenarios that involved "clinical situations in which they would expect the fear of a malpractice suit to have a *major* influence on their own or their colleagues' clinical decisions." The goal was to identify "the maximum extent to which defensive medicine affects clinical practice."[6]

The research team sent out the scenarios to a randomly selected sample of doctors in the three specialties, explaining that they designed the surveys with the specialty groups to study clinical decision-making (making no mention of malpractice in the explanation). The survey forms included descriptions of the scenarios and a list of possible responses. In nearly every scenario a perfectly acceptable response was to do nothing, according to the expert panels that designed the scenario. Alternatively, the doctor could order standard tests or procedures that would aid in the diagnosis.

The researchers tried to get at the question of defensive medicine in a variety of ways. Most directly, the survey forms asked doctors to indicate the reasons for their choice. Most of the surveys contained a list of potential reasons listed after each choice: medical indications, concerns about cost vs. benefit, malpractice concerns, patient expectations, and "other." The doctors were to place a single checkmark in the box for any reason that applied and a double check in the box for the "single most important reason."

The responses to these surveys suggest that doctors practice "defensively" less often than commonly believed. Ninety-five percent of the time the doctors chose to do nothing rather than order the test or diagnostic procedure. When they did choose the test or diagnostic procedure, the primary reason they gave almost all of the time was medical indications. In total, the doctors double-checked the malpractice concerns box in less than one half of one percent of the cases. In all but a very few of those cases, the doctors also checked the box for medical indications. This means that the doctors rarely said they chose a test or diagnostic procedure primarily because of concerns about medical malpractice and they almost never said they chose a test or diagnostic procedure purely because of concerns about medical malpractice.

Nevertheless, the surveys did suggest that there are areas with more defensive medicine (in the broad, nonpejorative sense of that term). Cardiologists were much more likely to double-check malpractice concerns for scenarios that presented a risk of heart attack (14 percent and 12 percent of the times they chose a test or procedure). Neurosurgeons were much more likely to double-check malpractice concerns for a scenario that presented a risk of brain injury (29 percent of the times they chose a test or procedure). And obstetrician-gynecologists were somewhat more likely to double-check malpractice concerns for a scenario that presented a risk of breast cancer (10 percent of the times they chose a test or procedure).

These are all potentially serious conditions, so it is possible that additional diagnostic tests or procedures would be beneficial. The surveys provide no basis for making any judgment about that. But there is one judgment that we can make: rates of defensive medicine differ from scenario to scenario. Finding defensive medicine in one area of medical practice does not necessarily tell us very much about what happens in another area. This will be important to keep in mind when we look at some of the other research.

The Office of Technology Assessment researchers did two things to confirm that doctors really were focusing on medical indications. First, they gave nearly half the doctors scenarios that were slightly different from the original scenarios. These "control" scenarios provided additional information about the case that would make it more likely that ordering the test or diagnostic procedure would be medically indicated. As would be expected if the doctors in fact were responding primarily to medical indications rather than risk of malpractice, the doctors were much more likely to choose the test or diagnostic procedure in the control scenarios. The difference was greatest in the scenario that presented the greatest immediate risk (chest pain) and with the diagnostic procedures that were most invasive (two gynecological procedures). This result corroborated the finding that medical indications, and not medical malpractice concerns, lay behind the doctors' responses to the scenarios.

Second, the researchers gave some doctors the original scenarios but without the specific list of reasons for choosing the test or diagnostic procedure. Instead, they simply provided a space in which the doctors were supposed to write down their reasons for their choices. These doctors chose the tests or diagnostic procedures at the same rate as the other doctors, but they were much less likely to list malpractice concerns as a reason. This result suggest that including "medical malpractice concerns" among the supplied list of reasons affected the responses of the other doctors and, therefore, that the number of tests and diagnostic procedures that would be ordered because of conscious medical malpractice concerns may be even lower than they found.

What was the OTA researchers' bottom line? Despite the fact that doctors say in opinion surveys that malpractice lawsuits affect how they practice, defensive medicine is not likely to explain very much of the huge growth in health-care expenses over the past quarter century.[7]

Comparative Hospital Record Analysis

Some researchers have tried to avoid the weaknesses of surveys by measuring defensive medicine directly. The earliest and most common approach uses hospital records to measure what doctors actually do and then compares that with the risk of medical malpractice faced in different areas and hospitals. Most of this research has looked at obstetricians, largely in response to increased rates of delivery by cesarean sections. Some doctors are concerned about the large growth in the rate of cesarean sections, and one common explanation for that growth is fear of medical malpractice.[8]

So cesarean sections are an obvious place to expect to find a high rate of defensive medicine.

Economists from Syracuse University conducted the first sophisticated research on cesarean sections.[9] They used records for all births in New York State in 1986, outside of New York City. The records contained information about the mother, the baby, the means of payment for the delivery, medical indications for the cesarean, other complications of the delivery, the doctor who delivered the baby, and the hospital. In addition, the leading medical malpractice insurance company in New York gave them a measure of the obstetrical malpractice risk in each county—the number of obstetrical malpractice suits per 100 doctors from 1975 to 1986.

The Syracuse researchers used a common and well-regarded statistical technique to measure the impact that each of these factors had on the likelihood of cesarean delivery. Their results were consistent with some of the conventional wisdom about cesarean deliveries—most important, the very strong role that a hospital's rate of cesarean deliveries plays in predicting whether any given birth will be by cesarean. But they did not find that a higher malpractice risk increased the rate of cesareans. In fact, higher malpractice risk very slightly decreased the chance of a cesarean delivery.

Researchers from the University of Washington conducted a similar study of how malpractice liability risk affected cesarean delivery rates in Washington State.[10] They measured medical malpractice claim risk at both the county level and for the individual physician. Looking at the same kinds of factors as the Syracuse researchers, they found no relationship between cesarean deliveries and either of these measures of malpractice risk.

Researchers from the Harvard Medical Practice Study, which we explored in chapter 2, also studied cesarean delivery rates in New York.[11] They took all of the childbirth records collected in the Harvard Medical Practice Study and pulled out information about each birth, including the hospital, the doctor, and the risk factors for the delivery. They also looked at a variety of measures of malpractice liability risk. Most significantly, they improved on the other hospital record research by creating hospital-level measures of malpractice liability risk. For example, they counted the number of obstetrical lawsuits against the hospital's staff during earlier years and divided that number by the number of doctors working out of the hospital. This allowed them to see whether hospital-specific differences in malpractice risk explained any of the difference in hospitals' rate of cesarean deliveries.

They found that differences in hospitals' malpractice risk did in fact explain some of the differences among hospitals. Controlling for all the other factors, a woman who entered a hospital with a high medical malpractice claim risk was about 30 percent more likely to have a cesarean section than a woman who entered a hospital with a low medical malpractice claim risk. This does not mean that these hospitals performed 30 percent more cesareans other hospitals. Instead it means that, if all other factors were equal—the risk factors, the region, the doctor—the claims history of the hospital made a significant difference. How big a difference is impossible to tell precisely from the published article, other than their researchers' conclusion that the effect was "not large." By comparison, the fact that a hospital was in a region with a high rate of cesareans increased the chance of cesarean delivery ten times more than the fact that the hospital had a high malpractice claim risk for that region.

Taken together, the hospital record research is consistent with the results of the clinical scenarios. The Harvard research suggests that there is some defensive medicine in obstetrical care, as would be expected from the high cost of birth injury claims and uncertainty regarding the benefits of cesarean deliveries. But the overall impact on practice patterns is not large. As we will see, later researchers have estimated that the total cost of defensive cesarean deliveries amounts to less than one half of one percent of all obstetrical charges.

The hospital record approach provides a more reliable measure of what doctors actually do. But this research cannot tell us whether the doctors' efforts are beneficial or wasteful. In addition, as the clinical scenarios showed, measuring the extent of defensive medicine in one area of medical practice may not tell us very much about the extent of defensive medicine in another area. With that said, the hospital record research does provide a useful corrective to the exaggerated claims about the extent and cost of defensive medicine.

Medicare Data-Mining

This next approach used a very promising research technique that involves extracting useful information from health insurance records. Stanford economists Daniel Kessler and Mark McClellan used Medicare rec-

ords to examine treatment patterns and compare how they varied according to medical malpractice risk. This approach is similar in many ways to
the hospital record research.[12] But the advantage of using Medicare records lies in the ability to tell whether the differences in treatment patterns
made any difference in the patients' health.

Health insurance data mining of this sort presents exciting possibilities
for evaluating all kinds of tests, procedures, and treatments—well beyond
the comparatively minor problem of defensive medicine. The possibilities
include evidence-based standards that could revolutionize the practice of
medicine, placing medicine more firmly in the realm of science and further
from the realm of art than it is today.

Kessler and McClellan's research focused on two very expensive and
very common heart conditions: heart attacks and ischemic heart disease
(coronary artery disease or coronary heart disease caused by narrowing of
the coronary arteries and decreased blood flow to the heart). They used
Medicare's huge database of payment records to measure the amount of
money spent on heart disease per patient in each state to see whether that
amount varied in any systematic way according to whether and when the
state adopted restrictive tort reforms. They reasoned that restrictive tort
reform reduces the threat of tort liability, and reducing that threat should
reduce the amount of defensive medicine. Thus, reductions in heart treatment expenses that could be directly linked to tort reform would represent
reductions in wasteful defensive medicine, as long as those reductions did
not lead to worse health outcomes.

They found that in states that enacted what they called "direct" tort reforms, meaning reforms that directly reduced malpractice liability, such as
caps on damages, heart disease expenses grew somewhat less from 1984 to
1990 than in other states. Controlling for inflation, heart disease expenses
grew about 24 percent in states that did not enact reforms during the 1985
to 1990 period, 17 percent in states that enacted reforms in 1985 to 1987,
and 22 percent in states that enacted reforms in 1998 to 1990. Altogether
heart disease expenses for the elderly grew 5 to 7 percent less in direct tort
reform states between 1985 and 1990. In addition, heart disease expenses
in states that enacted direct tort reforms before 1985 grew slightly faster
than expenses in states that did not enact these reforms, suggesting that
the tort reform savings declined after five years.

Significantly, the reductions in heart disease expenses did not harm patients. The researchers measured outcomes by using Medicare and Social Security records to count the number of heart disease patients who were readmitted to the hospital or died within one year after treatment. They found that there were only very small outcome differences between the states that enacted reforms and the states that did not enact reforms. For example, one-year mortality for heart attacks fell 5.39 percent in the direct tort reform states during the 1984 to 1990 period as compared to 5.46 percent in other states.

They drew two main conclusions from their results. First, changes in tort liability affect how health-care providers treat heart disease in elderly patients. Doctors in states that enacted direct tort reforms apparently were somewhat less likely to order expensive treatments in marginal heart disease cases. Second, the additional treatment provided to patients in states without tort reforms did not improve mortality rates in those states, suggesting that the additional treatment did not provide substantial benefits to the patients. Taken together, these results suggest that the additional heart disease treatment was wasteful defensive medicine.

Up to this point, Kessler and McClellan's analysis was exemplary. Heart disease was a sensible set of conditions to investigate for defensive medicine. Heart disease is the most expensive disease in the United States and the leading cause of death. Heart attacks are involved in more medical malpractice claims than any other condition except breast cancer and brain-damage in infants, and heart attack claims are also the third most costly kind of claim. Their statistical analysis appears to be excellent. I am using a similar approach in research that I am conducting on the effects of tort reform, and I found their explanations very instructive.[13]

What they did next, however, crossed the line between social science and advocacy. They used their solid, sensible analysis of heart disease expenses to generate an entirely speculative number that they should have known would have great—and greatly misleading—political effect. Without explaining how they calculated this number, they wrote: "If our results are generalizable to medical expenditures outside the hospital, to other illnesses, and to younger patients, then direct reforms could lead to expenditure reductions of well over $50 billion per year without serious adverse consequences for health outcomes."[14]

This is the source of the $50 billion number that former senators

McGovern and Simpson used in the quote that appears at the beginning of this chapter. McGovern and Simpson were entirely correct in referring to the study as "respectable." But the $50 billion number was anything but. Coincidentally or not, this number matches the defensive medicine number that the first President Bush used in his debates with Bill Clinton. Coincidentally or not, Dr. McClellan became the second President Bush's top health-care policy advisor and is now the head of the federal agency that runs the Medicare program.

Let me count the ways in which this $50 billion number is both fanciful and misleading.

First, the "if" in the sentence preceding the $50 billion number is a very big "if." Kessler and McClellan do not provide any basis for concluding that their results would apply outside the hospital, to other illnesses, or to younger patients. In fact, other research by Dr. McClellan suggests that heart disease in the elderly may be unusually prone to wasteful defensive medicine. Some of the leading treatments involve extremely expensive procedures that have very substantial benefits for some patients, but only slight benefits for others. As Dr. Kessler reported, two very expensive procedures—cardiac catheterization and bypass surgery—are "associated with essentially all the growth in hospital expenditures for heart attack treatment in the elderly in the past decade." And "at the margin more aggressive use of cardiac procedures at best leads to slight mortality benefits." Moreover, these slight benefits for the marginal patients appear to result not from the expensive procedures themselves, but rather from less expensive treatment provided along with those procedures.[15] In addition, the clinical scenario surveys I discussed earlier show that doctors are unusually attuned to malpractice concerns when there is a risk of a heart attack.

Second, Kessler and McClellan's own results show that tort reform has only a short-term effect on heart disease expense growth, and they admit that their "conclusions about long-term effects are speculative." In fact, heart disease expenses grew even faster in states that enacted tort reform before 1985 than in the states with no tort reform, suggesting that the savings may eventually disappear.

Third, while they acknowledge that medical malpractice lawsuits also provide an incentive for doctors to order beneficial treatments, they do not account for any of those benefits. They improved on the earlier defensive medicine research by isolating apparently wasteful expenses, but they did not make any effort to measure the injury-prevention effects of malpractice liability. Thus, their research does not provide even a remotely satisfactory basis for concluding that restrictive tort reform is in the public interest.

As this suggests, Kessler and McClellan jumped much too quickly from cause to cure. At bottom, their results follow from what Dr. McClellan proved in his earlier research: expensive treatments for heart disease do not appear to provide any real health benefit to the marginal patient. But McClellan did not publish his research until the mid-1990s, so the doctors who were ordering these treatments earlier could not have known just how small those marginal benefits were. The fact that doctors in the direct tort reform states were somewhat less likely to order these treatments is an interesting and significant result—because it proves that doctors respond to tort incentives. But restricting tort liability is a very strange solution to what is, at bottom, a medical management issue—overuse of expensive medical procedures.[16]

The Medicare Follow-Up Research: The Impact of Managed Care

In later research Kessler and McClellan investigated an alternative solution to overuse of expensive medical procedures—cost-control efforts by insurance companies, HMOs, or other managed care organizations. In an article published in 2002 they updated their earlier research to include four more years of Medicare records (1991 to 1994), and they took into account the new medical cost-consciousness attributable to managed care.[17] They found that something they called the "spillover effect" of managed care reduced heart disease expenses, without an appreciable affect on outcomes. They also found that the tort reform savings on heart disease expenses were only about half as large as they had estimated earlier. These more recent results confirm that medical management is a more effective way to reduce overuse of expensive medical technologies.

The key to understanding Kessler and McClellan's more recent research is in the way that they measured the effect of managed care. Medicare recipients can choose to enroll in HMOs that provide a broader range of benefits than ordinary Medicare. The theory is that the cost-control efforts of the Medicare HMOs allow them to provide more benefits at less cost—the idea behind managed care generally. Managed care has been controversial. But experts agree that the new cost-consciousness has significantly slowed the growth of health-care expenses in the United States.

Because Medicare pays a monthly fee to the HMOs for each of their Medicare-eligible members, Medicare did not at first collect the kind of detailed treatment records for the people in Medicare HMOs that they had for other people in Medicare. (Medicare has since started collecting that information, but not for earlier years.) As a result, Kessler and McClellan could not measure how managed care affected the heart disease expenses of people enrolled in the HMOs. Instead, they could only measure the "spillover effect" that managed care had on patients in traditional Medicare.

The idea that managed care would have a spillover effect makes sense, particularly for heart disease. Because heart disease involves intensive, hospital-based treatments, differences in hospital practice patterns will have a strong effect on heart disease expenses. Research on medical practice patterns shows that they vary widely from region to region and from hospital to hospital.[18] Because medical practice involves so much art, practice patterns evolve on a local level as doctors interact and learn from each other. Introducing a greater sense of cost-consciousness in one region but not another or in one hospital but not another would push the practice patterns in those two regions or two hospitals apart even for patients who are not in managed care plans.

Kessler and McClellan measured the spillover effect in a reasonable, but crude way. They divided the states into two groups: those in which the percentage of Medicare enrollees was above the median and all others. They counted states with above-median enrollments as "managed care" states, much as they treated states that enacted direct tort reforms as "tort reform" states. They found that heart disease expenses grew more slowly in the managed care states and that this managed care spillover effect was about the same size as the tort reform effect.

This approach almost certainly underestimated the ability of medical management to control heart disease expenses. First, it did not measure the effect on people enrolled in the managed care plans at all. Direct cost savings for a patient in a managed care plan should be even larger than the spillover effect on a patient in traditional Medicare. Second, states are not the best units of analysis for measuring the spillover effect of managed care. Medical practice patterns evolve at the hospital and the regional level, not the state level. The "managed care" states surely included hospitals and regions with a low percentage of patients in managed care. Likewise, many of the other states surely included hospitals and regions with a high share of patients in managed care. This means that measuring the spillover effect at the state level diluted that effect.[19]

Finally, the proportion of patients in Medicare managed care plans was very small at the beginning of the study period and amounted to only 10 percent of the patients by the end. If enrolling such a small percentage of people in managed care plans can have such a large effect on heart disease practice patterns, then the continued growth of managed care should have an even larger effect.

What is the bottom line? Tort reform does not reduce wasteful treatment for heart disease as much as Kessler and McClellan reported in their first study, and medical management does a better job at reducing the overuse of expensive medical procedures, without the negative consequences of restrictive tort reform.

The Birth Records Research

A second group of researchers has tried to measure wasteful defensive medicine directly at the other end of life. Researchers from the Urban Institute used information from the U.S. National Natality files to look at the rate of cesarean sections. The Natality files contain information from many states on the method of delivery, a measure of infant health called Apgar scores, medical risk factors, and complications of pregnancy for every baby born.[20]

Like the hospital record researchers, the Urban Institute researchers compared the rate of cesarean sections to medical malpractice insurance premiums. They improved on the earlier research by using the Apgar scores to evaluate the degree to which the defensive medicine improved infants' health. They found that cesarean sections were slightly more common in counties with higher medical malpractice premiums, but the health outcomes in those counties were no better than in other counties. These results suggest that the increased rate of cesareans represented wasteful defensive medicine.

The total cost of the extra deliveries was very low. The Urban Institute researchers estimated that cutting medical malpractice premiums in half would reduce the rate of cesareans by less than one half of one percent (from 15.18 percent to 14.71 percent). As they report, "Nationally this represents fewer than 17,000 cesarean sections or 3 percent of the approximately 540,000 primary cesareans performed every year." In dollar terms, the increased costs of these 17,000 deliveries amount to less than 0.3 percent of all obstetrical charges.

This research provides a healthy corrective to the exaggerated estimate Kessler and McClellan offered at the end of their first article on defensive medicine. The research shows that there is some wasteful defensive medicine in obstetrical care, but the rate is much lower than Kessler and McClellan found in the treatment of elderly heart disease patients. Taken together, the birth record research and the clinical scenario research tell us that the relatively high rate of wasteful defensive medicine Kessler and McClellan found in the treatment of elderly heart disease patients cannot be mindlessly applied to other medical conditions or to younger patients, providing yet another reason to reject their exaggerated estimate of the total costs of wasteful defensive medicine.

The Most Recent Research

Researchers from Dartmouth and the Congressional Budget Office have recently tried, unsuccessfully, to extend Kessler and McClellan's defensive medicine finding to other kinds of illnesses and to more recent years. The Dartmouth economists looked at both Medicare payment records and birth records to see whether treatment patterns changed in relation to medical malpractice risk. They used birth records to look at cesarean section rates and they used Medicare records to look at three different treatments for heart disease and two treatments for prostate conditions, as well as mammography. In addition, they also looked at the relationship between malpractice claims risk and the overall level of Medicare payments in the state.

In marked contrast to Kessler and McClellan, they found little or no relationship between malpractice claim risk and medical treatments. Only mammography was significantly related to malpractice risk, but the overall cost impact was trivial. As they conclude, "The fact that we see very little evidence of . . . dramatic increases in the use of defensive medicine in response to state malpractice premiums places the more dire predictions of the malpractice alarmists in doubt."[21]

The Congressional Budget Office also tried to extend the Kessler and McClellan findings. In connection with tort reform legislation proposed in 2003, the CBO looked at the effect of state tort reform on per patient spending by Medicare for a variety of illnesses as well as the overall per capita health-care spending in each state. Using Kessler and McClellan's methods, they "found no effect of tort controls on medical spending" and concluded that there would be no cost savings from a reduction in defensive medicine.[22]

This more recent research leaves us with one of several conclusions about the Kessler and McClellan result. Either the treatment of heart disease in the elderly is unusually susceptible to wasteful defensive medicine. Or the rise of managed care and increased cost-consciousness so changed practice patterns that defensive medicine became invisible in the latter half of the 1990s. Or increased expenses from the loss of the beneficial effects of tort liability offset the reduction in wasteful expenses for other kinds of medical treatment. Or, most likely, some combination of these.

In any event, whatever limited truth value there ever was in Kessler and McClellan's $50 billion number has by now completely disappeared.

WHAT DOES ALL THIS RESEARCH MEAN?

In combination, the defensive medicine research tells us that malpractice lawsuits probably do affect how doctors practice medicine, and some of what they do may not help patients. But the overall impact of this defensive medicine on health-care costs is not very large. This makes sense. Because most medical practice is based on tradition, not research, doctors cannot be certain about the benefits of much of what they do. In light of this uncertainty, it would hardly be surprising if medical practice evolved in the direction of providing greater care in the face of greater malpractice pressure and that some of that care would not be worth the extra cost. At the same time, however, the increased cost-consciousness of the managed care movement has pushed back, hard, in the opposite direction. Medical management appears to have washed out whatever minor impact the gradual risk in medical malpractice claim payments over the last fifteen years might have had on health-care costs.

The real problem the defensive medicine research points to is not in fact wasteful defensive medicine. The real problem is the same problem that Drs. Tancredi and Barondess wrote about nearly thirty years ago: too often, there is not enough evidence to guide doctors through their decisions. If doctors had a clear, evidence-based standard for deciding when to order a test or a procedure, then they could act with far more confidence. They would certainly be more confident that they were doing the right thing. And they should be more confident that they would not be held liable for any unfortunate result.

Building that confidence would take some work. Doctors have heard for too long and from too many people the myth that malpractice lawsuits have nothing to do with whether anyone made a mistake. But the gap between the myth and the reality does not mean we should cut back on liability. Instead, it means that we need to convince doctors to take the same evidence-based approach to understanding malpractice lawsuits that we would like them to take to medical practice.

As we saw in the last chapter, anesthesiologists have come the closest to adopting an evidence-based approach to both medical practice and malpractice lawsuits. They have become more confident, and much safer, as a result.

MOVING MORE SLOWLY FROM CAUSE TO CURE

Taking a few steps back, we can see that the question of defensive medicine really points to three different problems. First, at least some doctors are overusing expensive medical tests and procedures, sometimes because of a fear of liability. Second, there is too much art and not enough science guiding doctors in their work. Among other things, this second problem means we cannot measure the extent of the first. Third, doctors have anxieties about medical malpractice lawsuits that go well beyond the real risks that they face. In combination with the second problem (the lack of an evidentiary base for much of medical practice) these anxieties probably increase the extent of the first problem (overuse), though we cannot be sure.

The usual prescription for defensive medicine—cutting back on tort liability—is unlikely to solve any of these problems. Most obviously, cutting back on tort liability will not do anything to promote evidence-based medicine. If anything, that will have the opposite effect. Although malpractice lawsuits cannot promote the creation of evidence-based standards, they can help spread those standards. When there is good evidence that treatment X cures condition Y, fear of malpractice liability can help promote the spread of treatment X for condition Y.

Cutting back on tort liability might reduce the overuse of some tests and procedures, but both the research and common sense tell us that there are better solutions to that problem—solutions that would not throw out the tort law baby with the overuse bathwater. Fear of malpractice liability is only one among many possible reasons for ordering extra tests and procedures. Solutions that address the core problem—overuse—will be more effective than a solution that reduces just one of the causes.

Kessler and McClellan's later research showed that the spillover effects of early and small-scale managed care efforts were just as effective as tort reform in reducing overuse. And the more recent research suggests that managed care has been even more effective in reducing unnecessary care. The burgeoning "pay for quality" movement is even more promising. Like managed care, the basic idea of pay for quality is to change doctors' incentives so that ordering unnecessary tests and procedures hits them in the pocketbook. To his credit, Dr. McClellan is a big supporter of pay for quality in his role as the head of the Medicare program.

Although Kessler and McClellan may not have realized this, their research also teaches us that cutting back on tort liability will not solve the problem of doctors' anxieties. Kessler and McClellan showed that whatever effect tort reform has on defensive medicine wears off after time. Tort reform might have reduced defensive medicine in heart disease care for a while in the years before managed care, because it assuaged the heart doctors' anxieties. But because those anxieties were only very loosely connected to the real risk, they eventually started to return.

Evidence-based medicine has the potential to do much more to address doctors' anxieties. Good evidence about what works and what does not work should produce better results, reducing the risk of a bad result in the first place. Good evidence also should help reduce the fear of being second-guessed in the event of a bad result.

Evidence-based *risk management* also has the potential to address doctors' anxieties. Closed-claim files reviews can teach doctors what kinds of problems actually lead to malpractice lawsuits, so that they can respond to the risk rationally rather than through a generalized anxiety. In addition, participating in an evidence-based risk management effort may have real therapeutic potential—by giving doctors a way to assert control over what seems like an uncontrollable situation.

If doctors across the country gave as much of their time to risk management as they give to promoting tort reform, we might see some reductions in the amount of medical injuries, rather than just in doctors' legal responsibilities for medical injuries. This effort might correct doctors' mistaken sense that the best-paid and most prestigious professionals in the country are somehow the victims of a medical injury liability system that makes them responsible for only a very tiny fraction of their mistakes. If the anesthesiologists are any example, this effort might also lower doctors' malpractice insurance premiums.

EXPLAINING THE GAP BETWEEN MYTH AND REALITY

Having finished our review of the research, we are back to the question that the medical malpractice research always raises: why is there such an enormous gap between myth and reality?

Part of the answer here is unique to defensive medicine. From an individual doctor's perspective, all the other aspects of the myth involve judgments about other people: ungrateful patients, greedy lawyers, uneducated juries, judges and legislators who do not understand, and even those other doctors who make truly wrongful mistakes. By contrast, defensive medicine is something that even good doctors might do, doctors who do not make truly wrongful mistakes.

If we keep in mind the fact that doctors understand defensive medicine in the pejorative sense, we can see that defensive medicine is psychologically troubling in a way that a suit-happy plaintiff or a greedy lawyer is not.

I am no psychoanalyst, but you do not have to be to see some of the conflicts and anxieties caught up in the topic of defensive medicine. Imagining myself in the place of a doctor considering what to do in an uncertain case and reflecting on the possible malpractice risk, I can see how that risk could lead to concern about whether I have allowed this awful thing—the tort system—to influence me.

As a doctor I would know that much of what I do is art, not science. So whatever I do might not work. I would worry that there might be someone out there who really does know exactly what to do and who might some-day decide it was my fault if the patient does not get well. Getting a grip on myself, I might remember that because medicine is art and not science no one could be certain exactly what to do in this case. But then I would remember that there are people who think that they know much more than they do, and not a few of those people went to medical school. Suppose something goes wrong and a plaintiff's lawyer finds one of them. So I *am* at risk.

Okay. I am at risk. But what exactly do I do? I am even less certain about how to avoid a lawsuit than how to treat this patient, and I am not at all certain about that. And I really should not allow concerns about lawsuits to affect my medical judgment. But I am an educated, astute person and I know that unconscious concerns affect what I do. So maybe my judgment already is affected. In that case I need to step back and really think about what to do. But I do not really know for sure what to do, because medicine is an art not a science. Maybe there are people who know better . . .

I do not mean to suggest that this internal loop runs whenever a doctor is unsure about what to do. In fact, I think it probably does not run most of the time. Doctors shut it down by doing what they do and trying hard not to second-guess. If I am right, that explains why we do not actually find much defensive medicine despite the fact that doctors are convinced that defensive medicine is widespread. In the abstract, defensive medicine seems inevitable, but when doctors make decisions they just do what they do. And what they do is affected most strongly by who taught them, where they trained, and what the other doctors in their hospital and area are do-ing—with some adjustment at the margin for what they might have read in medical journals or heard at a conference.

Along with this psychological explanation for the gap between myth and reality, there is also a political explanation. Defensive medicine pro-vides a way to magnify the costs of tort liability and to promote the idea that tort liability bears the blame for the affordability crisis in health care.

The quote from former senators McGovern and Simpson at the begin-ning of this chapter illustrates how this is done. They write, "Reputable studies estimate that this 'defensive medicine' squanders $50 billion a year, enough to provide medical care to millions of uninsured Americans." This is literally correct, but completely misleading. The Kessler and McClellan study is reputable, even though their $50 billion number was not. And $50 billion in fact could buy a lot of health care for the uninsured. But there is no realistic way to use savings from reducing defensive medicine—if there were such savings—to provide insurance to the currently uninsured.

Many otherwise well-informed people nod their heads at statements like this because they make a superficial kind of sense, especially when combined with the other aspects of the medical malpractice myth. If you believe that malpractice lawsuits are random acts of violence against doctors who did nothing wrong, then it is easy to believe that what doctors do to avoid lawsuits is a waste of resources. If you believe that we have an epidemic of malpractice lawsuits, then it is easy to believe that the combination of the lawsuits and the defensive medicine explain the crisis of affordability in health care.

Of course, the fact that these things are easy to believe does not make them right. But it does help explain how people might believe so strongly in things that so clearly are not true. If we want to change people's minds, this is an important first step.

DR. BILL MAY BE GONE, BUT DR. JANE IS HERE TO SEE YOU

Frank Hamilton, a New York physician, claimed that between 1833 and 1856 "suits for malpractice were so frequent in the Northern states" that many men "abandoned the practice of surgery, leaving it to those who, with less skill and experience, had less reputation and property to lose."
—De Ville 1990

Outrageous liability rates are driving physicians from their practices, leaving patients vulnerable and the entire field of medicine in a state of turmoil.
—American Medical Association 2002

As the quotation from Dr. Hamilton shows, doctors have been complaining for over 150 years that malpractice lawsuits are driving them from their practices. Yet the medical profession continues to grow. Applications to U.S. medical schools increased in 2003 and 2004, reversing a downward trend that began in the mid-1990s, when medical malpractice premiums were also declining in real, inflation-adjusted terms.[1]

Despite the periodic complaints, no one has ever documented in systematic research that malpractice lawsuits prevent people from getting the medical care that they need. In fact, even the complaints often do not stand up to serious fact-checking. The Government Accounting Office recently checked stories from five states that the American Medical Association said were having a malpractice crisis and concluded: "Although some reports have received extensive media coverage, in each of the five states we found that the actual number of physician departures were sometimes inaccurate or involved relatively few physicians."[2]

As we will see, shortages of doctors do exist, but they come from rapid population growth in some parts of the country, a lack of health insurance and other problems that disproportionately affect rural areas and the poor, and from long-standing efforts to restrict the supply of doctors. As in any other walk of life, people continually enter and leave the medical profession, move from one part of the country to another, and change the balance of their working and nonworking lives.

In the middle of a highly politicized insurance crisis, some doctors place the label "fear of lawsuits" or "increased malpractice insurance premiums" on their decisions, and that might be what they really think—or in some cases are willing to let other people think. But in the big picture, access to medical care continues much the same regardless of lawsuits or doctors' insurance premiums. In fact, there are more doctors in the United States today, per capita, than ever before.

Consider my state of Connecticut, which the AMA says is one of the problem states. The AMA's Web site and the fact sheets it posts for doctors and legislators contain stories about Connecticut losing doctors, especially obstetricians, because of malpractice lawsuits and insurance premiums. But our commissioner of public health, Dr. J. Robert Galvin, recently testified to the Connecticut legislature that "according to the statistical people in physician licensing" this is not true. As he explained, "Physicians move around a lot, particularly younger physicians, and they move to different climates and they move to different ends of the profession. And so there's always some movement, but we have not seen demonstrable diminishment."

When pressed about obstetricians and gynecologists, he explained, "So some of it is perception, particularly with obstetrics and gynecology. . . . In all my years as a practitioner, what I found as obstetricians and gynecologists get older, they all want to do gynecological surgery. They don't want to deliver babies by and large because it's difficult and time consuming and a lot of night and weekend work."

Dr. Galvin closed his testimony on this topic with a story: "I had an acquaintance who left to go to Florida and said he didn't like it here and he had a lot of reasons as well. What he didn't like was the group he was in. What he did [like] was the fact that his wife's parents lived in Florida and he had a Florida license. . . . I had a professional colleague who left a very specialized practice to go into the ministry. It really didn't have much to do with malpractice or anything else, except that physicians tend to change. It's interesting, in other professions if you did 25 years and went on to something else—if you were a state police officer, people would say, 'Huh, he's doing something else.' So for a physician who started when he was 30 and left at 55, that should not be untoward. I stayed 40 years, but I'm from a different era."[3]

Of course, Dr. Galvin's story is just that, a story—not research. But, as we will see, his story is consistent with the research.

_____

LONG-TERM TRENDS IN THE SUPPLY OF DOCTORS

Any serious look at how medical malpractice lawsuits affect access to health care has to start by considering long-term trends in the medical profession. Otherwise we might mistakenly attribute to medical malpractice lawsuits something that has been going on for a long time. Dr. Galvin suggests that this is the case with the media reports about access to health care, and anyone who takes a careful look at the research will surely agree.

Until just a few years ago, the official word about the supply of doctors was that we were about to have too many doctors, not too few. Harvard Medical School professor David Blumenthal recently described the transformation in an elegant and insightful overview of the history of efforts to manage the supply of doctors. His article appeared in the *New England Journal of Medicine* in April 2004. The words "medical malpractice" do not appear anywhere in the article.

Dr. Blumenthal explains that until 1959 medical leaders believed that the number of doctors should grow with the overall population, not faster, and they limited the number of spots in medical schools accordingly. One indication of how sharply they restricted the number of doctors was how hard it was to get into medical school during that time. The expert view changed in 1959, however, when the surgeon general predicted that there would be a serious shortage of doctors. Universities responded by opening more medical schools. The number of U.S. medical school graduates doubled between 1965 and 1985. And it became much easier to get into medical school.

The pendulum began to swing back the other way in about 1980, when the Department of Health, Education, and Welfare (the old name for the Department of Health and Human Services) appointed an expert panel to report on the physician workforce. The experts concluded that there would be far too many doctors in the United States by the year 2000: about 150,000 too many, nearly one quarter of the number of doctors they expected to be practicing by then.

Congress responded by reducing federal funding for teaching medical students. But at the same time Congress increased the money available for training medical school graduates. As a result, medical schools expanded their internship and residency programs, filling them up in many cases with graduates of foreign medical schools. So the cut in funding for medical students did not in fact reduce the supply of doctors.

A series of expert panels and agencies explained this situation to Congress starting in the 1980s, always projecting that there would be far too many doctors by the year 2000. Congress finally acted in 1997, this time with a ceiling on how many residents the federal government would support.

As Dr. Blumenthal reports, "Almost as soon as Congress acted to moderate the expected glut of physicians, the expert consensus behind the prediction of an oversupply of physicians began to unravel." In other words, the pendulum began to swing yet again at the end of the 1990s. It swung with a vengeance once the year 2000 arrived, and everyone could see that the predicted glut of doctors had not materialized. Yes, there were as many doctors as the experts had predicted, but they were all more or less fully employed, and there were even shortages in some areas. For example, Dr. Blumenthal reports, "in the South and the West, where the population growth is most rapid, the supply of physicians and the medical-education capacity have not kept up." Other research has documented long-standing supply problems in rural areas and attributed that problem to inadequate financial opportunities for doctors, due at least in part to a lack of health insurance among people in rural areas.[4]

As Dr. Blumenthal explains, behind the recent swing of the pendulum lies a serious policy debate about how to decide how many doctors we need. The old view relied on expert opinions about how many doctors people needed, and what kind. The new view relies on statistical studies of how many and what kind of doctors people and their health insurers want and are willing to pay for.[5] Whether the expert-centered, paternalistic approach of the old view represented good health policy or not is a matter for debate. It is clear, however, that this approach kept the number of doctors from growing as fast as people voting with their health insurance dollars wanted.

That set the ground for doctor shortages in Nevada, the fastest-growing state in the country, at about the same time that the medical malpractice insurance crisis hit in 2002. And it also set the ground for the more persistent shortage of doctors in rural areas. Like most other Americans, doctors appear to prefer to live in suburban and urban areas. Limits on the supply of doctors mean that most medical school graduates can easily find work in the kinds of communities they prefer. They do not need to move to fast-growing areas in order to find well-paid work, nor do they need to move back to rural America, despite the physician shortages in both kinds of places.

MALPRACTICE LAWSUITS AND DOCTORS' CHOICE OF PRACTICE AND LOCATION

The big picture on physician supply shows that shortages result from long-term social and health policy trends. But that does not preclude malpractice lawsuits and premiums from also making a difference. Malpractice lawsuits and insurance premiums represent costs of practicing medicine. An increase in the price of malpractice insurance amounts to a cut in doctors' hourly wages, and an increase in the frequency or intensity of malpractice lawsuits affects doctors even though insurance companies pay their attorneys' fees and any settlements or verdicts. I would expect these increases to affect doctors' decisions, much like other declines in wages or practice conditions.

Precisely how declines in practice conditions affect doctors is unclear, however. On the one hand, reducing financial or other rewards could reduce doctors' willingness to work. On the other hand, reducing the financial rewards could actually increase the amount that they work, in order not to suffer a cut in income. There is evidence in both directions.[6]

If financial incentives do affect doctors' decisions (and a great deal of research in other areas suggests that financial incentives have a big effect on doctors), then it makes sense that changes in malpractice insurance premiums would affect doctors' decisions about what and where to practice, at least at the margin. In fact, there is some evidence that this is the case, particularly for rural doctors.

The Dartmouth economists I mentioned in the last chapter, Katherine Baicker and Amitabh Chandra, looked at the impact of malpractice risk on doctors' decisions about whether and where to practice.[7] They examined on a state-by-state basis the relationship between several measures of malpractice risk (insurance premiums, the number of payments made on behalf of doctors, and the amount of the payments) and the number of doctors per capita over the period from 1993 to 2001. When they looked at all doctors, they did not find a significant relationship between the amount of premiums and the number of doctors, either in general or by specialty. But when they considered rural physicians separately, they did find an impact: "a 10% increase in malpractice premiums results in a 1% decrease in all rural MDs per capita, and almost a 2% decrease in older rural MDs." This suggests that a malpractice insurance crisis could exacerbate the long-standing problem of keeping enough doctors in smaller and poorer rural areas. This makes sense. Anything that reduces the already low financial rewards of practicing in those areas seems bound to affect physician supply.

Baicker and Chandra also found a statistically significant, and in some cases substantial, relationship between the number of malpractice lawsuits per doctor and the number of some kinds of doctors. They report, "Younger and older doctors in general and in ob-gyn seem to respond to increases in the number of cases (as do younger ob-gyns and older internists in particular)." A 10 percent increase in the number of paid cases would result in a nearly a 2 percent decrease in the number of doctors under thirty-five and a little over a 1 percent decrease in the number of doctors over age fifty-five.

While this latter result is very interesting, we should keep in mind the fact that the number of paid claims per doctor has remained steady or even declined over the past ten years. Thus, this finding does not corroborate the AMA's story about the effect of the insurance crisis on doctors. Baicker and Chandra conclude, "Overall, these results provide weak evidence that some physicians on the margins of their careers make entry and exit deci-

sions in part based on the size and number of malpractice payments."
Again, the evidence was strongest for rural doctors.

When we think about the impact of medical malpractice lawsuits and
premiums on doctors' decisions, we must not lose sight of what we learned
in chapter 2. Because of the large gap between the amount of malpractice
and the comparatively small number of malpractice claims, more malpractice lawsuits and higher malpractice premiums may well be a very
good thing. In this sense, the issue of how medical malpractice lawsuits
affect access to health care is just like the issue of defensive medicine we
considered in chapter 6. As with defensive medicine, the important question is not only whether there is an effect on doctors' behavior (after all,
that is one of the goals of tort law), but also whether there is any impact on
patient health.

For example, surveys conducted by the American College of Obstetricians and Gynecologists suggest that some obstetrician-gynecologists gave
up the obstetrical part of their practice when malpractice premiums shot
up.[8] ACOG conducted these surveys as part of an effort to publicize the
negative effects of the insurance crisis, so there is good reason to take them
with a grain of salt. Nevertheless, it makes sense that rapid increases in
premiums would lead obstetrician-gynecologists to become more specialized, particularly when they practice as a group.

Obstetrician-gynecologists who do not deliver babies pay much lower
malpractice premiums because they do not face the risk of very expensive
"bad baby" lawsuits. Malpractice insurance premiums are the same for a
doctor no matter how many babies she delivers, so increasing malpractice
insurance premiums encourages obstetrician-gynecologist groups to fun-
nel the obstetrical work to a smaller number of doctors. Concentrating the
delivery work in the hands of a smaller number of doctors spreads the costs
of fewer large premiums over more deliveries and therefore increases the
income of the group. (At the same time, it seems likely to further increase
the price of the insurance on a per-doctor basis, because there are fewer
doctors exposed to birth-related claims.) A close look at the anecdotal information offered by the medical societies is consistent with this concen-
tration effect. The stories about obstetricians and family practitioners who
have given up delivering babies disproportionately feature doctors who
had not been delivering very many babies each year.

If in fact the malpractice insurance price increases shifted the delivery of babies to higher volume, more specialized obstetricians, we need to ask, "Was that good or bad?" The short answer is we do not know. I predict that the overall impact was good, for two reasons. First, particularly in a group practice, the doctors will have an incentive to give the job of delivering babies to the doctors who do that job best. Second, research in other areas suggests that "practice makes perfect," so that doctors who deliver more babies may have better outcomes.[9] But I am speculating—as are the people in the medical societies.

What is lacking is serious research. Did the malpractice insurance price increases in fact shift deliveries to fewer, higher volume doctors? Do doctors who deliver more babies have better outcomes? Did this leave some pregnant women without access to care? Has the decline in the number of rural doctors harmed rural patients' health? Or has it improved the economic foundation of the practices of the doctors who remained? Has it done both? These are all important questions, but, to the best of my knowledge, we do not have solid answers to any of them.

RESEARCH ON MALPRACTICE LAWSUITS
AND ACCESS TO MEDICAL CARE

Economists have begun conducting research that may help us reach a better-informed judgment about how malpractice lawsuits affect access to health care. The research to date includes the Kessler and McClellan research on heart disease we looked at in chapter 6, as well as two studies on infant health. All three studies examine whether tort reform has had any effect on patient health.

Before describing the research, I should emphasize one point that I may not have made clear enough in the last chapter: why there is so much economic research on the impact of tort reform. The reason is not because of economists' ideological views about tort reform, whether for or against. Economists and other serious researchers study the effect of tort reform because it gives them a way to study how law affects behavior.

Unlike in medicine, there is no way to run a controlled experiment in law. Doctors have reasonably good reasons to believe that the human body responds to medicine and other treatment the same way in experimental conditions as elsewhere. And scientists can design medical research that carefully isolates and measures the impact of a new medicine or treatment.

Not so with law. I have designed laboratory experiments that study how changing a legal rule affects behavior, and I have very little confidence that we know how our results apply outside the psychology laboratory.[10] We simply cannot create in the psych lab the precise conditions that people face outside the lab. And we do not know enough about human behavior to be confident that we are studying the right components of decisions in the lab. The psych lab research is promising and important, but it is a long way from providing the clear answers to focused questions that at least some of the medical research provides.

State tort reform comes as close as possible to a kind of a natural experiment that, for the moment at least, is a more promising way to study whether and how legal rules affect behavior. A state tort reform provides a shock to an existing system that allows researchers to study the difference it makes. For example, if medical malpractice lawsuits really do leave "patients vulnerable and the entire field of medicine in a state of turmoil," as the AMA says, then states that place restrictions on malpractice lawsuits should have better health-care outcomes than other states. Separating the difference that tort reform makes from everything else that is going on is not a simple task, but the economists whose work we began to look at in the defensive medicine chapter have refined their statistical tools for this purpose.

When considering this research we have to remember that no single study can provide a definitive answer to questions about the impact of law on society. As with the jury research I reviewed in chapter 4, we can only be confident that researchers have found something real when different kinds of research, conducted by different research teams, come to similar conclusions. A striking statistical result, different from all the rest, is probably suspect, unless we have good reason to believe that all the other research was seriously flawed.

When it comes to the impact of restrictive tort reform on health care, the research has not yet reached critical mass. Nevertheless, all the research that has been done so far points in the same direction: tort reform does not improve health-care outcomes. If anything, the research suggests that at least some kinds of tort reforms might have a detrimental effect on health, consistent with the injury-prevention role of malpractice lawsuits.

RESEARCH ON TORT REFORM
AND HEALTH-CARE OUTCOMES

There are three high-quality studies that consider the impact of tort reform on patient health. The first is the Kessler and McClellan heart disease study we discussed in the last chapter. The other two look at infants.

Kessler & McClellan research on mortality from heart disease.[11] Kessler and McClellan studied the relationship between tort reform and heart disease treatment among elderly Medicare patients. They found that "direct" tort reform that limited doctors' liability (such as caps on damages) reduced the overall intensity of heart disease treatments without an appreciable effect on patient health. Although there was in fact a "statistically significant" difference between the mortality rates in the tort reform and non–tort reform states, the difference was very small. (Statistical significance means only that we can be very confident that the results are solid, not that the effect was large.) Heart attack patients in the direct tort reform states were slightly more likely to die in the year after their heart attacks than in the other states. For example, one-year mortality for heart attacks fell .05 percent less in the direct tort reform states during the 1984 to 1990 period than in other states (a 5.39 percent decline as compared to a 5.46 percent decline). Although the negative effect of tort reform on health was very small, this result suggests that tort reform at the very least does not clearly improve patient health.

The Urban Institute research on prenatal care.[12] The Urban Institute research team we discussed in chapter 6 also studied the relationship between tort reform, prenatal care, and infant health. Using the same U.S. National Natality files that they used for their research on cesareans, they found that differences in malpractice risk do in fact seem to make a small difference in the percentage of mothers who receive timely prenatal care. The difference was larger for black mothers than for white mothers, and larger for less educated and unmarried mothers. The difference did not have an appreciable effect on infant health, however (measured by low birth weight and Apgar scores).

To give readers a sense of the size of the tort reform difference, they estimated that cutting medical malpractice premiums in half "would reduce the percentage of unmarried white women obtaining late prenatal care by between 2.3 and 3.8% points and the percentage of unmarried black women obtaining late prenatal care by between 3.5 and 4.5% points." It would take far more radical tort reforms than are presently on the political table to cut premiums in half. This suggests that more politically realistic tort reform options would be unlikely to have much of an impact on prenatal care. In any event, they concluded that the effects of even the radical tort reform on prenatal care would be "small enough that they would not be expected to have a detectable effect on average infant health." Thus, like Kessler and McClellan's results, the Urban Institute results do not support the AMA's claim that rising malpractice insurance premiums threaten public health.

Klick and Stratmann research on infant mortality.[13] Economists Jonathan Klick and Thomas Stratmann studied the relationship between tort reform, the number of doctors, and infant mortality, also on a state-by-state basis. They found mixed evidence regarding the effect of tort reform on the number of doctors. States with caps on damages had a statistically significant, but small (3 percent), increase in the number of doctors per capita, while states with other tort reforms had a statistically significant, but small, decrease in the number of doctors per capita. For example, states that limited lawyers' fees had about 2 percent fewer doctors, all other things being equal.

Klick and Stratmann also found mixed evidence on infant mortality. On the one hand, when they controlled for all their variables they found that none of the tort reforms led to any improvements in infant health. On the other hand, states that enacted one specific kind of tort reform—a rule that prevents plaintiffs from including insured health-care costs in their medical malpractice damages (commonly known as collateral source reform)—had significant *increases* in infant mortality: 3 percent for white babies and between 5 percent and 8 percent for black babies.

Collateral source reform may reduce the frequency of medical malpractice lawsuits by making lawyers less willing to take cases involving injuries that lead to large medical expenses but little long-term disability; the resulting decline in malpractice claim pressure may lead doctors to be less careful. My interviews with personal-injury lawyers support the idea that collateral source reform could reduce claim frequency,[14] but Klick and Stratmann's result is unusual and striking enough that we need to confirm it in other research before drawing strong conclusions. Needless to say, however, this result hardly suggests that tort reform improves patient health.

Klick and Stratmann also reported some intriguing partial results that linked caps on damages with lower black infant mortality, an effect that may be concentrated in poorer rural areas. This result disappeared when they considered "state effects" in their statistical analysis, meaning that the result may be due to unique characteristics of the states that enacted the caps, rather than the caps themselves. In discussions, Jonathan Klick speculated that the negative effect of malpractice pressure might be strongest in rural areas because of the long-standing problem with physician supply. As he explained, this "rural effect" would be consistent with the results of the Dartmouth and Urban Institute research: "The doctors who practice in the middle of nowhere are the ones who are the marginal cases, so they will be very responsive to practice costs. For people in these areas, having marginally fewer doctors may really affect the provision of their healthcare."

If Professor Klick is right—and he would be the first to say that their research does not provide a clear answer—tort costs would be more in the nature of the straw that broke the camel's back than the fundamental underlying cause of the problem. Tort reform would be an inefficient and indirect way to address that problem, especially because the lion's share of the financial benefits of tort reform would go to doctors in urban and suburban areas that do not have problems with physician supply.

THE RESEARCH IN CONTEXT

For the moment, the Klick and Stratmann findings should be regarded as intriguing and potentially important. Until other researchers looking at other kinds of data are able to confirm them, we should withhold judgment.

Nevertheless, considered as a whole, this early research on malpractice and access to care does suggest a preliminary conclusion: increased medical malpractice pressure, whether through higher premiums or more law-suits, has a small but positive effect on patient health, consistent with the prevention goal of malpractice lawsuits, unless that increased pressure means that patients lose access to truly necessary care. There is some evidence that increased malpractice pressure can reduce the number of doctors, and possibly affect patient health, in areas with long-standing physician supply problems, including some rural areas in the United States. As this suggests, the real health problem stems from the demographic trends and public policy decisions that created the physician shortage.

HORROR STORIES AS A POLITICAL STRATEGY

In light of these research results, it is hardly surprising that the AMA is focusing on horror stories rather than research in its campaign for tort reform.[15] As the quotation from Dr. Hamilton at the beginning of the chapter shows, this is not the first time that doctors have told stories about leaving practice as part of a campaign for limits on malpractice liability. American Bar Foundation researchers Stephen Daniels and Joanne Martin made this same observation (and also quoted Dr. Hamilton) when they studied the rhetoric of organized medicine during the last medical malpractice insurance crisis, in the 1980s.

As Daniels and Martin explained, stories about doctors leaving practice play a critical role in the medical malpractice debate, transforming what would otherwise be a private pocketbook matter for doctors into a crisis that affects health care for everyone. As a result of their research, they concluded that stories about obstetricians are the most important of all. To illustrate their point, they described an Insurance Information Institute advertising campaign from 1986 that featured an advertisement with the headline "The Lawsuit Crisis Is Bad for Babies."

Featuring a large picture of a woman holding a baby, the ad said, "A medical survey shows one out of every nine obstetricians in America has stopped delivering babies. Expectant mothers have had to find new doctors. In some rural areas women have had to travel elsewhere to give birth. How did this happen? It's part of the lawsuit crisis."

As Daniels and Martin write, "The image almost defines the essence of innocence and helplessness. Those who harm children—especially infants—are seen as the epitome of callousness, if not outright evil. Innocence at risk demands our attention and action so that the evil at hand can be eradicated. There is great political advantage, then, in making malpractice reform a solution to the long-standing public health problems related to the ob/gyn field."[16]

The parallels between the rhetoric of the 1980s and today are striking. As it did in the eighties, the tort reform campaign today focuses on access to health care. (President Bush's January 2005 Collinsville address: "And so, physicians are faced with a terrible choice: give up medicine entirely, or to move to another place where they can afford to practice medicine.") As before, the campaign features obstetricians, babies, and mothers. (President Bush's Collinsville address: "Pregnant women have to travel longer for checkups. . . . You wouldn't get an OB/GYN to come here. It's affecting rural medicine.") As before, the campaign takes long-standing problems and uses them to agitate for policy goals that have little or nothing to do with the real problems. (President Bush's Collinsville address: "I proposed a hard cap on non-economic damages." And "Congress needs to pass joint and several liability reform.")

As Daniels and Martin report, "The focus on the poor and/or rural residents seems to be a result of the fact that there was a preexisting literature on the problem of delivering medical care to these communities—all of which was independent to and predated the malpractice debate." They conclude, "In short, the more specific problems of care for the poor and those living in rural areas and their literatures were appropriated for an entirely different policy purpose—to promote change in the civil justice system by offering malpractice reform as a solution for those problems."[17]

This could have been written, almost word for word, today.

<hr>

THE DECLINE OF PART-TIME, HIGH-RISK
MEDICAL PRACTICE: BAD OR GOOD?

Despite the lack of research supporting the AMA's claims about access to health care, I am convinced that rising medical malpractice insurance rates have played at least some role in one significant trend that we would not expect to show up in the research that we reviewed. This is the trend toward increased specialization and the related decline of the generalist with a part-time, high-risk practice.

As far back as the 1970s, generalist doctors have been giving up obstetrics and surgery, at least in part to avoid the higher malpractice premiums that go with delivering babies or performing surgery. Family practitioners long ago largely gave up those practice areas in urban and suburban areas; some family practitioners reportedly are giving up surgery and obstetrics in rural areas today as well. Within the practice of obstetrics and gynecology itself, doctors may also be increasingly specializing, with fewer doctors who deliver babies part-time.[18]

"Insurance Crisis Hastens Long-Term Trend" is not exactly a rallying cry for tort reform, especially when it not clear whether the trend is good or bad. A recent survey of obstetricians in South Carolina, reportedly the first research of this kind, found that most obstetricians in both urban and rural settings believed that family practitioners should not provide obstetrical services. Younger obstetricians were more likely to give this opinion than older obstetricians, meaning that resistance to family practitioners delivering babies will grow over time.[19]

As this survey research shows, many obstetricians support the declining role of family doctors in obstetrical care. This suggests that we need to be careful how we evaluate organized medicine's current concern for family physicians who deliver babies. Especially in light of the trend toward specialization throughout the medical profession, this concern has at least the appearance of a newly convenient, or, better yet, a recently rediscovered means to a long desired end.

Some comments that Urban Institute researchers offered in connection with defensive medicine bear notice here: "Reducing defensive medicine does not seem to be the primary motivation for tort reform. The medical community's support for tort reform seems grounded at least as much in self-interest as in selfless concern for reducing medical spending. Tort reform was invented to respond to the mid-1970s 'crisis' in availability of liability insurance, not the longer standing complaints about defensive medicine. Since then, organized medicine has consistently promoted legal reform, but the rationale has varied with the legislative era, much as other proposed policy solutions have taken on new rationales over time. Medical practitioners are fully entitled to lobby policy makers in their own interest, like attorneys and everyone else, but policy makers are entitled to consider the nature of their lobbying."[20]

So, too, with access to care. If encouraging family practitioners to deliver babies or increasing access to health care for rural and poor Americans *really* were the desired policy goals, and not simply the best available justifications for a long-favored political goal, would tort reform be the proposed solution? Solving the access problem requires more doctors and better health insurance for the underserved, not tort reforms that would provide a financial benefit to doctors for rich and poor, town and country, alike.

How to improve opportunities for family practice lies far beyond my expertise, but I feel confident that tort reform will not reduce obstetricians' wish for a monopoly over obstetrics. Adjusting insurance payment formulas would have much more impact on opportunities for family practice than would tort reform. If family practitioners in fact get equally good results as obstetricians, with fewer cesareans and other complications,[21] Medicaid and private insurance companies should be interested. On the other hand, maybe the obstetricians are right. In any event, tort reform is a sideshow in the debate over the role of family practice, not the main event. The people who are trying to make tort reform the main event do not really care about family practitioners.

A FINAL WORD ON MALPRACTICE LAWSUITS, ACCESS TO HEALTH CARE, AND THE MEDICAL MALPRACTICE MYTH

This concludes my efforts to expose the medical malpractice myth. Chapter 2 demonstrated that there is more far medical malpractice than there are malpractice lawsuits, and that medical malpractice lawsuits are not increasing. Chapter 3 explained how we got a malpractice insurance crisis without an increase in malpractice lawsuits. Chapter 4 laid out the evidence showing that most people who are injured by medical malpractice do not sue and, when people do sue, the legal system does a good job of filtering out the weaker claims. Chapter 5 made the positive case for malpractice lawsuits. Chapter 6 demonstrated that defensive medicine is a trumped-up charge. And this chapter has shown that, once again, the evidence does not support organized medicine's claims. There are isolated access problems, but they do not really have anything to do with malpractice lawsuits.

As we have seen, in most cases a real problem lies buried somewhere in the rhetoric. That is a requirement for good political spin. There has to be *something* at the center of the web. You cannot admit that you are peddling a solution in search of a problem. In the next chapter we will review what the research tells us are the real problems with medical malpractice law-suits and then consider some evidence-based solutions.

8 EVIDENCE-BASED MEDICAL LIABILITY REFORM

One very clear conclusion emerges from the research on medical malpractice and medical malpractice lawsuits: The real medical malpractice problem is medical malpractice. It is not pretty to say, but doctors and nurses make *preventable* mistakes that kill more people in the United States every year than workplace and automobile accidents combined. Any research-driven approach to medical liability reform must start with this fact firmly in mind.

The evidence shows that the fundamental problem with medical malpractice lawsuits is almost exactly the opposite of what the medical malpractice myth would have us believe. The problem is not that there are too many claims; the problem is that there are too few. And, because our health-care system does such a poor job of giving injured patients the information they need to tell whether their injuries were due to malpractice, too many patients have to file lawsuits to find out.

If we were to base proposals for liability reform upon the available evidence, we would make it easier to bring a claim. Such evidence-based reform also would provide a way for injured patients to find out what caused their injuries without having to bring a lawsuit, so that they could make better informed decisions about whether to bring one. In addition, evidence-based liability reform would encourage doctors and other health-care professionals to take responsibility for, and learn from, their mistakes. It would also address the real malpractice insurance problems discussed at the end of chapter 3.

This chapter offers an evidence-based alternative to the myth-based reforms that have dominated the medical malpractice policy debate. In the first part of the chapter I provide a conceptual blueprint for a state statute to be called the Patient Protection and Healthcare Responsibility Act. The tone of the description is more technical than most of the rest of the book. Readers who do not need to understand the details should be able to get by with the text boxes that set out the main points. I find that it is helpful to have an overall sense of the statute before delving too deeply into any one part.

In the second part of the chapter I go back through the four parts of the proposal more slowly. I explain the research behind each part, and I address some of the complications and potential objections.

For most readers, the most important things to take from this chapter are, first, a general understanding of the goals of the reforms and, second, an appreciation for the fact that both the reforms and the goals grew out of the research. I don't have an ideological commitment to these particular reforms, and I don't think anyone else should, either. But we should have a commitment to the goals: reducing patient injuries, improving the accuracy of medical malpractice claiming, improving patient compensation, and reducing the disruption that the insurance cycle imposes on doctors. These reforms represent my best shot at achieving these goals. Whatever their other strengths and weaknesses might be, these reforms are much more likely to meet the goals than anything that grows out of the medical malpractice myth.

I harbor no illusions that a statute like this will be enacted overnight, or ever in this precise form. But I do hold out the hope that we can learn from studying these evidence-based reforms and from comparing them with the tort reform ideas that have emerged from the medical malpractice myth.

THE PATIENT PROTECTION AND HEALTHCARE RESPONSIBILITY ACT

The Patient Protection and Healthcare Responsibility Act (PPHRA—"Pippra") has four goals that track the real problems that the research has identified:

- The research tells us that there is too much medical malpractice. Thus, the first goal is to reduce the amount of medical malpractice.
- The research tells us that injured patients cannot adequately evaluate whether their injuries are the result of medical malpractice.

Thus, the second goal is to give patients information they need to make that evaluation.
- The research tells us that most people injured by medical malpractice are not compensated. Thus, the third goal is to improve compensation for medical injuries.
- Finally, the research tells us that the boom-and-bust insurance cycle causes the medical malpractice insurance crises that are so disruptive for doctors. Thus, the fourth goal is to moderate the effect of this cycle on doctors.

There are four parts to the act. The first part sets up a medical-injury disclosure and enforcement process. Disclosure should help reduce injuries and improve patients' ability to evaluate whether their injuries were preventable. The second part contains an apology and early-offer procedure for medical malpractice lawsuits. The third part contains a supplemental no-fault patient-compensation insurance program with modest benefits. The fourth part creates a new insurance requirement that should protect doctors from the worst effects of the insurance cycle.

I will discuss potential objections and complications after I describe the main ideas. As will be obvious, there are many important details to be worked out. Nevertheless, we can evaluate the basic concepts before getting to the details.

The PPHRA Disclosure Requirement

PPHRA would require health-care providers to inform any patient (or the person responsible for the patient) whenever they realize the patient has suffered an adverse health-care event, or an event that possibly was an adverse health-care event. Providers would have to tell the patient (a) what happened, (b) what the preferred outcome would have been, (c) how what happened differed from the preferred outcome, and (d) what they or others could have done differently to increase the chance of getting the preferred outcome. This disclosure must be oral and in writing. When health-care providers tell patients that they suffered a *possible* adverse event, they would have to tell the patients again if they decided that the event was actually an adverse event.

It is important to note that this disclosure requirement is only a more

PPHRA Disclosure Provisions

- Must disclose—orally and in writing—any adverse and possible adverse events to patient, Department of Public Health, and patient's health insurer.
- Obligation is on all health professionals providing care.
- DPH has strong enforcement powers, including audit.
- Nondisclosure means that the adverse event will be treated as negligent in any medical malpractice claim.

detailed version of what doctors are already supposed to do under the AMA's code of medical ethics, as I will explain shortly. A health-care provider could satisfy this disclosure obligation merely by telling the patient or responsible person directly or by receiving a copy of a written disclosure from another provider, together with proof that the patient or responsible person received and understood it. The obligation would fall on every professional involved in the care, not just the physician in charge. In most cases the right person to make the disclosure to the patient would be the physician in charge, but everyone involved would have an obligation to make sure that happens. The consequence for not disclosing would potentially be severe: if the patient brings a civil action, the adverse health-care event will be regarded as resulting from the negligence of any health-care provider who had an obligation to disclose it but did not do so.

The act would also require health-care providers to provide information regarding adverse or possible adverse health-care events to the Department of Public Health and to the health insurance company or other entity paying for the affected patient's health care, in a form that the department would develop for this purpose. The Department of Public Health (DPH) would be responsible for collecting and analyzing the event reports. After taking appropriate measures to protect the privacy of patients, the DPH would make the information from the reports available to the public in a form that would promote patient-safety research and awareness. I am not wedded to giving this responsibility to state departments of public health. That agency would be a logical choice in Connecticut, but other states may have another more appropriate agency.

DPH would be responsible for ensuring compliance with the disclosure requirements and would administer an auditing program with unannounced audits of patient records and verification from patients that disclosures were received and understood. DPH would be authorized to develop and require health-care providers to adopt reasonable procedures to ensure compliance with the disclosure obligations. DPH also would be authorized to assess fines on noncompliant providers. Persistent noncompliance would be grounds for withdrawal of the license to practice.

As part of the enforcement effort, DPH would be authorized to work with health-care payment organizations to develop electronic and other procedures for matching disclosures to events and for audit planning. In connection with this effort, DPH would be authorized to require the payment organizations to provide patient treatment data to DPH.

Obviously, the definitions of "adverse health-care event" and "possible adverse health-care event" would be very important. I suggest starting with the definitions used in the hospital record-based research, such as the Harvard Medical Practice Study discussed in chapter 2. The Harvard researchers defined an adverse event as "an unintended injury caused by medical management rather than by the disease process."

As reflected by the disagreements among reviewers in the research effort and by the Tony Sabia case discussed in chapter 4, it is not always easy to make judgments about cause. For example, causation can be hard to judge when there is a delayed diagnosis of a condition that might well have resulted in death or disability anyway. Requiring providers to disclose possible adverse events relieves them from having to resolve difficult causation issues when deciding whether and what to disclose, and it also means that patients will be informed more often. If there is a reasonable possibility that medical management made the patient's condition worse, the provider must disclose that fact. The patient would then be able to consider whether to consult another doctor or take other steps to obtain additional information.

In addition to providing a broad general definition of adverse health-care events and possible adverse health-care events, the act would direct DPH to develop lists of adverse and possible adverse events, based on the analysis of the reports and the patient-safety literature. For example, a postoperative infection is at least a possible adverse event, and a sponge left in the body would certainly be an adverse event. The definitions of adverse

PPHRA Apology and Restitution Incentive
- Provider apologizes and offers restitution.
- If offer is refused and if verdict is less than 20 percent above offer, plaintiff receives the lesser of the offered amount and the verdict, minus the attorneys' fees the defendant incurred from the date of the offer.

health-care event and possible adverse health-care event should become more precise over time as providers and DPH develop more experience with the reporting system. As a result, patients with adverse outcomes will have a better understanding of the causes of those outcomes, and there should be fewer lawsuits filed in situations in which there was no medical management injury or no negligence. Even more important, the reports and the DPH analysis would provide useful patient-safety feedback for providers.

The PPHRA Apology and Restitution Incentive

The act would create a new apology and restitution procedure that would give providers and patients an incentive to settle cases early. The procedure would work as follows. A health-care provider who apologizes and acknowledges fault for a medical injury would be able to offer restitution for that injury within a reasonable time after it becomes possible to know the extent of the patient's injuries and future losses. Significantly, the apology would be an admission of liability. The patient would then have a reasonable time to consider whether to accept the offer. If the patient rejects the offer, the case would proceed to trial, but the only question at trial would be the amount of the patient's damages.

The incentive comes from a rule about what happens if the patient does not accept the offer. If the patient rejects the offer, the patient will become responsible for the defendant's litigation expenses, including attorney fees, from the time of the offer until the end of the trial, unless the verdict is at least 20 percent more than the offer. In addition, the plaintiff can recover more than the amount of the offer only if the verdict at trial is at least 20 percent more than the offer. If the verdict is less than 20 percent above the offer, the plaintiff gets the lower verdict amount.

The incentive would be most effective in speeding up claims in which the defense team knows that liability is relatively clear. As the closed–claim research we reviewed in chapter 4 revealed, a large percentage of the paid claims involve cases that insurance company experts regarded as "indefensible." Speeding up the resolution of those claims offers obvious savings of time and expense. In addition, as ethicist Lee Taft explains in a thoughtful recent essay introducing this incentive idea, apology and restitution offer therapeutic benefits to both health–care providers and patients.[1]

The PPHRA Supplemental No-Fault Compensation Provision

PPHRA would create a new no–fault patient–compensation program with modest benefits principally intended to provide compensation for, and an incentive to avoid, moderate injuries. Any patient injured by an adverse health–care event would be entitled to compensation for that injury from insurance purchased by the responsible health–care provider(s) according to a schedule to be established by the Department of Public Health. (Once again, I am not wedded to that agency being given this responsibility. In many states, there may be another, more appropriate, agency.) The schedule would compensate patients for reasonable health–care and rehabilitation expenses not covered by other insurance or benefit plans, as well as for lost wages or services not recoverable from other sources, up to a maximum amount for an adverse event (or series of related events).

PPHRA Patient Compensation Program
- Designated health-care providers must obtain insurance (or make acceptable self-insurance arrangements).
- Insurance benefits are paid to any patient injured by an adverse event caused by the provider.
- Benefits cover uninsured medical expenses and wage losses, after a deductible and up to a maximum per injury according to a schedule to be established by DPH.
- Maximum benefit per injury will not exceed $50,000.
- DPH will create an administrative enforcement process modeled on workers' compensation and Social Security disability.

The size of the maximum amount would be set by the legislature. My suggestion would be to set a relatively low amount, for example $50,000 or $80,000, and to minimize interference with the current tort approach. In addition, there should be a period of disability or an amount of health and rehabilitation expenses that would be uncompensated and that would function like an insurance deductible to discourage very small claims. The goal here would be to avoid the problem of our automobile accident compensation system, in which the research tells us too much money is spent on minor injury claims.[2]

The act would direct the Department of Public Health to set up an administrative procedure for determining eligibility and compensation under the new no-fault liability. The administrative procedure would be modeled on workers' compensation and Social Security benefit procedures. Patients would be allowed to have the assistance of an attorney or patient advocate at any hearing, at their own expense. The legislature might consider having state-paid advocates available for patients with earnings below a certain amount.

The PPHRA Insurance Requirement

PPHRA's medical liability insurance provisions adopt the "enterprise insurance" approach I described at the end of chapter 3. The act would require hospitals and comparable organizations (such as nursing homes, rehabilitation centers, and surgery centers) to obtain liability insurance (or comparable protection) for all the medical professionals who provide services using the organization's facilities. The insurance would cover the professionals for all claims relating to services provided, or to be provided, in the organization's facilities. For example, an obstetrician would be covered for claims relating to a particular pregnancy by the insurance provided by the hospital in which the doctor delivered, or planned to deliver, the baby. The insurance would cover traditional tort claims and it would also provide the patient-compensation benefits just described.

Doctors with both office and hospital practices would still need to purchase their own medical liability insurance policies to cover their office practice. Most serious medical malpractice suits, especially for obstetricians, involve services that are provided in a hospital. This means that the premiums for the personal medical liability insurance of a doctor with a

PPHRA Insurance Provisions

- Hospitals and other designated organizations must purchase insurance covering claims made against a health professional arising out of care provided or to be provided in a facility of the organization.
- Insurance will provide $2 million per occurrence per professional, in addition to defense costs, and will be primary for covered claims.
- If patient compensation program is adopted, this insurance will cover those benefits as well.

substantial hospital practice would be much less than it is now, even with the new patient-compensation benefits.

Of course there would be important details to be worked out (such as the amount of protection for each doctor, whether a hospital can purchase a single policy for all its doctors, and whether a hospital may fulfill the insurance obligation through alternatives to traditional liability insurance). And undoubtedly there would be some initial difficulties in figuring out which claims are covered by which insurance policies. But these are technical problems that would be easy to resolve. In the long run, organization-based medical liability insurance makes more sense from both a tort and insurance perspective, as I will explain shortly.

CONSIDERING THE PATIENT PROTECTION
AND HEALTHCARE RESPONSIBILITY ACT

The basic framework of PPHRA should now be clear. The act would create a new disclosure obligation with a strong enforcement system. The act would create a procedure to encourage apologies and early settlements in cases involving clear liability, and it would create a new no-fault compensation program that would be especially important for moderate injuries, which are almost completely ignored at present. And the act would shift more of the responsibility for medical liability insurance to hospitals and comparable health-care organizations, which are better able to manage the volatility of the insurance underwriting cycle.

This is a completely different approach to medical liability reform than the damage caps and other tort reforms offered by the White House and the AMA. This approach would do a much better job than those tort reforms at meeting the stated objectives of compensating more patients who are injured by medical injuries and encouraging fewer "invalid" claims.

Of course, it seems likely to make medical liability insurance more expensive, particularly for hospitals and comparable health-care facilities. But more expensive is not always bad. Medical liability insurance may cost more after PPHRA, but we would have safer health care, better compensation for patient injuries, and a fairer distribution of insurance premiums.

In addition, it is vitally important to remember that PPHRA only "costs" more from the perspective of medical providers, who would like us to ignore the lion's share of the injury costs, which injured patients presently bear. Taking a broader, more public-minded perspective, we can easily see that PPHRA would not increase the costs of medical injuries. Instead it would shift more of those costs to organizations that are in a good position to prevent injuries in the first place. That should cut costs, not increase them.

The Disclosure Requirement

It is hard to argue with the proposition that patients are entitled to know what happened to them, particularly when the result is not what their doctors intended. In fact, the American Medical Association medical ethics code requires doctors to tell their patients about both good and bad outcomes. The general principal is "a physician should at all times deal honestly and openly with patients." More specifically, "Situations occasionally occur in which a patient suffers significant medical complications that may have resulted from a physician's mistake or judgment. In these situations, the physician is ethically required to inform the patient of *all the facts* necessary to ensure understanding of what has occurred." As the ethics code emphasizes, "Concern regarding legal liability which might result following truthful disclosure should not affect the physician's honesty with a patient."[3]

In light of the Institute of Medicine report, *To Err Is Human,* and the research reviewed in chapter 2, it became obvious by the late 1990s, if not earlier, that doctors in fact were not fully disclosing medical injuries, particularly preventable injuries.[4] In response, the Joint Commission on

Accreditation of Healthcare Organizations (JCAHO—"Jayco"), a private organization that accredits hospitals, began in 2001 requiring hospitals to adopt policies to ensure that the lead doctor on a case discloses any "unanticipated outcomes" to the patient. But JCAHO almost immediately backed off from a literal reading of the new disclosure requirement by suggesting that it would be checking to see only that hospitals were disclosing "sentinel events," JCAHO's term for the most serious injuries or death.[5]

PPHRA improves on the JCAHO rule in many ways, all of which are designed to ensure that patients actually receive the information doctors have long been obligated to provide them. First, the scope of the disclosure is much broader, and PPHRA creates a procedure that will provide increasingly specific guidance about what must be disclosed. Significantly, PPHRA puts a publicly accountable government agency in charge, not an unaccountable private association or professional society.

In addition, PPHRA imposes the obligation on all the professionals involved in the care, as well as the organization. Providers can fulfill this obligation only by disclosing the event themselves or by receiving a signed document showing that someone else already adequately informed the patient. This means that no one involved in the adverse event can simply assume that someone else will inform the patient or the patient's family. It also means that a senior professional will be less likely to silence lower-ranking professionals involved in the care.

PPHRA requires the disclosure to be both oral and in writing. The writing requirement will improve the accuracy and precision of the disclosure, and it will provide a greater opportunity for providers to reflect on and learn from the adverse event. It also will provide a record that the patient can use to decide what to do. Patients can easily become confused about a disclosure that is not written down, and doctors can too easily gloss over or rush through uncomfortable details in a spoken explanation. We make banks and credit card companies put their interest rates and fee information in writing. Adverse health-care events can be much more complicated to understand than interest and fees. And they are much more important.

PPHRA requires the information to be given to the Department of Public Health so that DPH can study adverse events and improve patient safety. Quality improvement requires the measurement of adverse out-

comes as well as continuous efforts to learn from them. If we do not ap-
point a central agency to count and analyze adverse events, providers will
never know how their safety and outcome records compare to other providers, where there is room for improvement, and whether they are getting
any better.

Just as important, PPHRA directs DPH to create a serious auditing system to enforce the disclosure requirement. No auditing system can ensure
one hundred percent compliance, but it can ensure that providers set up
and generally follow systems for reporting adverse events. In addition,
PPHRA treats the failure to disclose as an admission of negligence. This
makes it much less likely that providers will withhold information in individual cases with very bad outcomes. No auditing system, alone, can eliminate that possibility, because the odds of any particular case being audited
will always be very low. Arguably the rule would not have any effect on
someone who wanted to cover up a negligent mistake. But it is rare that
everyone involved in a patient's care makes a culpable mistake, so the rule
places pressure on the other people involved to disclose the adverse event
to the patient.

It is easy to think of any number of potential objections to the PPHRA
disclosure requirements. But a moment's reflection should be enough to
realize that all or most of these objections will fall into one of two cate-
gories: "government is bad" and "doctors know best." Self-regulation has
not worked to ensure that health-care professionals disclose adverse
events. If we are serious about safety improvement, there is no realistic alternative to a publicly administered and enforced adverse-event reporting
system.

Someday we will have such a system. Although I doubt that we will get
that system because of a desire to improve the accuracy of medical malpractice claiming, there is no doubt that mandatory, strongly enforced,
adverse-event disclosure would do far more to improve the accuracy of
claiming than any of the tort reforms currently on the political table. Giving patients reliable, detailed information would allow them to make much
better decisions about whether to file a medical malpractice claim.

As we saw in chapter 4, the research shows that even an informal and
seemingly ineffective hospital complaint process could significantly improve the ability of patients to judge the merit of potential lawsuits. Why?

Because that process gave patients access to information about what happened to them. Reliable adverse-event reporting, backed up by state auditing, would provide even better information to patients and, thus, improve the accuracy of patient claims even more.

The Apology and Restitution Incentive

I am tempted to defend the apology and restitution incentive simply by referring readers to the essay by ethicist Lee Taft that introduced the idea of linking an apology to an attorneys' fee-shifting incentive.[6] But of course that would defeat the purpose of a book like this, which is supposed to pull together research and ideas, not send people off to the library.

When I first read about Taft's idea, I immediately connected it with the closed-claim research described in chapter 4. The closed-claim research shows that in a substantial percentage, probably a majority, of the paid malpractice claims the insurance companies' own experts believe that the health-care provider was liable. The closed-claim research also shows that insurance companies paid bigger settlements in those clear liability cases than in cases involving uncertain liability. In combination, these two facts mean that a substantial percentage of the medical malpractice claim dollars—certainly much more than half—is paid in clear liability cases. Anything that significantly speeds up the resolution of those kinds of cases offers a real improvement in the efficiency of the medical malpractice claiming process, as it actually exists.

Research that I worked on with Northwestern University law professor Albert Yoon strongly suggests that Taft's idea would work. We studied the effect of a similar settlement incentive that New Jersey put in effect in 1994. We found that it speeded up settlements and reduced litigation expenses.[7]

The New Jersey settlement incentive involved what is known as the "offer of judgment" rule. In federal court and in most state courts, this rule allows defendants to make an offer of judgment to the plaintiff much like the restitution offer Taft proposes, but without the apology. If the plaintiff accepts the offer, that settles the case, as in Taft's proposal. If the plaintiff rejects the offer, there is a potential consequence, as in Taft's proposal. The difference is that the offer-of-judgment consequence usually is negligible. If the jury does not award the plaintiff more than 80 percent of what the defendant offered, the plaintiff has to pay the defendant's court costs, which include docket fees and printing costs and other trivial expenses that the defendant has to pay to the court during the lawsuit.

Court costs do not ordinarily include attorney fees, and therefore the offer-of-judgment rule does not give a defendant the possibility of recovering attorneys' fees from a plaintiff who turns down a good offer. That is where the New Jersey rule is different, however. In New Jersey the defendant can recover attorney fees from the time of the offer until trial, just like in Taft's proposal. (New Jersey also allows plaintiffs to make offers of judgment, which is not a part of Taft's proposal.) But until September 1994, New Jersey capped the total amount of attorneys' fees that could be shifted at $750 per case, so the rule did not in fact provide a very big incentive.

That situation changed in 1994, however, when New Jersey removed the $750 cap. Albert Yoon and I studied how that change affected New Jersey tort cases. We were able to get access to tort claim records from 1992 to 1997 from a very large company that sold insurance in New Jersey and the surrounding states. When we analyzed those records, we found that New Jersey tort cases settled more quickly after the change—nearly two and a half months quicker on average—and the insurance company on average spent $1,200 less on its own attorneys per claim as a result. Plaintiffs' lawyers presumably also spent less time on each case, but the insurance company records did not contain that information.

There is good reason to believe that Taft's proposal would have a much larger effect on medical malpractice claims than the New Jersey rule had on the claims we studied. The claims we studied were personal auto and homeowners' insurance claims. The average amount paid in cases with a payment was just over $36,000; the average fee paid to the defense lawyer was just over $5,000; and the average duration of the litigation was less than three years. Medical malpractice lawsuits are much bigger and generally take longer to resolve, so there is much more room for savings.

In addition, PPHRA provides a stronger incentive to accept the offer than the New Jersey rule. Under PPHRA, a plaintiff who rejects an offer of restitution has to pay the defendant's attorney fees unless the jury award is at least 20 percent *more* than the defendant's offer. By contrast, under the New Jersey rule the plaintiff has to pay the defendant's attorney fees only if the verdict is at least 20 percent *less* than the defendant's offer. The

PPHRA approach makes it much more likely that the plaintiff will have to pay the defendant's fees, and therefore increases the incentive to accept the restitution offer.

These are good reasons to support Taft's proposal. But he defends his idea with a very different, and to my mind more profound, reason. Taft argues, convincingly, that apology and restitution offer therapeutic benefits to both doctor and patient. As he observes, "Undisclosed error interrupts the essential ingredient of trust between doctor and patient and disrupts the doctor's sense of integrity. Although the error itself relates to physical harm, the lack of apology disrupts the moral dimension of the doctor's relationship with the patient, the broader medical community, and himself."[8] Apology and restitution help repair the break in the moral order and, thus, promote the corrective justice goal that forms the moral underpinning for medical malpractice law. And, from a practical perspective, the relationship between the doctor and the patient, along with the therapeutic benefits of apology and restitution, makes it much more likely that the offer will be accepted in a medical malpractice case than in the auto and homeowners' cases Albert Yoon and I studied.

Based on his own experience with medical malpractice lawsuits and on research on the effect of apologies in malpractice lawsuits, Taft argues that doctors should be willing to apologize even without an incentive. He cites jury research suggesting that juries award lower damages in cases in which the doctor has apologized and shows genuine remorse. Other research shows that plaintiffs are also willing to accept smaller settlements in that situation. Nevertheless, so much fear and distrust have built up among doctors and their defense lawyers over the years that the incentive probably is necessary.

I am told that some plaintiffs' lawyers do not like Taft's idea and that they find the incentive too one-sided. I imagine they think it would reduce the value of their best cases without offering enough to injured patients in return. I think they are wrong. The apology is an admission of liability, whether the plaintiff accepts the offer of restitution or not. That is a very substantial benefit to the plaintiff. Also, faster settlements benefit injured patients at least as much as doctors. And, perhaps most important, the research shows that plaintiffs are looking for more than money. They want answers to what happened, and they also want the kind of moral closure

that a sincere apology can help to provide. In addition, widespread acceptance of the apology and restitution framework could reduce the stigma of
medical malpractice claiming. That result offers very clear benefits to injured patients and their lawyers.

Lee Taft's idea is just one among many constructive ideas about how to
improve the resolution of medical malpractice claims. I included it in
PPHRA because I find the corrective justice implications particularly appealing, and because there is research suggesting that it really will work.
But, as with the disclosure concept, my main objective here is to illustrate
the difference between evidence-based medical liability reform and the
tort reform ideas that emerge from the medical malpractice myth. There
are plenty of ways to reform tort law so that medical malpractice lawsuits
come closer to achieving their deterrence, compensation, and corrective
justice goals, as long as you support the idea that lawsuits have a legitimate
role to play in achieving those goals and as long as you are willing to pay attention to the evidence.

*Supplemental No-Fault Compensation
for Adverse Healthcare Events*

No-fault compensation for medical injuries turns out to be an idea that
lots of people like in theory but almost no one likes in practice. Health-care
providers like no-fault in theory because it feels less adversarial and more
consistent with the therapeutic nature of their calling. They do not like it
in practice, however, because it threatens to open a floodgate of claims and
dramatically increase their insurance premiums. All it takes is one look at
what U.S. business pays for workers' compensation insurance to cool the
medical no-fault ardor of almost any health-care administrator. Workplace
accidents injure far fewer people than medical malpractice. Yet, as I explained in chapter 1, workers' compensation premiums in the United
States for 2003 were five times as large as medical malpractice insurance
premiums.

Patient advocates like no-fault compensation in theory because it offers
the promise of quick, no-hassle compensation. Patient advocates do not
like it in practice, however, once they realize that they still have to prove
that medical treatment caused the patients' injuries and that no-fault damages are not enough to pay for the skilled advocates and experts needed
to overcome health-care providers' causation defenses in serious-injury

cases. Also, medical injuries are very different from workplace accidents, so workers' compensation may be a poor model. Among other differences, workers know what to expect in the workplace, and they generally have a good idea exactly what happened to them in a workplace accident. If they do not know, they usually have ways to find out. Patients do not.

In short, no-fault medical-injury compensation is an old idea whose time has never come. There are two very limited no-fault medical-injury programs in the United States, one in Virginia and one in Florida. Both apply only to a narrow range of birth injuries. Neither is widely regarded as a success.

So why do I include a no-fault compensation concept in PPHRA?

There are two reasons. The first is to provide a contrast with the AMA. The AMA has launched an all-out effort to cut back on tort liability, in part on the grounds that tort lawsuits do not compensate enough injured patients, without offering a serious proposal to increase the number who are compensated.

The second reason is that the approach to no-fault compensation laid out in PPHRA is worth serious examination, notwithstanding the general lack of enthusiasm for no-fault today. The PPHRA concept is different from the Virginia and Florida programs and the massive tort replacement systems suggested in the past.

Unlike the Virginia and Florida birth injury programs, PPHRA's no-fault compensation would be most important for medical injuries that are ignored by medical malpractice lawyers today. Serious birth injuries are one area where the claiming rate already is reasonably high, and doctors' fears about liability are real. We do not need a new no-fault compensation system to boost the rate of serious-injury, high-value claims. The PPHRA disclosure program would increase the accuracy of serious-injury claims, and it might help obstetricians and other high-risk specialists emulate the risk management success of the anesthesiologists. That would be improvement enough for the high-value injuries that are the main focus of medical malpractice lawsuits today.

Where we do need streamlined, administrative no-fault compensation is for smaller-value claims. Different lawyers have different cutoffs for different kinds of malpractice claims, but we can tell from the closed-claim research that very few lawyers are taking very many malpractice cases without the potential for a damage award of at least $200,000. Yet the research on medical malpractice reviewed in chapter 2 tells us that medical injuries are like auto and workplace injuries in one crucial respect. The severity of the injuries is like a pyramid—with many more low-value injuries than moderate-value injuries, and many more moderate-value injuries than high-value injuries. With few exceptions, medical malpractice lawsuits completely ignore at least the bottom three quarters of the medical-injury pyramid. That is where we need to focus some new deterrence and compensation energy.

Unlike the massive tort replacement programs proposed but never enacted in the past, PPHRA would be a small, supplemental program that would make no attempt at replacing tort liability. A $50,000 or even an $80,000 maximum award would ensure that the program did not compete with medical malpractice lawsuits, and it would encourage a new kind of patient advocate to build a career around representing people in lower-value claims in which the only question is whether the medical treatment caused the injury.

Currently, giving up tort liability for medical malpractice would be a very bad idea. There is no guarantee that no-fault would work well for high-severity injuries, especially because of the difficulty and expense involved in proving causation in many serious-injury cases. Patients do not have the direct access to evidence and the knowledge that workers can use to help prevent a cover-up in the workers' compensation context. At least for now, medical malpractice requires the large damages that tort lawsuits sometimes provide in order to motivate advocates to do the hard work needed to prove causation or get to the bottom of a cover-up. Nor are we ready to give up on a fault-based system for health-care providers who make truly awful mistakes, or who do awful things to hide their mistakes.

If you disagree with me about the benefits of tort liability, that is even more reason to get behind PPHRA, so that we develop some real experience with medical no-fault. Until there is a solid track record for medical no-fault, a comprehensive tort replacement program will be dead on arrival in any legislature in any state in the country.

Enterprise Insurance

The enterprise insurance concept in PPHRA is my answer to the medical malpractice insurance crisis. PPHRA would obligate hospitals and similar organizations to provide insurance covering all liabilities arising out of services performed, or to be performed, in their facilities.

I borrowed the name "enterprise insurance" from the concept of "enterprise liability." Enterprise *liability* reflects the idea that the best entity to bear the legal liability for medical injury is the "enterprise"—the organization that employs or at least potentially controls the medical professionals who provide patient care. Although individual doctors may make mistakes, those mistakes take place in an organization, and the people who run the organization are in the best position to design medical delivery systems that prevent mistakes or reduce their impact.

True enterprise liability has not caught on. Hospitals and HMOs resisted taking over the liability from doctors, and doctors resisted giving it up. It is not hard to imagine why the organizations did not leap to assume the liability. What might be harder to understand is why doctors refused to give it up. The answer is that doctors were afraid that giving up liability would mean losing control over patient care.

Enterprise *insurance* offers many of the benefits of enterprise liability, but without asking doctors to give up liability. With enterprise insurance, all the hospital or other enterprise has to do is provide insurance. Liability continues to rest firmly on the doctors' shoulders (except, of course, for mistakes by hospital personnel). But because the hospital has to pay for the doctors' insurance, it has a bigger incentive to design systems so that doctors make fewer mistakes, and so the mistakes that do happen have less serious results.

Enterprise insurance also makes more sense than individualized insurance as a strategy for dealing with the insurance underwriting cycle problems discussed in chapter 3. The individualized approach places too much of the burden of rapid premium increases on doctors in high-risk specialties and in high-risk locations. It would be one thing if doctors could simply raise the price of their services when insurance premiums go up, but the reality is that they cannot. Enterprise insurance shifts the burden of rapid and unpredictable insurance price increases to organizations better equipped to manage them.

Hospitals, nursing homes, rehabilitation centers, and other large health-care facilities provide a more diversified range of services than doctors and, thus, face more diversified risks. This greater diversity allows hospitals to spread the costs of liability insurance across both high- and low-risk services, so that the burden of suddenly increased premiums does not fall on a narrow range of higher-risk services, like obstetrical care.

Many medical schools and some HMOs and hospitals already provide liability insurance for their doctors.[9] As these organizations have found, they are better able to manage the volatility of insurance premiums than doctors are, and they are better able than their doctors to get insurance or to make alternative arrangements in difficult market conditions.

There are many possible objections to enterprise insurance, but they all have good answers. The objection that enterprise insurance would interfere with the health-care market may well be the easiest to answer. The health-care market already is so far from a world of free competition that our individualized approach to medical liability insurance is just as likely to be the result of a market failure. Given the superior ability of hospitals and other health organizations to obtain medical liability insurance, it is surprising that these organizations have not already assumed that responsibility on behalf of all the doctors who use their facilities.

Ironically, one important reason why hospitals are not already providing liability insurance to more doctors turns out to be the unintended consequence of a federal law that was supposed to improve the health-care market. Federal anti-kickback law prevents hospitals from paying doctors to bring patients to the hospital. The idea is that doctors should pick hospitals based on their best medical judgment, not on the share of the hospital bill or other benefits that the hospital is willing to kick back to the doctor. Because of this law, there is real concern that *voluntarily* providing liability insurance to doctors would be an illegal kickback, unless the doctors are hospital employees.

During the recent insurance crisis some hospitals wanted to provide insurance to private doctors in order to make sure that they could afford to keep practicing in the hospital. Some of those hospitals filed special requests with the U.S. Department of Health and Human Services to make sure that providing the insurance would not get them in trouble under the anti-kickback law. HHS gave the hospitals "advisory opinions" allowing them to provide the insurance, but I have read the letters and they are not encouraging for hospitals that would like to do this on a regular basis.[10]

A state law that *required* hospitals to provide liability insurance to doctors would completely eliminate the risk of federal prosecution for giving insurance to doctors. Hospitals would not be giving doctors insurance in return for their business; hospitals would be giving doctors insurance to comply with state law. This would not be a subterfuge. If every hospital has to provide the insurance, then the insurance will not affect doctors' choices about which hospital to use. On the other hand, it might make hospitals choosier about which doctors they allow to use their facilities. That would be a very good thing.

In the short term, enterprise insurance could provide a windfall to private doctors with high-risk, hospital-based practices, such as obstetricians. It also could be a difficult new burden for hospitals. But that windfall and burden would dissipate over time through adjustments in prices and reimbursement rates. In any event, the added burden should not be overstated. The insurance burden already is shifting to hospitals, both through contracting (e.g., hospitals, medical schools, and HMOs providing insurance to their employed doctors) and through plaintiffs' efforts to hold hospitals responsible for medical malpractice. The comparatively low value of doctors' insurance policies already encourages plaintiffs to target hospitals; that incentive will only get stronger if more doctors stop carrying insurance.

Enterprise insurance will increase hospitals' incentive to manage doctors, and that could reduce doctors' autonomy to some degree. But, the fact that the legal liability remains with the doctor helps the doctor retain moral authority over patient care. This is not to say that there will never be a conflict between doctors and the institutions that provide their insurance, but rather that enterprise insurance gives doctors more autonomy than would enterprise liability. In any event, the large number of doctors who already get their insurance through hospitals, HMOs, and medical schools are not rushing out to buy their own insurance. They seem to be managing fine with this privately arranged form of enterprise insurance.

Of course enterprise insurance will create some new administrative complications, but that should not be a reason to stick with an unsatisfactory situation. Objections about administrative complications almost always are makeweight arguments, hauled in to camouflage less savory interest-based objections, and this situation is no exception. Insurance companies that sell insurance mainly to doctors surely will oppose enterprise insurance, as will some hospitals, and both groups can be counted on to provide many reasons why it will be very difficult to put enterprise insurance in place. But those reasons will not be their real concern. If anything, putting all the doctors who practice in a hospital under a single insurance program would reduce the expense and complexity of arranging insurance and defending lawsuits. The insurance companies' real concern will be keeping the doctors' insurance business, and the hospitals' real concern will be avoiding the new expense.

There will in fact be some complications for doctors who practice inside and outside institutions, or who practice in more than one institution, and who therefore will be covered by more than one liability insurance policy—just like people who are covered by both their companies' auto insurance and their personal auto insurance. It will be necessary to draw lines about which policy pays for which kinds of claims, and there undoubtedly will be some gray areas. But this is no cause for alarm. Whenever insurance arrangements change, there is an initial flurry of disagreements, but then everyone learns how to deal with the new arrangements.

EVIDENCE-BASED LIABILITY REFORM
VS. MYTH-BASED LIABILITY REFORM

As should by now be clear, each part of PPHRA is evidence-based. The disclosure requirements are based on research that shows that doctors and hospitals do not in fact disclose adverse events and on research that shows that providing patients better information increases the accuracy of medical malpractice claims. Even more important, the disclosure requirements are designed to *produce* the kind of evidence that we need to reduce patient injuries and improve the quality of health care.

The apology and restitution incentive is based on two kinds of research. First, the closed-claim research shows that most malpractice claim payment dollars are paid in cases in which the insurance company's experts believe that the doctor in fact was negligent, suggesting that these cases are ripe for an apology. Second, the New Jersey research shows that this kind of incentive actually works.

The no-fault concept is based on the research showing that medical malpractice lawsuits almost always involve high-value injuries. Thus, a no-fault program with modest benefits would begin to fill a huge deterrence and compensation hole, without interfering with the current approach.

Finally, the enterprise insurance concept is based on research on the medical malpractice insurance underwriting cycle. That research shows that the malpractice insurance crises result from the boom-and-bust cycle, not short-term changes in medical malpractice lawsuits. That research also shows that the impact of the crisis falls disproportionately on doctors with hospital-based practices. It is also worth noting that the enterprise insurance concept is consistent with the emerging expert view that the best way to prevent medical malpractice is through a system approach.

The tort reform proposals that emerge out of the medical malpractice myth stand in sharp contrast. One good place to see those tort reform proposals is the White House Web site. The White House proposes "curbing lawsuit abuse with needed medical liability reform." The reform includes imposing a $250,000 cap on noneconomic damages and unspecified limits on punitive damages, eliminating lump-sum damage awards in favor of periodic payments, shortening the period after an injury in which a patient may bring a claim, and eliminating the legal rule that makes each defendant in a case responsible for all of the harm in the event that the other defendants do not have enough insurance or money to pay for their share.[11]

With one exception, the White House proposals have a clear and well-targeted aim: to reduce the number of high-severity, high-damage malpractice lawsuits, and to reduce the amount of damages that a severely injured patient can collect. The one exception is the punitive-damages proposal. Punitive-damage reform does not have very much to do with true medical malpractice lawsuits, which almost never involve punitive damages. Drug companies and medical device manufacturers are the real constituency for punitive-damages reform, not doctors and hospitals. This is the "hiding behind the doctor's white coat" side of medical malpractice reform that I mentioned in chapter 5.

These reforms attack tort law rules that English and American judges developed over hundreds of years in a carefully considered effort to balance the interests of plaintiffs and defendants. Plaintiffs' lawyers did not dream these rules up and impose them on the rest of the world. The rules emerged out of a long, deliberative process in which both sides of every case had full opportunity to be heard. If anyone was at a financial and tactical disadvantage in that process, it was plaintiffs, not defendants.

Not one of the White House proposals would improve the accuracy of malpractice claiming, increase the number of injured patients who will be compensated, or improve patient safety. Not one of the White House proposals will protect doctors from the next medical malpractice insurance crisis or provide real, immediate relief for doctors who deliver babies. What they will do, instead, is increase patients' share of the medical malpractice burden.

Of course the White House proposal does not say that. Instead it says, "Frivolous lawsuits and excessive jury awards are driving many health-care providers out of communities and forcing doctors to practice overly defensive medicine. This reduces access to medically necessary services and raises the costs of health care for all." For these reasons, "the President has proposed proven reforms, such as common-sense limits on non-economic damages, to make the medical liability system more fair, predictable and timely."[12]

This is the medical malpractice myth at work. As the research demonstrates, not one of these factual predicates is true. Not frivolous lawsuits. Not excessive jury awards. Not driving many doctors out of communities. Not overly defensive medicine. Not reducing access to medically necessary services. And not raising the costs of health care for all.

This is hardly to say that our current approach to medical liability and insurance is perfect. It is not. There are too few claims to provide an adequate safety incentive. Not enough patients are compensated. Patients get reliable information about what happened to them far too late in the process. And doctors are asked to bear too much of the medical liability insurance burden. If we want to address these real problems, we should start with the evidence, not the myth. Just as we need evidence-based medicine, we also need evidence-based medical liability reform.

Acknowledgments

I have had a great deal of help with this book. Law students Kathleen Santoro and John Maroney helped me collect, organize, and understand the research. University of Connecticut insurance librarian Yan Hong and her colleagues consistently came through on difficult requests. Other researchers generously shared their ideas and findings. Thank you to Bernard Black, Amitabh Chandra, Mark Geistfeld, David Hyman, Jonathan Klick, Michelle Mello, David Moss, William Sage, Charles Silver, Lee Taft, and, especially, Michael McCann and Neil Vidmar, who supported the project from start to finish and provided detailed comments and suggestions on the book manuscript. Friends and colleagues on all sides of the medical malpractice debates–doctors, insurance executives, trial lawyers, and patient-safety experts–were generous with their time and supportive of my effort to bring the research to a broader audience. My squash partners Peter Siegelman and Mark Silk put up with far too much conversation about medical malpractice myth and reality. Peter also read the manuscript and, like our law school colleagues Anne Dailey, Jeremy Paul, Jim Stark, and Carol Weisbrod, provided helpful comments.

The editors at the University of Chicago Press were superb. John Tryneski encouraged me to write the book and kept me on track throughout the process. Carol Saller's careful editing prodded me to clarify and streamline my prose. The University of Connecticut provided significant material and intellectual support, including a research leave without which I could not have stayed on the ambitious schedule that John Tryneski set for me.

Finally, my family supported me in countless ways throughout the research and writing process. In particular, my wife, Sharon, helped me conceive and execute the project in a way that we hope will be accessible to everyone who cares about health care in the United States.

Notes

CHAPTER 1

1. Mills 1977. For a description of this history see Studdert, Brennan et al. 2000 at 1647–48; and Mello and Brennan 2002 at 1599.
2. Mills 1978.
3. The leading exception was a technical law and economics analysis by Wharton professor Patricia Danzon. Danzon 1985.
4. Draper 2001. Avery 2003 and 2004 (multiple news stories). Eisley 2003.
5. Grady and Altman 2003. See also *Dallas Morning News* 2003.
6. *Los Angeles Times* 2003.
7. Langford 2004. Avery 2004.
8. Kohn et al. 2000.
9. Haltom and McCann 2004.
10. Galanter 1986, 1994, 2004. For a review of the research see Haltom and McCann 2004. For the latest research on auto accident claims see Browne and Schmit 2004.
11. All insurance numbers from *Best's Aggregates and Averages* (Best 2004), 165–70, 182–83.
12. AMA 2005.
13. Heinz et al. 1998 at 765. See also Dunworth and Rogers 1996.
14. Marjoribanks et al. 1996 at 174 and 176.
15. http://www.whitehouse.gov/news/releases/2005/01/20050105-4.html# (visited March 29, 2005).
16. Gawande 2002 at 7.
17. Ross 1970.
18. Gawande 2002 at 236–37.
19. Bassett et al. 2000 at 528.
20. Ibid.; Marjoribanks et al. 1996.

CHAPTER 2

1. Kohn et al. 2000.
2. Harvard Medical Practice Study 1990; Weiler 1991.
3. Connecticut Judicial Branch 2005.
4. Mills 1977.
5. Mello and Brennan 2002 at 1599; Mills 1977 at 2.
6. Mills 1977 at 8, 47, 49, and 53.
7. Mills 1977 at 100.
8. Danzon 1985 at 217–18.

9. Harvard Medical Practice Study 1990 at 6–7. The description of the review process is derived from Harvard Medical Practice Study 1990, chapter 5.

10. 1 = "Little or no evidence for management causation." 2 = "Slight to modest evidence for management causation." 3 = "Management causation not quite likely; less than 50–50 but close call." 4 = "Management causation more likely than not; more than 50–50 but close call." 5 = "Strong evidence for management causation." 6 = Virtually certain evidence for management causation." From form appended to chapter 5 of Harvard Medical Practice Study 1990.

11. "After having considered the factors in 8.1–8.7 you might have reassessed whether negligence occurred. If you feel that there is NO negligence, CHECK THE SPACE ON THE RIGHT AND GO TO Q. 11." Ibid.

12. For example, the first-stage review was verified only if the reviewer sent the record on to the second stage; the physician reviewers were asked to reconsider their opinions only if they concluded that there was evidence of negligence; and the physician reviewers were asked to provide a confidence rating only for an opinion that there was an injury caused by medical management and that the injury was caused by negligence, but not for an opinion that there was not.

13. Weiler et al. 1993 at 55.

14. Weiler et al. 1993 at 70.

15. Wilson et al. 1995 (Australia); Andrews et al. 1997 (Illinois).

16. Studdert, Brennan et al. 2000 at 1659.

17. Thomas, Studdert, Burstin et al. 2000.

18. Wilson et al. 1995.

19. Runciman et al. 2000; Thomas, Studdert, Runciman et al. 2000.

20. Thomas, Studdert, Runciman et al. 2000.

21. Ibid.

22. Wilson et al. 1995 at 461.

23. Schimmel 1964; Steel et al. 1981.

24. Schimmel 1964; Steel et al. 1981; Jahnigen et al. 1982 ; Chaudry et al. 2003.

25. Danzon 1985 at 22–24 (California); Localio et al. 1991 at 248 (New York); Studdert, Thomas et al. 2000 at 254 (Utah and Colorado).

26. Schnaue 2003.

27. Black et al., forthcoming.

28. Vidmar et al. 2005, at 335, 344–49.

29. Available at http//insurance.mo.gov/reports/medmal/sect/.

30. Danzon 1985; Weiler 1991; Weiler et al. 1993; Sloan et al. 1991 and 1993; Vidmar 1995.

31. Blendon et al. 2002.

32. Kaiser Family Foundation/Harvard School of Public Health 2005.

33. E.g., Danzon 2000.

34. Babcock and Lowenstein 1997.

35. Niebuhr 1960 at xi–xii.

36. Baker, et al. 2004; Baker and Simon 2002.
37. Begley, 2005. For collections of research on these topics see Kahneman et al. 1982; and Kahneman and Tversky 2000.
38. Margolis 1996.
39. Haltom and McCann 2004.

CHAPTER 3

1. Gron and Winton 2001.
2. Hanjani 2004.
3. Baker 2005.
4. Data for the charts in this chapter were taken from Best 2004 (and earlier editions).
5. The operating profit is the sum of the investment profit and the underwriting profit. The investment profit is the sum of the investment income plus capital gains realized during the year expressed as a percentage of the premiums earned during the year ([income + gains] ÷ premium × 100 percent). The underwriting profit is the sum of the premium earned during the year minus the underwriting and loss expenses incurred during the year, expressed as a percentage of the earned premium ([premium – expenses] ÷ premium × 100 percent).
6. Hunter 2002.
7. The rate of change was calculated using data from chart 1. Medical inflation data are from the Bureau of Labor Statistics annual Medical Care CPI reading (Bureau of Labor Statistics 2004). The rate of change for each year in chart 2 was computed by calculating the raw rate of change between year 1 and year 2 and subtracting from that rate the medical inflation rate for year 1.
8. Black et al., forthcoming.
9. E.g., Weiss 1985; Bradford and Logue 1998 and 1999.
10. Fitzpatrick 2004.
11. See, e.g., Scharfstein and Stein 1990.
12. See Harrington and Danzon 1994. For a general discussion of the winner's curse, see Thaler 1988.
13. E.g., Ross 1970 at 135.
14. Browne and Schmit 2004.
15. U.S. DHHS 2003.
16. Buffett 2002 at 9.
17. On the limited ability of investment income to explain insurance crises, see Harrington 2004; Logue 1996; Grace and Hotchkiss 1995; Doherty and Garven 2001.
18. Danzon 1985 at 222.
19. Kohn et al. at 26–27 (providing accident rates). Best 2004 at 165–70 (providing insurance premiums). The actuarial firm of Tillinghast–Towers Perrin estimates that the total costs of protection against medical malpractice, including captives, self-insurance, and other alternatives to traditional medical malpractice insurance, were $26.5 billion in 2003. Tillinghast–Towers Perrin 2004 at 18. Even that number is

only about 10 percent of the price for insurance against auto and workplace accidents.

20. Sage 2004 at 15.

21. See Geistfeld 2005; Wilson et al. 1995 at 470.

CHAPTER 4

1. Danzon 1985 at 22–24; Localio et al. 1991 at 248; Studdert, Thomas et al. 2000 at 254.

2. Localio et al. 1991 at 245 (New York); Studdert, Thomas et al. 2000 at 253 (Colorado and Utah).

3. Andrews et al. 1997 at 312; Andrews 1993 at figure 5. Farber and White 1990 (reporting that serious claims are generally litigated).

4. Haltom and McCann 2004.

5. E.g., Daniels and Martin 1995; Vidmar 1995.

6. See generally Daniels and Martin 1995, chapter 4.

7. Daniels and Martin 1995; Vidmar 1995; Vidmar et al. 2005.

8. See Vidmar et al. 2005.

9. See, generally, Baker 2004.

10. Clermont and Eisenberg 1992; Kalven and Zeisel 1966; Heuer and Penrod 1994.

11. Clermont and Eisenberg 2001; Baker and Born 2005.

12. Seabury et al. 2004; Daniels and Martin 1995.

13. Seabury et al. 2004 at 3.

14. Daniels and Martin 1995 at 82–83, 128–31, 137–46.

15. Ibid. at 60.

16. Vidmar et al. 1993; Vidmar 1995.

17. E.g., Taragin et al. 1992 at 781.

18. Black et al., forthcoming; Vidmar et al. 2005.

19. Taragin et al. 1992 at 784.

20. Ibid. at 782.

21. Hyman and Silver, forthcoming.

22. Cheney et al. 1989.

23. Because the published article uses percentages rather than absolute numbers, this is difficult, but not impossible, to figure out. Using figure 1 and the percentages given in the text on page 1601 of Cheney et al. 1989, we can compute that payments were made in 34 appropriate-care death cases, 25 appropriate-care disabling cases, and 104 appropriate-care nondisabling cases.

24. Thomas, Studdert, Runciman et al. 2000.

25. Waters et al. 2003.

26. Using figure 1 in Cheney et al. 1989 we can determine that there were 78 appropriate-care death cases and 82 appropriate-care disabling cases among the 1,004 lawsuits studied. Payments were made in 44 percent of these death cases (i.e., 34 cases) and 31 percent of these disabling cases (i.e., 25 cases).

27. Sloan and Hsieh 1990 at 1014, 1019; Sloan et al. 1993 at 98–113.

28. Spurr and Howze 2001 at 507; Farber and White 1994 at 778.

29. Rosenblatt and Hurst 1989 at 712.

30. Ogburn et al. 1988. See Baker, forthcoming, for further explanation of payments in nonnegligent cases.

31. Harris et al. 2003; Peeples et al. 2002 at 881–88.

32. Baker, forthcoming (critiquing Brennan et al. 1996). For some similar criticism see Spurr and Howze 2001 at 494.

33. Farber and White 1990 at 216.

34. Farber and White 1994 at 790.

35. Ibid. at 778.

36. Localio et al. 1991. As I explain in my article on the Harvard study, the research team eventually matched four other claims, but including those claims in the analysis does not make a material difference. Baker, forthcoming.

37. Harvard Medical Practice Study 1990 at 7–32.

38. These calculations can all be made using the table in Localio et al. 1991 at 248. See also Saks 1994.

39. E.g., Andrews 1993; Farber and White 1994; Lamb et al. 2003; Mazor et al. 2004. Cf. Cohen 2000.

40. These calculations can be made using table 3 in Localio et al. 1991 at 248.

41. Andrews et al. 1997 at 312. See also Andrews 1993 at figure 7 and at p. 5. For a recent update of the research, see Andrews 2005.

42. Werth 1998. Much of the discussion of Tony Sabia's case is adapted from Baker 2002.

43. Baker 2002 at 399.

44. See Haltom and McCann 2004 (tort reform stories). See ATLA 2005. Spurr and Howze 2001 is an important exception to research that draws a bright line between negligent and nonnegligent injuries.

CHAPTER 5

1. Blendon et al. 2002.

2. E.g., Studdert and Brennan 2001; Kohn et al. 2000; Mello and Brennan 2002.

3. Sage 2003.

4. Lubet 2003.

5. Hyman and Silver, forthcoming.

6. Hyman and Silver, forthcoming, citing Kohn et al. 2000 at 37; Studdert and Brennan 2001 at 227–28; Runciman and Tito 2003 at 978; and American Medical Association 2003.

7. Hyman and Silver, forthcoming.

8. Berens 2002.

9. Dolan and Altimari 2002; Herszenhorn 2002.

10. Hyman and Silver, forthcoming.

11. http://www.phri.org/news/news_inthenews06.asp.

12. *Hartford Courant* 2004. Dolan 2004.

13. Gawande 2002 at 89, 94, 100.

14. Waldman 2002c. *Hartford Courant* 2002b. Waldman 2002b. Waldman 2002a; Budoff 2002.

15. Overton 2002. Condon 2002a. Condon 2002b. *Hartford Courant* 2002a. Dolan 2002.

16. Connecticut Department of Public Health 2002.

17. *New York Times* 2002.

18. Mello and Brennan 2002.

19. Baker et al. 2004.

20. E.g., Holzer 1984; Carroll 2004.

21. See, e.g., Pham et al. 2005.

22. I am indebted to Cohen 1997–98 for the conceptual framework that follows.

23. Pierce and Cooper 1984. See also Hyman and Silver, forthcoming; Gaba 2000.

24. Cheney 1993 at 8.

25. Domino et al. 1999; Domino 1996.

26. Caplan et al. 1990. Pierce 1995.

27. Shoenbaum and Bovbjerg 2004.

28. Sloan et al. 1993.

29. Pace et al. 2004. From an outsider's perspective, collecting a share of the settlement can look unseemly, as if the lawyer is profiting from the patient's misfortune. But the patient suffered the misfortune long before the lawyer got involved, and this contingent fee approach provides the path to recovery. Contingent fees open up courts to people who otherwise would have no way to get a lawyer, and they focus lawyers on maximizing results for their clients See generally Bernstein 2004.

30. Baker 2001.

31. Vidmar 2005.

32. Cf. Holmes 1881 at 2 et seq.

33. Silver 2003.

34. Green 2005.

35. Bogus 2001 at 66 et seq.

36. Hickson et al. 1992; Forster et al. 2002; Mazor et al. 2004.

37. Bernstein 2004.

CHAPTER 6

1. Corrigan et al. 1996 at 277.

2. E.g., Zuckerman 1984 at 132.

3. E.g., Tancredi and Barondess 1978; Office of Technology Assessment 1994; Klingman et al. 1996; Kessler and McClellan 1997.

4. Zuckerman 1984; Kessler and McClellan 1997.

5. Tancredi and Barondess 1978 at 881–82.

6. Klingman et al. 1996 at 193.

7. Office of Technology Assessment 1994.

8. E.g., Rock 1988.
9. Tussing and Wojtoqycz 1992.
10. Baldwin et al. 1995.
11. Localio et al. 1993.
12. Kessler and McClellan 1996.
13. Yoon and Baker, forthcoming.
14. Kessler and McClellan 1996 at 387–88.
15. McClellan and Newhouse 1997 at 40 and 63.
16. De Ville 1998.
17. Kessler and McClellan 2002.
18. E.g., McClellan and Newhouse 1997.
19. By contrast, a state-level analysis makes more sense for tort reform because tort reform affects liability at the state level.
20. Dubay et al. 1999.
21. Baicker and Chandra 2004.
22. Congressional Budget Office 2003, 2004.

CHAPTER 7
1. American Association of Medical Colleges 2004.
2. GAO 2003 at 17.
3. Galvin 2005.
4. Rivo and Kindig 1996.
5. E.g., Cooper et al. 2002.
6. E.g., Rizzo and Blumenthal 1994.
7. Baicker and Chandra 2004.
8. Strunk and Esser 2004.
9. Halm et al. 2002.
10. See Baker et al. 2004.
11. Kessler and McClellan 1996 and 2002.
12. Dubay et al. 2001.
13. Klick and Stratmann 2004.
14. Baker 2001 at 312–13.
15. E.g., American Medical Association 2003.
16. Daniels and Martin 1995 at 96–97.
17. Ibid. at 99–100.
18. Topping et al. 2003
19. Ibid.
20. Bovbjerg et al. 1996 at 282n7.
21. See literature review in Topping et al. 2003.

CHAPTER 8
1. Taft 2005.
2. Conard et al. 1964.

3. LeGros and Pinkall 2002 (quoting AMA Code of Medical Ethics E-8.12).
4. Lamb et al. 2003. Mazor et al. 2004.
5. LeGros and Pinkall 2002. Bressler 2002.
6. Taft 2005.
7. Yoon and Baker, forthcoming.
8. Taft 2005 at 66.
9. See American Medical Association 1998; Haugh 2003; Larkin 2004. See also Sage 1997 at 174–75.
10. E.g., Office of the Inspector General, Advisory Opinion no. 04–19 (December 30, 2004).
11. See http://www.whitehouse.gov./infocus/medicalliability/ (last visited March 21, 2005).
12. Ibid.

References

American Association of Medical Colleges. 2004. U.S. medical school applicants, 1994–2004. Available at http://www.aamc.org/newsroom/pressrel/2004/applicants2004.pdf.

American Medical Association. 1998. What to consider when someone else is responsible for your insurance. In *Medical Professional Liability Insurance: The Informed Physician's Guide to Coverage Decisions.* Chicago: American Medical Association.

———. 2003. AMA statement to the Senate HELP Committee and the Senate Judiciary Committee, Re: Patient access crisis: The role of medical litigation. February 11.

———. 2005. *Physician characteristics and distribution.* Chicago: American Medical Association.

Andrews, Lori. 1993. *Medical error and patient claiming in a hospital setting.* Chicago: American Bar Foundation.

Andrews, Lori B., Carol Stocking, Thomas Krizek, Lawrence Gottlieb, Claudette Krizek, Thomas Vargish, Mark Siegler. 1997. An alternative strategy for studying adverse events in medical care. *Lancet* 349:309–13.

———. 2005. Studying medical error in situ: Implications for malpractice law and policy. *DePaul Law Review* 54:357–92.

ATLA. 2005. Faces of medical malpractice. Association of Trial Lawyers of America, *Consumer News for Families,* January 24. Available at http://www.atla.org/Focus/050124.aspx.

Avery, Sarah. Duke admits transplant error. 2003. *News and Observer* (Raleigh, NC). February 18.

———. 2003. Health fades, but hope lingers. *News and Observer* (Raleigh, NC). February 20.

———. 2003. Second transplant gives teen a chance. *News and Observer* (Raleigh, NC). February 21.

———. 2003. Brain damage dims hopes for Jesica. *News and Observer* (Raleigh, NC). February 22.

———. 2003. Jesica dies of brain damage. *News and Observer* (Raleigh, NC). February 23.

———. 2003. Fund set up in Jesica's name. *News and Observer* (Raleigh, NC). May 9.

———. 2003. Texas lawyer enters fray in teen's transplant death at Duke. *News and Observer* (Raleigh, NC). June 27.

———. 2004. Duke settles case of transplant gone wrong. *News and Observer* (Raleigh, NC). June 26.

Babcock, Linda, and George Lowenstein. 1997. Explaining bargaining impasse: The role of self-serving biases. *Journal of Economic Perspectives* 11:109–26.

Baicker, Katherine, and Amitabh Chandra. 2004. The effect of malpractice liability on the delivery of health care. NBER Working Paper 10709. August.

Baker, Tom. 2001. Blood money, new money, and the moral economy of tort law in action. *Law and Society Review* 35:275–319.

———. 2002. Real torts: Using Barry Werth's *Damages* in the law school classroom. *Nevada Law Journal* 2:386–402.

———. 2004. Insuring liability risks. *Geneva Papers on Risk and Insurance* 29:128–49.

———. 2005. Medical malpractice and the insurance underwriting cycle. *DePaul Law Review* 54:393–438.

———. Forthcoming. Reconsidering the Harvard medical malpractice study conclusions about the validity of medical malpractice claims. *Journal of Law, Medicine, and Ethics* 33 (3).

Baker, Tom, and Patricia Born. 2005. Connecticut civil appeals: Defendant's advantage. Working paper.

Baker, Tom, Alon Harel, and Tamar Kugler. 2004. The virtues of uncertainty in law: An experimental approach. *Iowa Law Review* 89:443–94.

Baker, Tom, and Jonathan Simon, eds. 2002. Risk, insurance, and the social construction of responsibility. In *Embracing risk: The changing culture of insurance and responsibility*, 33–51. Chicago: University of Chicago Press.

Baldwin, Laura-Mae, L. Gary Hart, Michael Lloyd, Meredith Fordyce, and Roger A. Rosenblatt. 1995. Defensive medicine and obstetrics. *JAMA* 274:1606–10.

Bassett, Ken L., Nitya Iyer, and Arminee Kacanjian. 2000. Defensive medicine during obstetrical care: A by-product of the technological age. *Social Science and Medicine* 51:523–37.

Begley, Sharon. 2005. People believe a "fact" that fits their views even if it's clearly false. *Wall Street Journal*, February 4.

Berens, Michael J. 2002. Infection epidemic carves deadly path: Poor hygiene, overwhelmed workers contribute to thousands of deaths. *Chicago Tribune*, July 21.

Bernstein, Anita. 2004. The enterprise of liability. *Valparaiso Law Review* 39:27–63.

Best, A. M. 2004 and earlier editions. *Best's aggregates and averages, property/casualty edition*. Oldwick, NJ: A. M. Best.

Black, Bernard, Charles Silver, David A. Hyman, and William M. Sage. Forthcoming. Stability, not crisis: Medical malpractice outcomes in Texas, 1988–2002. *Journal of Empirical Legal Studies*.

Blendon, Robert J., Catherine M. DesRoches, Mollyann Brodie, John M. Benson, Allison B. Rosen, Eric Schneider, Drew E. Altman, Kinga Zapert, Melissa J. Herrmann, and Annie E. Steffenson. 2002. Views of practicing physicians and the public on medical errors. *New England Journal of Medicine* 347:1933–40.

Blumenthal, David. 2004. New steam from an old cauldron: The physician supply debate. *New England Journal of Medicine* 350:1780–87.

Bogus, Carl. 2001. *Why lawsuits are good for America.* New York: New York University Press.

Bradford David F., and Kyle D. Logue. 1998. The effect of tax law changes on prices in the property casualty insurance industry. In *The Economics of property-casualty insurance,* ed. David Bradford, 29. Chicago: University of Chicago Press.

———. 1999. The influence of income tax rules on insurance reserves. In *The financing of catastrophe risk,* ed. Kenneth Froot, 275. Chicago: University of Chicago Press.

Brennan, Troyen A., Colin M. Sox, and Helen R. Burstin. 1996. Relation between negligent adverse events and the outcomes of medical-malpractice litigation. *New England Journal of Medicine* 335:1963–67.

Bressler, Harold J. 2002. Patient safety standards: Analyzing the JCAHO revisions. *Journal of Health Law* 35 (2) (Spring 2002): 179–88.

Browne, Mark J., and Joan T. Schmit. 2004. Patterns in personal automobile third-party bodily injury litigation: 1977–1997. Working Paper. September 7. Available at http://ssrn.com/abstract=588481.

Bovbjerg, Randall R., Lisa C. Dubay, Genevieve M. Kenney, and Stephen A. Norton. 1996. Defensive medicine and tort reform: New evidence in an old bottle. *Journal of Health Politics Policy and Law* 21:267–88.

Budoff, Carrie. 2002. Prescription error bill heads to governor. *Hartford Courant,* April 30.

Buffett, Warren E. Letter to shareholders. Available at http://www.berkshirehathaway.com/letters/2001pdf.pdf.

Caplan, Robert A., Karen L. Posner, Richard J. Ward, and Frederick W. Cheney. 1990. Adverse respiratory events in anesthesia: A closed claim analysis. *Anesthesiology* 72:828–33.

Carroll, Roberta, ed. 2004. Risk management handbook for health care organizations. 4th ed. San Francisco: Jossey-Bass.

Chaudry, Sarwat I., Kolawole A. Olofinboba, and Harlan M. Krumholz. 2003. Detection of errors by attending physicians on a general medicine service. *Journal of General Internal Medicine* 18:595–600.

Cheney, Frederick W. 1993. ASA closed claim project: Where have we been and where are we going? *ASA Newsletter* 57:8–22.

Cheney, Frederick W., Karen Posner, Robert A. Caplan, and Richard J. Ward. 1989. Standard of care and anesthesia liability. *JAMA* 261:1599–1603.

Clermont, Kevin, and Theodore Eisenberg. 1992. Trial by jury or judge: Transcending empiricism. *Cornell Law Review* 77:1124–74.

Cohen, George M. 1997–98. Legal malpractice insurance: A comparative analysis of economic institutions. *Connecticut Insurance Law Journal* 4:305–50.

Cohen, Jonathan R. 2000. Apology and organizations: Exploring an example from medical practice. *Fordham Urban Law Journal* 27:1447–48.

Conard, Alfred F., James N. Morgan, Robert W. Pratt, Jr., Charles E. Voltz, and

Robert L. Bombaugh. 1964. Automobile accident costs and payments: Studies in the economics of injury reparation. Ann Arbor: University of Michigan Press.

Condon, Garret. 2002a. Hospital says nitrous oxide removed. *Hartford Courant*, January 19.

——. 2002b. St. Raphael Hospital reopens cardiac room. *Hartford Courant*, January 24.

Congressional Budget Office. 2003. *Cost estimate for H.R. 5, the help efficient, accessible, low-cost, timely healthcare (HEALTH) Act of 2003.* Washington, DC: CBO.

——. 2004. *The effects of tort reform: Evidence from the states.* Washington, DC.: CBO.

Connecticut Department of Public Health. 2002. Letter to hospital of St. Raphael. In the author's possession.

Connecticut Judicial Branch. 2005. Civil cases added by case type for the years 1989–90 to 2003–04. Wethersfield, CT.

Cooper, Richard A., Thomas E. Getzen, Heather J. McKee, and Prakash Laud. 2002. Economic and demographic trends signal an impending physician shortage. *Health Affairs* 21:140–54.

Corrigan, Jacqueline, Judith Wagner, Leah Wolfe, David Klingman, and Philip Polishuk. 1996. Medical malpractice reform and defensive medicine. *Cancer Investigation* 14:277–84.

Dallas Morning News. 2003. Hospitals sued over transplant; family says 1-year-old died after receiving liver of the wrong blood type. March 12.

Daniels, Stephen, and Joanne Martin. 1995. *Civil juries and the politics of reform.* Evanston: Northwestern University Press.

Danzon, Patricia A. 1985. *Medical malpractice: Theory, evidence, and public policy.* Cambridge: Harvard University Press.

——. 2001. Liability for medical malpractice. In *Handbook of Health Economics*, vol. 1, ed. A. J. Culyer and J. P. Newhouse, 1349–1404. New York: Elsevier.

De Ville, Kenneth Allen. 1990. *Medical malpractice in nineteenth-century America.* New York: New York University Press.

——. 1998. Act first and look up the law afterward? Medical malpractice and the ethics of defensive medicine. *Theoretical Medicine and Bioethics* 19:569–89.

Doherty, Neil A., and James R. Garven. 2001. Insurance cycles: Interest rates and the capacity constraint model. *Journal of Business* 68:383–404.

Dolan, Jack. 2002. Hospital agrees to pay fine in 2 deaths. *Hartford Courant*, November 1.

——. 2004. One doctor, two comas. *Hartford Courant*, June 20.

Dolan, Jack, and Dave Altimari. 2002. Court order silences victims: Hospital sues over families' comments. *Hartford Courant*, July 26.

Domino, Karen B. 1996. Closed malpractice claims for awareness under anesthesia: a closed claim analysis. *ASA Newsletter* 60 (6): 15.

Domino, Karen B., Karen L. Posner, Robert A. Caplan, and Frederick W. Cheney. 1999. Airway injury under anesthesia. *Anesthesiology* 91:1703–11.

Draper, Melissa. 2001. Illness spurs resurgence of hope. *News and Observer (Raleigh, NC)*, November 2.

Dubay, Lisa, Robert Kaestner, and Timothy Waidman. 1999. The Impact of malpractice fears on cesarean section rates. *Journal of Health Economics* 18:491–522.

———. 2001. Medical malpractice liability and its effect on prenatal care utilization and infant health. *Journal of Health Economics* 20:591–611.

Dunworth, Terence, and Joel Rogers. 1996. Corporations in court: Big business litigation in U.S. federal courts, 1971–1991. *Law and Social Inquiry* 21:497–592.

Eisley, Matthew. 2003. Mistake alleged in blood match. *News and Observer (Raleigh, NC)*, February 16.

Farber, Henry S., and Michelle J. White. 1990. Medical malpractice: An empirical examination of the litigation process. *RAND Journal of Economics* 22:199–217.

———. 1994. A comparison of formal and informal dispute resolution in medical malpractice. *Journal of Legal Studies* 23:777–806.

Fitzpatrick, Sean M. 2004. Fear is the key: A behavioral guide to underwriting cycles. *Connecticut Insurance Law Journal* 10:255–74.

Forster, Heidi P., Jack Schwartz, and Evan DeRenzo. 2002. Reducing legal risk by practicing patient-centered medicine. *Archives of Internal Medicine* 162:1217–19.

Gaba, David M. 2000. Anesthesiology as a model for patient safety in health care. *British Medical Journal* 320:785–88.

Galanter, Marc. 1986. The day after the litigation explosion. *Maryland Law Review* 46:3–39.

———. 1994. Real world torts: An antidote to anecdote. *Maryland Law Review* 55:1093–1160

———.2004. The vanishing trial: An examination of trials and related matters in federal and state courts. *Journal of Empirical Legal Studies* 1:459–570.

Galvin, J. Robert. 2005. Testimony of Commissioner, Connecticut Department of Public Health, before the Insurance and Real Estate Committees of the Connecticut General Assembly, February 10. Broadcast on CT-N Channel 20, February 11, 06:44 PM, and transcribed by Video Monitoring Services of America.

GAO. 2003. *Medical malpractice: Implications of rising premiums on access to health care.*. Washington, DC: GAO-030836.

Gawande, Atul. 2002. *Complications: A surgeon's notes on an imperfect science.* New York: Henry Holt.

Geistfeld, Mark. 2005. Medical malpractice insurance and the (il)legitimate interest of the medical profession in tort reform. *DePaul Law Review* 54:439–62.

Grace, Martin F., and Julie L. Hotchkiss. 1995. External impacts on the property-liability insurance cycle. *Journal of Risk and Insurance* 62:738–54.

Grady, Denise and Lawrence K. Altman. 2003. Suit says transplant error was cause in baby's death, *New York Times*, March 12, A23.

Green, Michael. 2005. Letter to the editor. *Wall Street Journal*, January 16.

Gron, Anne, and Andrew Winton. 2001. Risk overhang and market behavior. *Journal of Business* 74:591–612.

Halm, Ethan A., Clara Lee, and Mark Chassin. 2002. Is volume related to outcome in health care? A systematic review and methodologic critique of the literature. *Annals of Internal Medicine* 137:511–20.

Haltom, William, and Michael McCann. 2004. *Distorting the law: Politics, media, and the litigation crisis.* Chicago: University of Chicago Press.

Hanjani, George H. 2004. Mutuality and the underwriting cycle: Theory with evidence from the Pennsylvania fire insurance market, 1873–1909. *Social Science Research Network* (February). http://ssrn.com/abstract=519603.

Harrington, Scott E. 2004. Tort liability, insurance rates, and the insurance cycle. In *Brookings-Wharton Papers on Financial Institutions,* ed. Robert Litan and Richard Herring. Washington, DC: Brookings.

Harrington, Scott E., and Patricia Danzon. 1994. Price cutting in liability insurance markets. *Journal of Business* 67:511–38.

Harris, Catherine T., Ralph A. Peeples, and Thomas B. Metzloff. 2003. Who are those guys? An empirical examination of medical malpractice plaintiffs' lawyers. Wake Forest University Public Law Research Paper no. 03–09. April. http://ssrn.com/abstract=399640.

Hartford Courant. 2002a. Commentary. Deaths at St. Raphael, January 20.
———. 2002b. Editorial. Rx for pharmacy blunders. February 17.
———. 2004. Editorial. Remove derelict doctors. July 8.

Harvard Medical Practice Study. 1990. *Patients, doctors, and lawyers: Medical injury, malpractice litigation, and patient compensation in New York: The report of the Harvard Medical Practice Study to the State of New York.* Cambridge: Harvard University.

Haugh, Richard. 2003. Surviving medical malpractice madness. *Hospitals and Health Networks Magazine* (May), 47.

Heinz, John P., Robert L. Nelson, Edward O. Laumann, and Ethan Michelson. 1998. The changing character of lawyers' work: Chicago in 1975 and 1995. *Law and Society Review* 32:751–75.

Hensler, Deborah R., M. Susan Marquis, Allan F. Abrahamse, Sandra H. Berry, Patricia A. Ebener, Elizabeth G. Lewis, E. Allan Lind, Robert J. Maccoun, Willard G. Manning, Jeannette A. Rogowski, Mary E. Vaiana. 1991. *Compensation for accidental injuries in the United States.* Santa Monica: RAND.

Herszenhorn, David M. 2002. Hospital drops legal action to stem tide of bad publicity. *New York Times,* July 27.

Heuer, Larry, and Steven Penrod. 1994. Trial complexity: A field investigation of its meaning and effects. *Law and Human Behavior* 18:29–51.

Hickson, Gerald, Ellen Wright Clayton, Penny B. Githens, and Frank A. Sloan. 1992. Factors that prompted families to file medical malpractice claims following perinatal injuries. *JAMA* 267:1359–63.

Holmes, Oliver Wendell, Jr. 1881. *The common law.* Boston: Little Brown.

Holzer, James F. 1984. Current concepts in risk management. In *Analysis of anesthetic mishaps*, ed. Ellison C. Pierce, Jr., and Jeffrey B. Cooper. Boston: Little Brown.

Hunter, J. Robert. 2002. Consumer advocate challenges insurers on "Crisis" in med mal market. *National Underwriter: Property and Casualty / Risk and Benefits Management Edition* (October 7): 10.

Hyman, David A, and Charles M. Silver. Forthcoming. The poor state of health quality in the U.S.: Is malpractice part of the problem or part of the solution? *Cornell Law Review*. Working paper version available at http://ssrn.com/abstract =526762.

Jahnigen, D., C. Hannon, L. Laxson, and F. M. LaForce. 1982. Iatrogenic disease in hospitalized elderly veterans. *Journal of American Geriatric Society* 30 (6): 387–90.

Kahneman, Daniel, Paul Slovic, and Amos Tversky, eds. 1982. *Judgment under uncertainty: Heuristics and biases.* Cambridge: Cambridge University Press.

Kahneman, Daniel, and Amos Tversky, eds. 2000. *Choices, values and frames.* Cambridge: Cambridge University Press.

Kaiser Family Foundation/Harvard School of Public Health. 2005. Survey. Available at http://www.kff.org/kaiserpolls/pomro111105pkg.cfm.

Kalven, Harry, Jr., and Hans Zeisel. 1966. *The American jury.* Boston: Little Brown.

Kersh, Rogan, and William M. Sage, eds. Forthcoming. *Medical malpractice and the U.S. healthcare system.* New York: Oxford University Press.

Kessler, Daniel, and Mark McClellan. 1996. Do doctors practice defensive medicine? *Quarterly Journal of Economics* 111:353–90.

———. 1997. The effects of malpractice pressure and liability reforms on physicians' perceptions of medical care. *Law and Contemporary Problems* 60:81–106.

———. 2002. Malpractice law and health care reform: Optimal liability policy in an era of managed care. *Journal of Public Economics* 84:175–97.

Klick, Jonathan, and Thomas Stratmann. 2003. Does medical malpractice reform help states retain physicians and does it matter? *Social Science Research Network* abstract (October). Accessed at http://ssrn.com/abstract=453481.

Klingman, David, A. Russell Localio, Jeremy Sugarman, Judith Wagner, Philip T. Polishuk, Leah Wolfe, and Jacqueline A. Corrigan. 1996. Measuring defensive medicine using clinical scenario surveys. *Journal of Health Politics, Policy, and Law* 21:185–205.

Kohn, Linda T., Janet M. Corrigan, and Molla S. Donaldson, eds. 2000. *To err is human: Building a safer health system.* Washington, DC: National Academy Press.

Lamb, Rae M., David M. Studdert, Richard M. J. Bohmer, Donald M. Berwick, Troyen A. Brennan. 2003. Hospital disclosure practices: Results of a national survey. *Health Affairs* 22 (2) (March-April): 73–83.

Langford, Terri. 2004. Hospitals settle transplant suit: 1-year-old died days after getting part of father's liver. *Dallas Morning News*, October 6.

Larkin, Howard 2004. Homegrown: Liability insurance. *Hospitals and Health Networks Magazine* 78 (3) (March): 44.

LeGros, Nancy, and Jason D. Pinkall. 2002. The New JCAHO patient safety standards and the disclosure of unanticipated outcomes. *Journal of Health Law* 35 (2) (Spring 2002):189–210.

Localio, A. Russell, Ann G. Lawthers, Joan M. Bengtson, Liesi E. Hebert, Susan L. Weaver, Troyen A. Brennan, and J. Richard Landis. 1993. Relationship between malpractice claims and cesarean delivery. *JAMA* 269:366–73.

Localio, A. Russell, Ann G. Lawthers, Troyen A. Brennan, Nan M. Laird, Liesi E. Hebert, Lynn M. Peterson, Joseph P. Newhouse, Paul C. Weiler, and Howard H. Hiatt. 1991. Relation between malpractice claims and adverse events due to negligence, results of the Harvard Medical Practice Study III. *New England Journal of Medicine* 325:245–51.

Logue, Kyle. 1996. Toward a tax-based explanation of the liability insurance crisis. *Virginia Law Review* 82:895–959.

Los Angeles Times. 2003. Put light on medical errors, March 18.

Lubet, Steven. 2003. Like a surgeon. *Cornell Law Review* 88:1178–97.

Margolis, Howard. 1996. *Dealing with risk: Why the public and the experts disagree on environmental issues.* Chicago: University of Chicago Press.

Marjoribanks, Timothy, Mary-Jo Delvecchio Good, Ann G. Lawthers, and Lynn M. Peterson. 1996. Physicians' discourses on malpractice and the meaning of medical malpractice. *Journal of Health and Social Behavior* 37:163–78.

Mazor, Kathleen M., Steven R. Simon, and Jerry H. Gurwitz. 2004. Communicating with patients about medical errors: A review of the literature. *Archives of Internal Medicine* 164:1690–97.

McClellan, Mark, and Joseph P. Newhouse. 1997. The marginal cost-effectiveness of medical technology: A panel instrumental-variables approach. *Journal of Econometrics* 77:39–64.

McGovern, George, and Alan K. Simpson. 2002. We're reaping what we sue. *Wall Street Journal,* April 17.

Mello, Michelle M., and Troyen A. Brennan. 2002. Deterrence of medical errors: Theory and evidence for malpractice reform. *Texas Law Review* 80:1595–1637.

Mills, Don H., ed. 1977. *Report on the Medical Insurance Feasibility Study.* Sacramento: California Medical Association and California Hospital Association.

———. 1978. Medical insurance feasibility study: A technical summary. *Western Journal of Medicine* 128:360–65.

Niebuhr, Reinhold. 1960. *Moral man and immoral society: A study in ethics and politics.* New York: Scribner.

New York Times. 2002. Hospital where 2 died says it failed to shut a gas line. January 19.

Office of Technology Assessment. 1994. *Defensive Medicine and Medical Malpractice.* Washington, DC: U.S. Government Printing Office.

Ogburn, Paul L., Thomas M. Julian, Doris C. Booker, Marilyn S. Joseph, Julius C. Butler, Preston P. Williams, Mark L. Anderson, Ann C. Shepard, Susan L. Ogburn, William C. Preisler, and Mark D. Wood. 1988. Perinatal medical negligence closed claims from the St. Paul Company, 1980–1982. *Journal of Reproductive Medicine* 53:608–11.

Overton, Penelope. 2002. Error kills two patients: Hospital of St. Raphael says women got anesthetic instead of oxygen. *Hartford Courant,* January 17.

Pace, Nicholas M., Daniela Golinelli, and Laura Zakaras. 2004. Capping non-economic awards in medical malpractice trials: California jury verdicts under MICRA. Santa Monica: RAND.

Peeples, Ralph, Catherine T. Harris, and Thomas B. Metzloff. 2002. The process of managing medical malpractice cases: The role of standard of care. *Wake Forest Law Review* 37:877–902.

Pham, Hoangmai H., Kelly Devers, Sylvia Kuo, and Robert A. Berenson. 2005. Health care market trends and the evolution of hospitalist use and roles. *Journal of General Internal Medicine* 20 (2) (February): 101–7.

Pierce, Ellison C., Jr. 1995. The 34th Rovenstine Lecture. Available at http://www.gasnet.org/societies/apsf/history/rovenstine34–1.php.

Pierce, Ellison C., Jr., and Jeffrey B. Cooper, eds. 1984. Analysis of anesthetic mishaps. Boston: Little Brown.

Rivo, Marc, and David Kindig. 1996. A report card on the physician work force in the United States. *New England Journal of Medicine* 334:892–96.

Rizzo, John A., and David Blumenthal. 1994. Physician labor supply: Do income effects matter? *Journal of Health Economics* 13:433–53.

Rock, Steven M. 1988. Malpractice premiums and primary cesarean section rates in New York and Illinois. *Public Health Reporter* 103:459–63.

Rosenblatt, Roger A., and Andy Hurst. 1989. An analysis of closed obstetric malpractice claims. *Obstetrics and Gynecology* 74:710–14.

Ross, H. Laurence. 1970. *Settled Out of Court.* Chicago: Aldine.

Runciman, William B., Alan F. Merry, and Fiona Tito. 2003. Error, blame, and the law in health care: An antipodean perspective. *Annals of Internal Medicine* 138:974–79.

Runciman, William B., Robert K. Webb, Stephen C. Helps, Eric J. Thomas, Elizabeth J. Sexton, David M. Studdert, and Troyen A. Brennan. 2000. A comparison of iatrogenic injury studies in Australia and the USA II: Reviewer behavior and quality of care. *International Journal for Quality in Health Care* 12:379–88.

Sage, William M. 1997. Enterprise liability and the emerging managed health care system. *Law and Contemporary Problems* 60 (Spring): 159–210.

———. 2004. Understanding the first malpractice crisis of the 21st century. In *Health Law Handbook,* ed. Alice G. Gosfield. 1. Minneapolis: West.

———. 2004. The forgotten third: Liability insurance and the medical malpractice crisis. *Health Affairs* 23:10–21.

Saks, Michael. 1994. Medical malpractice: Facing real problems and finding real solutions. *William and Mary Law Journal* 35:693–726.

Scharfstein, David S., and Jeremy C. Stein. 1990. Herd behavior and investment. *American Economic Review* 90:465–79.

Schimmel, Elihu M. 1964. The hazards of hospitalization. *Annals of Internal Medicine* 60:100–10.

Schnaue, Frank. 2003. In search of affordable insurance. *United Press International,* June 27.

Seabury, Seth A., Nicholas M. Pace, and Robert T. Reville. 2004. Forty years of jury verdicts. *Journal of Empirical Legal Studies* 1:1–25.

Shoenbaum, Stephen, and Randall R. Bovbjerg. 2004. Malpractice reform must include steps to prevent medical injury. *Annals of Internal Medicine* 140:51–53.

Silver, Charles. 2003. Class certification and blackmail. *New York University Law Review* 78:1357–1430.

Sloan, Frank A., Randall R. Bovbjerg, and Penny B. Githens. 1991. *Insuring medical malpractice.* New York: Oxford University Press.

Sloan, Frank A., Penny B. Githens, Ellen Wright Clayton, Gerald B. Hickson, Douglas A. Gentile, and David F. Partlett. 1993. *Suing for medical malpractice.* Chicago: University of Chicago Press.

Sloan, Frank A., and Chee Ruey Hsieh. 1990. Variability in medical malpractice payments: Is the compensation fair? *Law and Society Review* 24:997–1040.

Spurr, Stephen J., and Sandra Howze. 2001. The effect of care quality on medical malpractice litigation. *Quarterly Review of Economics and Finance* 41:491–513.

Steel, Knight, Paul M. Gartman, Caroline Crescenzi, and Jennifer Anderson. 1981. Iatrogenic illness on a general medical service at a university hospital. *New England Journal of Medicine* 304:638–42.

Strunk, Albert L., and Linda Esser. 2004. View of the 2003 ACOG survey of professional liability. *ACOG Clinical Review* 9 (6): 1, 13–16 (November–December 2004).

Studdert, David M., and Troyen A. Brennan. 2001. Toward a workable model of "no-fault" compensation for medical injury in the United States. *American Journal of Law and Medicine* 27:225–52.

Studdert, David M., Troyen A. Brennan, and Eric J. Thomas. 2000. Beyond dead reckoning: Measures of medical injury burden, malpractice litigation, and alternative compensation models from Utah and Colorado. *Indiana Law Review* 33:1643–86.

Studdert, David M., Eric J. Thomas, Helen R. Burstin, Brett I. W. Abar, E. John Orav, and Troyen A. Brennan. 2000. Negligent care and malpractice claiming behavior in Utah and Colorado. *Medical Care* 38:250–60.

Taft, Lee. 2005. Apology and medical mistake: Opportunity or foil? *Annals of Health Law* 14:55–94.

Tancredi, Laurence R., and Jeremiah A. Barondess. 1978. The problem of defensive medicine. *Science* 200:879–82.

Taragin, Mark I., Laura R. Willett, Adam P. Wilczek, Richard Trout, and Jeffrey L. Carson. 1992. The influence of standard of care and severity of injury on the resolution of medical malpractice claims. *Annals of Internal Medicine* 117:780–84.

Thaler, Richard H. 1988. Anomalies: The winner's curse. *Journal of Economic Perspectives* 2:191–202.

Thomas, Eric J., David M. Studdert, and Troyen A. Brennan. 2002. The reliability of medical record review for estimating adverse event rates. *Annals of Internal Medicine* 136:812–16.

Thomas, Eric J., David M. Studdert, Helen R. Burstin, E. John Orav, Timothy Seena, Elliott J. Williams, K. Mason Howard, Paul C. Weiler, and Troyen A. Brennan. 2000. Incidence and types of adverse events and negligent care in Utah and Colorado. *Medical Care* 38:261–71.

Thomas, Eric J., David M. Studdert, William B. Runciman, Robert K. Webb, Elizabeth Sexton, Ross McL. Wilson, Robert W. Gibberd, Bernadette T. Harrison, and Troyen A. Brennan. 2000. A comparison of iatrogenic injury studies in Australia and the USA I: Context, methods, case mix, population, patient and hospital characteristics. *International Journal for Quality in Health Care* 12:371–78.

Tillinghast–Towers Perrin. 2004. *U.S. tort costs: 2004 update.* Accessed May 11, 2005, at http://www.towersperrin.com/tillinghast/publications/reports/2003_Tort_Costs_Update/Tort_Costs_Trends_2003_Update.pdf.

Topping, Daniel B., William J. Hueston, and Phyllis MacGilvray. 2003. Family physicians delivering babies: What do obstetricians think? *Family Medicine* 35:737–41.

Tussing, A. Dale, and Martha A. Wojtoqycz. 1992. The cesarean decision in New York State, 1986. *Medical Care* 30:529–40.

U.S. DHHS. 2003. *National Practitioner Data Bank Public Use Data File,* March. Rockville, MD: U.S. Department of Health and Human Services, Health Resources and Services Administration, Bureau of Health Professions, Division of Practitioner Data Banks. Available at http://www.npdb-hipdb.com/publicdata.html.

Vidmar, Neil. 1993. Empirical evidence on the "deep pockets" hypothesis: Jury awards for pain and suffering in medical malpractice cases. *Duke Law Journal* 43:217–66.

Vidmar, Neil. 1995. *Medical malpractice and the American jury: Confronting the myths about jury incompetence, deep pockets, and outrageous damage awards.* Ann Arbor: University of Michigan Press.

Vidmar, Neil, Paul Lee, Kara MacKillip, Kieran McCarthy, Gerald McGwin. 2005. Uncovering the "invisible" profile of medical malpractice litigation: Insights from Florida. *DePaul Law Review* 54:315–56.

Waldman, Loretta. 2002a. Prescription errors stir debate: Bill would require mistakes to be reported. *Hartford Courant,* March 4.

———. 2002b. Sons sue pharmacy in mother's death. *Hartford Courant,* February 28.

———. 2002c. Wrong Rx has fatal result: Botched prescription causes overdose. *Hartford Courant,* February 13.

Waters, Teresa M., David M. Studdert, Troyen A. Brennan, Eric J. Thomas, Orit Almagor, Martha Mancewicz, and Peter P. Budetti. 2003. Impact of the National Practitioner Data Bank on the resolution of malpractice claims. *Inquiry* 40:283–94.

Weiler, Paul C. 1991. *Medical malpractice on trial.* Cambridge: Harvard University Press.

Weiler, Paul C., Howard H. Hiatt, Joseph P. Newhouse, William G. Johnson, Troyen A. Brennan, and Lucian L. Leape. 1993. *A measure of malpractice.* Cambridge: Harvard University Press.

Weiss, Mary. 1985. A multivariate analysis of loss reserving estimates and property-liability insurers. *Journal of Risk and Insurance* 52:199–21.

Werth, Barry. 1998. *Damages: One family's legal struggles in the world of medicine.* New York: Simon and Schuster.

White, Michelle J. 1994. The value of liability in medical malpractice. *Health Affairs* 13:75–87.

Wilson, Ross McL., William B. Runciman, Robert W. Gibberd, Bernadette T. Harrison, Liza Newby, and John D. Hamilton. 1995. The quality in Australian health care study. *Medical Journal of Australia* 163:458–71.

Yoon, Albert, and Tom Baker. Forthcoming. A market solution to civil litigation? An empirical study of offer-of-judgment rules. *Vanderbilt Law Review.*

Zuckerman, Stephen. 1984. Medical malpractice: Claims, legal costs, and the practice of defensive medicine. *Health Affairs* 3:128–33.

Index